Pakistan and Afghanistan

Pakistan and Afghanistan

Resistance and Reconstruction

Marvin G. Weinbaum

Westview Press

BOULDER • SAN FRANCISCO • OXFORD

Pak Book Corporation

LAHORE • ISLAMABAD • KARACHI

This Westview softcover edition is printed on acid-free paper and bound in library-quality, coated covers that carry the highest rating of the National Association of State Textbook Administrators, in consultation with the Association of American Publishers and the Book Manufacturers' Institute.

Published in 1994 in the United States of America by Westview Press, Inc., 5500 Central Avenue, Boulder, Colorado 80301-2877, and in the United Kingdom by Westview Press, 36 Lonsdale Road, Summertown, Oxford OX2 7EW

Distributed in Pakistan by Pak Book Corporation, 21 Queen's Road, Lahore

Library of Congress Cataloging-in-Publication Data
Weinbaum, Marvin G., 1935–
    Pakistan and Afghanistan : resistance and reconstruction / Marvin
G. Weinbaum.
      p.   cm.
    Includes bibliographical references and index.
    ISBN 0-8133-8807-4 (U.S.)
    ISBN 969-8133-09-7 (Pakistan)
    1. Pakistan—Foreign relations—Afghanistan.   2. Afghanistan—
Foreign relations—Pakistan.   3. Afghanistan—History—Soviet
occupation, 1979–1989.   4. Refugees—Pakistan.   5. Refugees—
Afghanistan.   I. Title.
DS383.5.A3W45   1994
327.54910581'09'048—dc20   93-49473
                                                                                                           CIP

Printed and bound in the United States of America

The paper used in this publication meets the requirements
of the American National Standard for Permanence of Paper
for Printed Library Materials Z39.48-1984.

10   9   8   7   6   5   4   3   2   1

To the Memory of Louis Dupree

Contents

Preface and Acknowledgments

This book grows out of almost a quarter century of scholarly interest and personal fascination with the people and politics of Pakistan and Afghanistan. Over much of that time, I have tried to be a discerning observer of the critical part played by Pakistan in helping the Afghan mujahidin to sustain their resistance, ultimately prevailing over the Soviet Union and the communist government in Kabul. I have been anxious to understand the influence of the conflict on Pakistan, particularly to weigh the refugees' impact on the host society. More recently my attention has been drawn to Pakistan's continuing role in the struggle by the victorious forces to establish political authority and legitimacy, and rehabilitate their liberated country. It is impossible to take note of these developments without also asking what the consequences are for Pakistan and the region if the Afghans succeed or fail to rebuild their state and its economy.

As a political scientist, I have a strong inclination to look for generalizations that can be drawn from the political events under study. The implications for conflict resolution and political integration cross-nationally in the region or wider developing world are of particular interest. What patterns of action are found, for example, that could instruct our study of resistance movements, political refugees, and the politics of rehabilitation and reconstruction? Also, how do they inform us about the policies of small states when they find themselves caught up in regional conflicts and a global competition, and face chronic problems of protecting both territorial integrity and domestic political integration? How can they profit from the status of client state without compromising traditional security concerns? And, of course, since ethnic fractionalization cum nationalism in Afghanistan follows a post-cold war phenomenon registered globally, there is a natural interest in gaining some insights into what precipitated this outcome and how a modus operandi might be reached that preserves the state or manages relations among de facto or de jure separate political entities.

On inspection, the events that began with the Soviet invasion and ended with attempts to form an Islamic government in Kabul often seem *sui generis*. One has only to point to the character of the Afghans and their resistance to communism, to Pakistan's international role, and to the competition between Moscow and Washington to find much that is not only time bound but seems to have little application to or meaning in

x   Preface and Acknowledgments

other settings. Even in the Afghans' ethnic and sectarian divisions, no good parallels are to be found. Thus, despite the dramatic force of the events, no overarching theories or testable hypotheses about major power behavior and guerrilla warfare are indicated.

All the same, the book will suggest, if we need to be reminded, that the West has regularly underestimated the will and capacity of resistance movements. The Afghan experience is a good illustration of how peoples who differ along significant social lines can rally together in the face of common external enemies. It will also show that leaders who are dedicated, able, and ruthless, in this instance among the Islamists or the communists, can defy predictions about their staying power and political reach. Pakistan may be a textbook case of how to maneuver in gaining access to military, economic, and political resources from the West, mainly the United States. In its response to the Soviet invasion of Afghanistan, Pakistan's policies inform us about how client states can also maneuver their patrons, succeed in maintaining older ties, and mitigate, as in the case of the Soviet Union, the provocations that alliances may create.

Surely, there is much in the events described here that humbles us in our ability to make predictions. Few of us were convinced that the Soviets would ever relinquish their grip. Nor were we then or now very confident in our expectations about how power would configure once the Islamic forces had taken power. Indeed, we seem most to have underestimated the power and influence of the more universal Islamic factors and overestimated the constraints of traditional authority figures and norms.

Not until the conflict was in its end-game, moreover, was there sufficient appreciation of the potential impact in ideas and personnel on the rest of the region. The victory of the mujahidin may indeed have been a catalyst in the eventual breakup of the Soviet Union. But it may also be of major consequence in the radicalization of much of the Middle East. The Afghan war may influence the possibilities for democracy and territorial integrity in Pakistan and immediately affect the chances of a compromise settlement on the Kashmir issue. The latter may of course be critical in determining whether Pakistan and India, as nuclear states, are going to realize a modus vivendi for the foreseeable future.

Materials for this book were gathered during several visits to Pakistan. One more lengthy stay, from late 1989 through mid-1990 in Peshawar, was made possible by a Fulbright award designated for the study of Afghan refugees. Briefer research trips to Pakistan took place in 1982, 1985, 1988, 1992, and 1993. The full roster of Pakistanis and Afghans who helped shape my ideas and provided many of the findings for this study would be too lengthy to present. But high on the list would be such people as Mushahid Hussain, Hedayat Arsala, Abdul Aziz Farough, Rahimullah Yousefzai, Sabahuddin Kushkaki, Nasim Jawad, Sajjad Hayder, Baba Momand, Abdul Rashid, Suliman Shah, Haji Syed Daud, Nasim Zehra Akhlaque, Hussain Momand, Farid Hakim, Mawahid Hussain Shah, Yusuf Nuristani, Brigadier (retd.) Noor Husain, and Mohammad Idris. Naim Majrooh and, earlier, his martyred father, Sayd Majrooh, warrant special appreciation. Particular recognition must also go to Imtiaz Bokhari, Fazil ul-Rahman, Tariq Husain, Mohammad Umar Khan, and Najam Rafique at the Center for Strategic Studies in Islamabad. Among academics whom I first met in Pakistan I want to single out for thanks Rasul Bakhsh Rais, Moonis Ahmar, Pervaiz Cheema, Naim Qurishi, Ijaz Galani, Ashraf Ghani, Hasan-Askari Rizvi, Azmat Hayat, and Rasul Amin.

This book would surely have not been possible without the assistance and encouragement of large numbers of officials with the U.S. Consulate in Peshawar, the U.S. Embassy in Islamabad, and the U.S. Agency for International Development in Peshawar and Islamabad. I especially profited from discussions with Jerry Feierstein, Craig Karp, Dan Larson, Terry Pflaumer, Brad Hanson, Jonathan Addison, Larry Crandal, Al Nehoda, and Hank Cushing. Invaluable support in so many ways was provided by the U.S. Educational Foundation in Islamabad and its principal figures, Peter Dodd and Ali Imram Afaqi. The same should be said about Lela Margiou and Jay Gurian of the U.S. Information Service in Peshawar. And for their long-time assistance and friendship, Amanullah and Imtiaz with the U.S. Embassy in Islamabad deserve mention and thanks. In the expatriate and relief aid community, I want to acknowledge Peter Rees, Stephen Mastny, Carla Brissman, Joe Steele, Andrew Wilder, the late Dominique Vergos, and Nancy Dupree. I also owe much to Richard and Nancy Newell, with whom my wife and I shared the Fulbright House in Peshawar. The Newells have been for more than 20 years a source of insight about Afghanistan and have provided strong encouragement for this project. Closer to home, I wish to acknowledge my colleague at the University of Illinois, Mobin Shorish, for helping me toward a better understanding of the Afghans.

Also in the United States, for their helpful comments on earlier or preliminary versions of the manuscript, former Ambassador to Pakistan Robert Oakley, Ambassador to the Afghan Interim Government Peter Tomsen, Howard Wirsing, Leo Rose, and Chris and Eliza Van Hollan deserve mention. Incalculable are the years of discussion with the late Arnold Raphel, a good friend and extraordinary diplomat. For permission to use materials published in another version, I wish to thank the editors of the *The Middle East Journal, Asian Survey*, and the now regrettably ended American Universities Field Staff *Reports.*

As in so many other of my writing projects, I do not know how much I would have accomplished without the editorial assistance and support of my wife. Though Peshawar is always a difficult city for a Western woman, Francine was with me for most of my stay in 1989–90. She used the time productively and creatively in teaching English at the North-West Frontier Province (NWFP) Agricultural University and also becoming involved in U.S. Information Service/American Center activities. For assistance in formatting the book, I am greatly thankful to Phyllis Koerner, Merrily Shaw, and Debra Anderson.

The dedication of this book to the late Louis Dupree acknowledges that among the many people who have inspired and instructed me about the region over the years, he was clearly at the forefront. Dupree's writings were for most of us interested in Afghanistan—before it took international center stage—rich in detail and color. Through the 1960s and 1970s, Dupree's American Universities Field Staff *Reports* were often about all that a scholar had to turn to for secondary source material. The hospitality shown to those visiting him and Nancy at their house in Kabul is legendary. Louis' interpretations and commentary reflected not only his storehouse of information but his ever-playful, irreverent humor. Above all, it was his love of scholarship and deep affection for the culture and people of the region that we noted and admired. Regrettably, he failed to live to witness the fall of Kabul to the mujahidin, although he would have been greatly saddened to see the diminishment of the Afghan state and the continued suffering of its citizens.

Marvin G. Weinbaum
University of Illinois at Urbana-Champaign

Pakistan and Afghanistan

1

Historical Backdrop

There has been much to distinguish Pakistan and Afghanistan. They are unequal in economic status and dissimilar in their total ethnic composition and constitutional makeup. Pakistanis like to stress their obligations to the Afghan people for reasons of faith and history, but the relationship between governments of the two countries has never been cordial. Despite a steady interchange of people and goods, strains existed long before the communist coup in Kabul in April 1978 and the Soviet invasion of Afghanistan in December 1979. Most of their disagreements have been traceable to the colonial-fashioned border between the two countries. Economic resentments and provocation, and cross-border political agitation have sustained tensions. Aside from national interests, the very ethos of the two states stand in some contrast.

The ideal and rationale of the Pakistani state is an Islamic consensus that is expected to transcend geographic and ethnic divisions. Traditionally, the Afghan state has found its legitimacy in satisfying and balancing the interests of competitive ethnic and tribal communities. The relationship between ethnicity and politics has, then, been virtually reversed from one state to the other. As Raja Ehsan Aziz writes: "While Pakistan upheld the Islamic basis of national unity, de-emphasizing ethnic-regional differentiation at home and championing Pan-Islamism internationally, the Afghan politics of survival revolved largely around Pakhtun ethnicity including Pakhtun tribal support. [In addition, the two] were structured differently and placed at very dissimilar levels of development."[1]

Under the Monarchy

A history of antagonism and discontinuities in relations began not very auspiciously shortly after Pakistan's creation in 1947 when

Afghanistan's delegation to the United Nations alone cast its votes against Pakistan's admission to the world organization. The Kabul government's antagonism toward the new country carved from British India focused on the disputed international borderline drawn by Sir Mortimer Durand in 1893. Once Afghanistan obtained its independence in foreign affairs from the British in 1919, Afghan leaders rejected the border which they felt had unfairly separated the Pashtuns, Afghanistan's largest ethnic group, from their brethren living in India's northwest frontier. The call was for the British and their Pakistani successors to give independence to the Pashtun population or, alternatively, to permit it to join the Afghan state.

Tension between the two states continued over the next few years. In 1949 it flared up with the accidental bombing of a village on the Afghan side of the border. Despite an apology from the Pakistan government, overtures were rejected. In large measure because of these political differences, Afghanistan failed to receive requested military assistance from the United States in the late 1940s and again in the mid-1950s. Pakistan, in a defensive arrangement with the West designed against the Soviet Union, had won the right to block the arming of its antagonistic neighbor. Especially with the advent of the cold war, Pakistan, the more powerful, appeared as a preferred partner in Washington's strategic policy of containing the Soviets.

The cause of Pashtunistan became especially popular under the influence of Mohammad Daoud, cousin of the Afghan monarch, first as Afghan minister of war and then, beginning in 1953, as prime minister. The ruling royal family held Pakistan responsible for Afghanistan's economic woes and security problems. Above all, the championing of a separate state for Pashtuns detached from Pakistan conveniently served as a response to what was perceived as Pakistan's efforts to dominate its neighbor and as a means for the Kabul government to extend its popularity with its own influential Pashtuns, whose tribes dominated the border areas.

Over his ten years as prime minister, Daoud's insistence on pressing the issue brought reaction in Pakistan in the form of economic embargoes and the closing of diplomatic missions. The border was closed in 1950 and again in 1955, leaving landlocked Afghanistan without its most accustomed trade route—to the port of Karachi. By 1960, relations had reached a low point, and the possibility of a general war emerged from the military incursions, propaganda campaigns, and economic retaliations.

Limited fighting occurred in 1960 and 1961 in the tribal border areas leading to a break off in relations in September 1961 (diplomatic ties had been severed in 1957 as well). Border traffic was closed, including the free movement of Pashtun nomads who regularly crossed the 1,500 mile border in their seasonal migrations. This halt in traffic with its accompanying hardship to the Afghan economy did not end until June 1963. It pointed up the strong dependence of Afghanistan on Pakistan but also forced some transfer of this dependence to the Soviet Union. Moscow gave strong encouragement for the Afghan regime to lean on its northern neighbor both for military equipment and a trade outlet. When Daoud was finally forced to resign in March 1963, it was in large measure over the royal family's tiring of the Pashtunistan issue and its impact on Afghan economy and society.

While Pakistan has looked longingly at Afghanistan as a natural friend and ally, based mainly on shared Islamic beliefs and some common ethnic identifications, Afghanistan has viewed Pakistan with the suspicion that goes with dependence on a wealthier neighbor who, consciously or not, adopts a patronizing attitude—viewing Afghans as a simple folk who require guidance. Whatever the reasons, the two countries' relationships never became wholly stable and normal, and thus contrasted with Pakistan's successes with Iran and Turkey. Even the 1963 Tehran agreement reopening the Pakistan-Afghanistan border was only a short-term arrangement for restoring diplomatic ties, not one for developing a more predictable and smooth relationship.

With the border reopened and formal relations restored, Afghanistan, under a new democratic constitution established in 1965, took a more relaxed view of Pakistan. Iran's Mohammad Reza Shah had been a middleman in the restoration of diplomatic ties. The period of relative normalcy between the countries coincided with increased preoccupation inside Afghanistan with parliamentary and electoral politics. The Pashtunistan issue was relegated to the sidelines in this experiment with representative, though not effective, government. The Kabul authorities officially sided with Pakistan in its 1965 war with India, a fact that surprised many, given the commonalty of disputes based on territory that India and Afghanistan had with Pakistan. Six years later, when India had entered the war against Pakistan in the country's east wing, Afghan leaders again refrained from taking advantage of an Islamabad government preoccupied by the conflict.

Considerable progress in normalizing relations between Kabul and Islamabad seemed likely late in the democratic period which ended with the monarchy's fall in July 1973. Pakistan's prime minister Zulfikar Ali Bhutto had apparently gotten along with Afghan king Zahir Shah, whom Bhutto had visited shortly after taking office in Islamabad. Afghanistan, under the leadership of prime minister Mosa Shafiq, had concluded its controversial Helmand waters agreement with Iran, and was ready to work out an agreement with Bhutto. Authorities in Kabul only wanted some assurances that the Pakistanis would respect Pashtun culture in the country's North-West Frontier Province (NWFP) and adjacent tribal areas. (Over a longer period Pakistan had tried to keep its Pashtuns loyal through preferential development expenditures to the NWFP and the recruitment into the armed forces of men from the tribal areas.) In the months before its fall, the Shafiq government signaled that it had no strong economic demands. Bhutto was amenable so long as a political understanding with Pakistan's Pashtun champion Abdul Wali Khan was on track. However, when that failed to work and Bhutto cracked down on the province, the rapprochement failed.

Daoud's Republic

The return of Daoud to power in 1973 following a leftist military coup convinced Pakistan's leaders that tensions would again rise. Daoud referred to the Pashtunistan issue in his initial address after assuming power on July 17, 1973. But the topic was not pushed again until the Lahore Summit Conference of Islamic States in February 1974, where the issue was raised to the discomfort of several attending heads of state.

Bhutto's anxieties over the issue were understandable. Pakistan had less than two years earlier lost its east wing to Bangladesh. Bhutto had his mind most of all on the looming insurgencies in the NWFP and Baluchistan. In the 1970 elections, Bhutto's People's Party had swept the Punjab and Sind but failed to win a single seat in the two provinces bordering on Afghanistan—where popular support appeared to go to pro-autonomy parties. The 1973 constitution, which vested considerable power in the provinces, recognized the need to respond to local demands. Even while constitutionally allowing for greater autonomy, Bhutto's aim was to bring the NWFP under fuller government control.

Bhutto believed that much of the tension in the NWFP early in 1974, where over 70 explosions occurred in Peshawar and its vicinity, was the responsibility mainly of saboteurs trained by the Afghans. He insisted that the Afghan regime was in fact behind all the troubles on the frontier. The Pakistan government was in particular angered by the sanctuary and financial assistance given to Baluch separatists in Daoud's Afghanistan. Determined not just to neutralize the Afghan campaign, Bhutto sought to devise counter measures that would deter Daoud. The plan was to create pressures within Afghanistan that could be used to reduce Daoud's urge to pursue the Pashtunistan issue. Daoud's government would be shown its vulnerability and the high price of any designs on Pakistan.[2] An anti-Kabul propaganda center whose goal was to destablize Daoud's new regime was established in Pakistan. But Bhutto had more direct action in mind.

There had been at least two attempted coups against the Daoud regime in 1974 from leftist factions in the military. Pakistan denied its involvement. Within a year, however, the collusion of the Islamabad governments with enemies of the Daoud government was unmistakable. Going beyond the traditional policy of supporting tribal dissidents in the border areas as a means to counter Afghan irredentism, Bhutto agreed to give protection and military training to Afghan Islamists whose explicit aim was to overthrow the regime in Kabul.[3] When leading radical Islamists, Gulbuddin Hekmatyar and Kabul University Professor Burhanuddin Rabbani, fled to Pakistan in 1974, Bhutto welcomed them, quickly recognizing how these young activists and their followers could suit Pakistan's aims. Between 1973 and 1977, Pakistan trained an estimated 5,000 dissidents in secret military camps, most of them young Muslim dissidents and sympathizers.[4] The military's General Nasirullah Barber is credited with creating an organized Afghan resistance.[5] Aid was also channeled to the dissident Afghan Hazara community in central Afghanistan.

Hekmatyar was formerly a firebrand fundamentalist student at Kabul University. Ironically, it was Daoud's overthrow of Zahir Shah that had made Hekmatyar's political career possible. Hekmatyar had been imprisoned for the murder of a left-wing student and was released with the fall of the monarchy. Also among those fleeing to Pakistan when Daoud deposed the monarchy was a young engineering student, Ahmad Shah Masoud. He joined the Muslim youth movement in exile headed by Professor Rabbani but returned to Afghanistan in 1975 to organize forces against the Daoud regime.

Several local insurrections were planned. The best known uprising against the Daoud government occurred in the Panjshir area north of Kabul on July 21, 1975. The insurgency was put down after a few days, and many of its participants were captured. Daoud accused Pakistan of fomenting the uprising. There was good evidence, despite the denials, that the Bhutto government was responsible for arming and financing the rebels, even for the timing of the incident.[6] The surviving militants took refuge in Peshawar, where they were allowed to organize their followers and open offices. In Pakistan, the Islamists enjoyed support from Bhutto's People's Party, the military, and the religious parties; the Afghan insurgents could also count on Saudi Arabian sources for money.[7] Not unimportantly for Bhutto, the Afghan Islamist elements opposed Daoud on the desirability of creating an independent Pashtunistan. Their ideas of popular Islam had little place for ethnic or tribal nationalism. Hekmatyar's Hezb-i-Islami (Islamic Party), from the outset the preferred group of Pakistan's military, rejected not only the nationalist ideology of Pashtunistan but, in the name of Muslim solidarity, the political axis between Kabul and New Delhi.

There was little resemblance between the Afghan religious hard-liners, devoted to building mass followings, and Pakistan's major religious party, the Jama'at-i-Islami, never successful in mobilizing large numbers of voters. Yet Bhutto's policies giving aid and comfort to the Afghan Islamists coincided with the aims of Pakistan's conservative religious elements, which were displeased with Daoud's left-leaning politics and his crackdown on Afghanistan's religious groups. Bhutto, by his willingness to protect Afghan dissident religious elements, was also very likely trying to solidify closer relations between Pakistan and Saudi Arabia.[8] These policies, moreover, coincided with those of Iran's Shah. The Tehran government was anxious about the Afghan government's Soviet connections and Kabul's anti-monarchic views. Revived assistance by Daoud to Pashtuns, but especially dissidents in Baluchistan in their fight for autonomy if not independence, also had implications for Iran's restive Baluch population. The Shah, in fact, applied military and economic pressures, including the deportation of many Afghan laborers from Iran, eventually forcing Daoud to seek reconciliation with Tehran.[9] For both Bhutto and Iran's Shah, the return of former king Zahir Shah would have been desirable.

The Afghan government responded with retaliatory propaganda aimed specifically at Bhutto.[10] Daoud tried to make things more difficult for Pakistan by stepping up aid to rebels in Pakistan's Baluchistan. Still more, the Kabul government used what means it had to aggravate political squabbles in Pakistan's NWFP.[11] Yet, in little more than a year after the failed Panjshir rebellion, the prospects for bilateral relations had greatly improved.

By 1976, Daoud no longer saw the advantage in pursuing the Pashtunistan policy, and Bhutto came to realize the possibility of weakening Afghanistan's close ties to India and the Soviet Union. He sought to convince the Afghans that the two countries were historically linked and that Afghanistan had a bright future if it put aside old suspicions and sought cooperation with Islamabad. An agreement on Pashtunistan was close to completion in early 1977. Daoud's decision to undertake a state visit to Pakistan in March 1977 provides clear evidence that he had modified his hard-line stand on Pashtunistan. The Afghan president was prepared, de facto, to recognize the Durand Line as the international boundary. To show good faith, Afghanistan would no longer allow Baluch and Pashtun guerrillas to use the country as a sanctuary. In return, Bhutto promised to implement the guarantees of regional autonomy in Pakistan's 1973 Constitution. Bhutto offered to release Wali Khan and other imprisoned National Awami Party leaders from the NWFP and Baluchistan—including Ataullah Mengal, Khair Baksh Marri, and Ghaus Bakhsh Bizenjo, whose detainment since 1973 had set off an insurrection in Baluchistan still ongoing in 1977. There was even some discussion that Pakistan might agree to train Afghan officers. These understandings were the concrete measures that were expected to rapidly accelerate Daoud's shift to the right in domestic and foreign policies.[12]

No less critical to the shift were policies of Iran's Shah. Beyond once again offering his good offices to effect a normalization, the Shah promised $3 billion in development aid to Afghanistan. The financial assistance was significant not only for its size—more than the country had received from all donors over a 30-year period—but for the promised construction of a rail line between Kabul and the Iranian border, directly linking Afghanistan to the Persian Gulf, and offering the Afghans an alternative to the lengthy road route that ran to Karachi. Iran had its own objectives, of course. Afghanistan was to be induced to reduce Soviet influence, which had become more pronounced after the 1973 coup.

The incentives presented were welcomed in Kabul. Daoud was determined to distance himself further from the Afghan leftists who had brought him to power. Without necessarily alienating Moscow, he sought to create alternatives to the Soviets, who not only had penetrated the Afghan economy and military but were also making broad inroads into the culture and society. Better relations with his Muslim neighbors would provide a counterweight and, above all, improve chances for massive financial support from the rich Arab oil-producing states, an aim not unlike the economic salvation sought by Bhutto. At the same time, Daoud expected ties with India could probably be maintained as well.

The normalization did not go smoothly. Daoud had difficulty delivering on a promise to return to Pakistan those Baluchis and Pashtuns given sanctuary in Afghanistan. In Daoud's March 1977 visit to Islamabad as well as to Delhi and Riyadh, he met with Baluch representatives and informed them that their followers would have to leave Afghanistan by the end of April.[13] However, several thousand Baluch refugees resisted being repatriated to Pakistan. Also, a number of the key figures in the two major opposition movements refused to go along with the agreement, leading to splits within these groups. The Baluch opposition leaders, it had been expected, would be brought into a broad government coalition where they would adopt a less militant position on the Baluch separatism and Pashtunistan.

Negotiations between Daoud and Bhutto were nevertheless close to success when Bhutto's regime unexpectedly lost its legitimacy in the irregularities alleged in Pakistan's March 1977 National Assembly elections. By July 1977, after months of street demonstrations, the prime minister had been removed from office by General Zia ul-Haq. General Zia restated the desire for brotherly ties with Afghanistan, and Daoud signaled to Zia the same willingness to shelve the Pashtunistan issue, although he balked at demands for formal acceptance of the Durand Line.[14] Also, even with the improved relations, Daoud had not eased up on his enemies among the religious right. In February 1978, a court trial of 25 Afghans held for treason pointed an accusing finger at fundamentalist groups operating out of Pakistan.[15] In any event, before a final agreement could be reached, Daoud was himself ousted in the communist coup of April 1978.

The Communist Era Begins

Initially at least, there was an attractiveness for Kabul's new Marxist regime in the cause of Pashtunistan, especially because of its anti-Pakistani thrust. The dominant and more Pashtun-dominated Khalqi faction in control in Kabul was anxious to "sidetrack popular discontent by adventurism in foreign policy."[16] At one point Hafizullah Amin, the foreign minister and preeminent Khalqi leader, is alleged to have brought up with the Indian envoy to Kabul the prospect of a secret pact to divide Pakistan.[17] While not anxious for a major war, this policy suited the Soviets, who were involved in instigating a deterioration of Afghan relations with Pakistan as a means of increasing the Kabul government's dependence.

For a time, Pakistani border settlements came under shelling from the Afghan side. Yet under President Mohammad Taraki, the Afghan regime failed to press the Pashtunistan issue. In fact, relations with Pakistan seemed on the upgrade; General Zia visited Kabul late in 1978, and Taraki promised a return visit. Even after the Amin-ordered murder of Taraki in September 1979 and Amin's succession to the presidency, serious overtures were made to normalize relations. Amin was desperate to consolidate his power, not only against a growing domestic resistance to the regime but before the Soviets—whose plans he had foiled— succeeded in his removal. If Pakistan would agree to withdraw its support for the armed dissidents, Amin appeared ready to accept explicitly the Durand Line.

Standing in the way of any real improvement in relations was the spreading insurgency against the communist regime, begun in summer 1978, and Pakistan's policy of harboring the resistance parties and allowing them to acquire weapons. The Pakistan military helped the resistance in its civil war against the Kabul government by establishing bases in Miran Shah, Parachinar, Momand, and Bajaur agencies inside Pakistan. Islamabad also allowed the mujahidin or holy warriors to set up offices in Peshawar. Many Afghan groups did so, joining the already present Hezb-i-Islami, Jamiat-i-Islami (Islamic Society) and Harakat-i-Enqilab-i-Islami (Islamic Revolutionary Movement). Ahmad Shah Masoud, one of many guerrilla commanders inside Afghanistan, affiliated his band of fighters with Rabbani's Jamiat-i-Islami.

Pakistan had also become involved in conflict through admitting Afghan refugees—over 150,000 by the summer of 1979, and double that number prior to the Soviet invasion in late December. Massive international assistance had not yet begun, but Saudi Arabia, in support of several religious parties among the Pakistanis and Afghans, was already giving financial help to the resistance fighters and refugees in Pakistan. As seen by Islamist activists across the region, Afghanistan was essentially a heathen state, and Pakistan had assumed the role of ideological bastion, destined to further both the Afghan and Muslim cause.

Notes

1. *Central Asian Survey*, Vol. 7, nos. 2/3 (1988), p. 155.

2. Abdur Rehman Gariftar, *Frontier Post* (Peshawar), August 21, 1989.

3. Barnett R. Rubin, "Afghanistan: The Fragmentation of a State and Chances for Reconstruction," a paper written for the U.S. Institute of Peace, September 1989, p. 8.

4. Girardet, *Afghanistan; the Soviet War* (New York: St. Martin's Press, 1985), p. 166.

5. Khawar Malik, *Frontier Post* , February 7, 1992.

6. Girardet, *Afghanistan*, p. 167. Also, Mushtahid Hussein, *Frontier Post*, September 17, 1989.

7. Oliver Roy, *The Nation* (Lahore), May 7, 1989.

8. Rubin, *Afghanistan: The Fragmentation*, p. 8.

9. Hafizullah Emadi, "Durand Line and Afghan-Pak Relations," *Economic and Political Weekly*, July 14, 1990, pp. 15–16.

10. Louis Dupree, *AUFS Field Staff International*, South Asia Series, Vol. 18, no. 8, (September 1974), p. 13.

11. Lawrence Ziring, *Pakistan: The Enigma of Political Development* (Boulder: Westview Press, 1980), p. 148.

12. Selig Harrison, *Foreign Policy*, no. 41 (Winter 1980-81), p. 168. Also *Far East Economic Review*, January 30, 1981, p. 33.

13. Fred Halliday,"Revolution in Afghanistan," *New Left Review* (December 1978), p. 31.

14. Henry S. Bradsher, *Afghanistan and the Soviet Union* (Durham, N.C.: Duke University Press, 1983), p. 63; also A. Samad Ghaus, quoted by Bruce Amstutz, *Afghanistan; The First Five Years of Soviet Occupation* (Washington, D.C.: National Defense University Press, 1986), p. 490, note 100.

15. Anthony Hyman, *Afghanistan Under Soviet Domination, 1964-1981* (New York: St. Martin's Press, 1982), p. 71.

16. Ibid., p. 158.

17. Bradsher, *Afghanistan and the Soviet Union*, p. 122.

2

The Strategic Stakes

Without Pakistan there could have been no Afghan resistance movement and little prospect for its success against the Soviets. The sanctuary of Pakistan allowed the mujahidin to organize military operations, and the Islamabad government gave them largely unhindered cross-border access. Pakistan became a conduit for multinational arms deliveries to those fighting in Afghanistan. It also helped the many resistance parties coalesce into something of a distinct political force. Pakistan was indispensable in drawing international attention to the mujahidin cause and led the condemnation of the Soviet armed intervention in international fora. In negotiations leading to the withdrawal of Soviet military forces, Pakistan assumed a pivotal role. Pakistan's open border enabled more than 3.2 million Afghans to find refuge and relief aid in camps and, unrestricted in their movement, to participate in the economy of Pakistan's cities.

Pakistan's championing of the resistance struggle and its embrace of refugees was also purposeful, with geostrategic and domestic imperatives motivating Pakistan's leaders to pursue several major objectives during the course of the war. Yet much to their disappointment and frustration, these goals were at times incompatible. The first goal was the removal of Soviet forces from Afghanistan. Pakistan's military planners worried about the possibility of facing a coordinated attack from Afghan and Soviet troops on one front and the Indian military on the other. Even if an armed communist invasion of Pakistan was a remote possibility, intimidation was not. There was deep concern that Moscow, through material support, would instigate ethnic separatist movements in Pakistan's Baluchistan and the North-West Frontier provinces.

The second objective was the early return of Afghan refugees. The government in Islamabad facilitated and supplemented the massive international aid program that sustained the refugee community, and a broad consensus held that the Afghans be allowed to stay until they could return with security. Managing the burden of refugees, however, left Pakistan dependent on continuing help from the international community. Increasingly, moreover, Pakistanis viewed Afghan exiles as having an undesirable impact on their economy and society. The Afghan resistance groups and the community of refugees were held responsible in large measure for a breakdown of law and order, and economic dislocations. The Afghan issue also punctuated the domestic political dialogue, sharpening an already bitter discourse.

Third, the Afghan involvement contributed to regime survival by helping to neutralize General Zia ul-Haq's critics. Many doubt that the martial law regime would have lasted so long without the war and the international assistance it attracted. Almost overnight, Zia became an international statesman. As the country's president, he led Pakistan from its diplomatic isolation of the late 1970s to international leadership in the resistance to armed aggression. In return for the risks and obligations Pakistan claimed to have incurred in its unwavering support for the Afghan resistance, the Islamabad government received generous financial and diplomatic backing. As the war dragged on, Pakistan's role as conduit for arms and administrator of humanitarian aid carried some liabilities; but these were outweighed by the benefits—the leakage of dollars and goods into Pakistan's domestic economy. The expanding economy, bolstered by foreign assistance programs, enabled the Zia regime to win public tolerance if not wide popularity. With this assistance, especially from the United States, Zia could both buy off and suppress his opposition.

Fourth, a dedicated anti-communist, Zia intended to use the war and Pakistan's role as a front-line state to defend Islam against Soviet-sponsored communism. Indeed, at times it seemed that Zia would not be content with merely aiding Afghan Muslims, but was driven by a mission to extend the struggle across the Oxus to the Soviet Central Asian republics. Elements in Pakistan's military encouraged the view that militant Muslim movements spawned by the Afghan conflict could eventually reach in and destabilize the republics. Perhaps more important, the future alliance with an Islamic government in Kabul, together with similar understandings with Iran and possibly even Turkey, gave promise of new offensive options against India through broad military coordination. A cooperative Afghanistan could provide Pakistan, always vulnerable to superior Indian military forces, with the military assests and strategic capabilities presumably possible through greater geopolitical depth.

The fifth, and perhaps paramount aim for Pakistan's policy makers, was the desire to block the revival of Afghan nationalism and gain recognition of the international boundary. President Zia hoped to realize this outcome through the creation of a postwar Afghanistan that, while not necessarily a client state, would feel beholden to Pakistan. Afghan leaders would focus their energies on reconstruction and be preoccupied with Islamic goals in lieu of ethnic and tribal ambitions. A friendly government would also have no truck with New Delhi. Zia felt that by standing at the forefront in the war, Pakistan had won the right to a regime of its choice in Kabul.

Because the Afghan war was, above all, a national security issue, the Pakistani military assumed a leading role. With support of Afghan resistance forces meant to be disguised when possible, it was necessarily a clandestine operation. As such, the major responsibility fell to Pakistan's military intelligence division, the Inter-Service Intelligence (ISI). The ISI's assignment to implement policy was understandable. Less predictable was Islamabad's willingness to allow it to also design Pakistan's Afghan policy.

Pakistan's Resolve

Until the Soviet military intervention in December 1979, Afghanistan had appeared to Pakistan as largely a political irritant, a petulant and resentful neighbor. Afghan irredentism, represented by the call for a Pashtunistan, while potentially a challenge to Pakistan's national integrity, was considered manageable. Economically and militarily, Afghanistan was no match for Pakistan. Pakistan's adversarial relations with India and domestic regional instability posed more serious problems for the country's national security. The deployment of tens of thousands of Soviet troops, together with the arming of a government of Moscow's own making in Kabul, altered this picture by presenting what was perceived to be a geostrategic threat to Pakistan, involving its security and national integrity. In the minds of some, the Soviets planned to use Afghanistan as a stepping stone to the Indian Ocean in the legendary Russian quest for a warm water port.

If, indeed, these were the intentions of the Soviet Union, then the presumed route was through Pakistan's Baluchistan port of Gwadar and hence, perhaps, to the control of the oil wealth of the Persian Gulf. In their worst moments, Pakistani planners could imagine having to fight a two-front war. In this scenario Pakistan's army would face a pincer movement as the Soviets and their Afghan allies were joined by traditional adversary India. Even if the Soviets had no intention of making a direct move against Pakistan, the danger existed that a war that dragged on could easily spill over, drawing in Pakistan as a combatant. A victory by the communists would leave a permanent threat on the border, especially since it was likely to include an indefinite Soviet military presence in Afghanistan.

Once the Soviet military became bogged down in fighting the Afghan resistance, the possibility of a frontal attack on Pakistan diminished—if it had ever existed. More likely than outright aggression against Pakistan was the possibility of the country's becoming the victim of subversion aimed at weakening its resolve on Afghanistan, mainly with threats of abetting provincial secessionist movements. Most serious was the possible assistance to ethnic groups with long-standing grievances against the central government. Likely candidates were dissident elements in the Sindh and pro-communist Baluch nationalists. A strategy based on infiltration of arms and subversives, even if it did not succeed in dismembering the country, would question the regime's ability to maintain law and order, and undermine its authority.

The settlement of the refugees, most of them in the NWFP, posed another kind of threat to the country's prosperity and security. Many in Pakistan feared the long-term effect on the society of having to absorb the refugees, who might play a disruptive role in the country's politics. A heavily armed resistance and large refugee community could raise the level of violence in politics and everyday life. By intensifying ethnic feelings, displaced Afghans, in coalition with Pakistan's Pathans (called Pashtuns in Afghanistan), could conceivably acquire a domestic political voice which, if denied, could increase separatist thinking. Pakistan's vulnerability to ethnic pressures for greater autonomy in the NWFP seemed especially real in view of the military-run government's questionable legitimacy in the absence of a popular electoral mandate.

Pakistan's determination to oppose communist domination of Afghanistan and willingness to block any Soviet military adventures represented strategic objectives convergent with those of the United States. In effect, Pakistan assumed the role of strategic ally in an effort to contain and, if possible, defeat the Soviet Union. For Washington, the Afghan conflict appeared as the latest, surely one of the most serious battles in a cold war intensified by Brezhnev's increasingly aggressive policies in the Third World. Pakistan felt little of the same military and ideological rivalry with the Soviets. Nevertheless, the Pakistani military saw itself as filling a role resulting from the lack of a countervailing force in the region, especially while the United States and Iran were preoccupied with their confrontation. In remaining steadfast against the perceived enemies of Islam, Pakistan's leaders were aware that they could be establishing a precedent and strengthening the will of countries in the Persian Gulf region, possibly the next Soviet targets. Rather than directly confront the Soviet Union, Pakistan could funnel military assistance to the mujahidin and give them sanctuary. The Islamabad government had no intention of being drawn into a shooting war with the Soviets or their Afghan clients; as mentioned, it hoped to reap benefits from Moscow's threat, mainly by obtaining foreign aid for Pakistan's deteriorating defense capabilities without becoming an extension of the war's battleground.

Hesitation on Pakistan's part did not reflect any doubts about the country's necessary adversarial role, at least for General Zia. He believed firmly that the Soviet presence in Afghanistan constituted a threat not only to Pakistan but to the entire region, including Iran and even India. But whatever the invasion meant to others, Zia felt that no other country had a larger stake in the outcome. On a personal level, security concerns aside, Zia's dedication in opposing the Soviet military intervention was rooted in deeply felt Islamic beliefs and the moral obligation to give aid to those contending against an "aggressive godless creed."[1] The Pakistani leader might well have pursued the course of assisting the Afghan mujahidin without outside help. His regime was always proud to announce that it had stood up against the Soviet invasion a year and a half before a formal U.S. aid package was initiated. Still, Zia was anxious to maximize international support, to avoid assuming the risks and costs alone. If at all possible, he did not want the war to be seen abroad as solely Pakistan's responsibility.[2]

To its credit, Pakistan succeeded in building and holding together through the 1980s an international consensus against the Soviet invasion. Islamabad yearly carried overwhelming majorities in the U.N. General Assembly condemning Soviet actions and, in effect, sanctioning Pakistan's stand in the war. In the first of these resolutions, in January 1980, an emergency session of the General Assembly voted 104 to 18 with 13 abstentions. Support for Pakistan's position increased further. By 1983 Pakistan spearheaded a resolution sponsored by 44 other countries that had 116 in favor of an immediate withdrawal of foreign troops. The number of countries voting in support increased to 122 in 1985 and did not decline through the decade. Although Pakistan indicated that through the United Nations it was ready to open talks on a settlement, and these discussions began in 1982, the Islamabad government maintained its refusal to recognize the regime in Kabul and therefore to negotiate directly with the Afghan government. Above all, Pakistani officials insisted that a negotiated peace should not reward the Soviets for their invasion.

Islamabad successfully countered attempts by the regime in Kabul to gain a sympathetic hearing elsewhere. Despite intense lobbying, the Afghan communists failed to make much headway in gaining diplomatic recognition from countries in the 101-member Non-Aligned Movement. Pakistan also stymied the Kabul government in the Organization of the Islamic Conference (OIC), blocking its claim to the Afghanistan seat. At an OIC meeting soon after the Soviet invasion, Pakistan enunciated and won adoption of the four pillars on which it rested its Afghan policy over the 1980s: Soviet withdrawal, return of Afghan refugees, free choice of a government by the Afghans, and the institution of a nonaligned government in Afghanistan.

Continued diplomatic and material support for Pakistan, the refugees, and the mujahidin could not be taken for granted, however. For all the moral support Pakistan seemed to have mustered against the communists, only Egypt and Saudi Arabia had actually broken relations with the Kabul regime. Not only was much of this international support "hollow and ritualistic," Pakistan could not help but observe inconsistencies even among the Americans. including more deferential policies toward the Soviet Union.[3] International fatigue was bound to set in should the conflict continue indefinitely, especially were disunity among mujahidin elements to become more visible.

Any erosion of international approval for Pakistan's position would certainly have been viewed as a significant setback. It also remained imperative for Islamabad that while it mobilized anti-communist forces, it not forfeit Pakistan's credentials as a nonaligned country. Supported by Moscow, the Kabul regime had used its emissaries to mount a full-scale campaign, mainly in the Third World, to break the back of the body of support for the resistance cause. Privately, the Soviets pressed several Islamic countries friendly to Pakistan to convince the Islamabad government to adopt a more conciliatory approach in peace negotiations.

The Allies

Not long after its creation in 1947, Pakistan assumed a major role in Washington's design to contain the Soviet Union. Linked to the CENTO and SEATO defense pacts in the 1950s, Pakistan importantly bridged U.S.-supported defenses across much of Asia. Later, the Nixon Administration even went so far as to pronounce Pakistan the centerpiece in U.S. policies in the region. Pakistan's pivotal role seemed most confirmed when it helped to facilitate Washington's opening to China in 1971. Once the Shah's regime in Iran was gone, west of Saudi

Arabia there was no pro-Western state clear to Thailand. Pakistan was perceived in some quarters as taking over at least in part Iran's military role in southwest Asia as well as serving as protector of the royal family of Saudi Arabia.[4]

The notion that the Afghan invasion represented the international advance of communism meant that the long-held containment policy could finally be put to a direct test. The timing of the test could not have seemed more inappropriate; leading up to the Soviet invasion, U.S.-Pakistan relations had deteriorated to an all-time low. A year earlier, Pakistani authorities were believed to have badly mishandled and possibly even been complicit in a mob attack that destroyed the American Embassy in Islamabad. American lawmakers strongly disapproved of Pakistan's nuclear program and were uneasy about supporting a regime that had refused to schedule democratic elections since coming to power in July 1977. Washington's pleas to spare the life of former Prime Minister Bhutto, executed in April 1979, had been ignored.

The Carter Administration had imposed a ban on aid to Pakistan in April 1979, a cutoff ostensibly mandated by a reading of the Symington Amendment that required the stoppage of aid where a country's nuclear development ran counter to U.S. polices on proliferation. The United States had also refused to consider a re-scheduling of payments due on Pakistan's external debt and had used its influence to harden the position of other international financial institutions involved in negotiations with Pakistan.[5] Distrust for the United States was meanwhile high over Washington's Middle East policy. With Pakistan's Arab ties strengthened during the 1970s, governments in Islamabad took new interest and showed greater public concern for Islamic issues, naturally including the Palestinian cause.

If the strategic objectives of the United States and Pakistan happened to converge over Afghanistan, they were nonetheless hardly identical. The Carter and then Reagan administrations viewed the Afghan conflict as the latest, most serious battle in the cold war which had been intensified through the late 1970s by Brezhnev's more aggressive policies in the Third World. Pakistan posed a major obstacle to Soviet ambitions, though it may not have been a primary target of communist adventures. Washington's policy sought to bolster Islamabad's poorly disguised assistance to the Afghan resistance though arms deliveries. The United States also hoped to firm up Pakistan's military in order to stiffen its resolve to oppose the Soviets and Afghan communists diplomatically. Initially, at least, there was little thought that the mujahidin might actually prevail; it was enough to keep the resistance alive. Important to this purpose was a substantial U.S. contribution to the international effort to support Pakistan's ability to host Afghan refugees.

Direct military and economic assistance was meant to express Washington's appreciation for Pakistan's tough, unyielding stand. The first offer of aid by President Carter was ridiculed by General Zia. The $400 million over a two-year period was viewed as a paltry sum in view of Pakistan's perceived need and the extent of the obligations to be taken on. A more attractive six-year aid package totaling $3.2 billion in economic and military assistance, including the symbolically important sale of forty F-16A fighter-bombers, was provided in 1981 by the Reagan Administration. Aid was renewed in a second package in 1987 that was scheduled to last six years and held a mix of $1.74 billion in military sales credits on concessional terms and $2.28 billion in economic aid, all on a grant basis. At this level of assistance, Pakistan became the third largest recipient of U.S. aid after Israel and Egypt. Washington also had no choice but to allow Pakistan to siphon off some of the largesse intended for the mujahidin. This process began even before the bilateral aid package was put together, when just weeks after the Soviet invasion, the CIA, drawing on Egyptian goodwill and their stockpiles of Soviet weapons of all varieties, began funneling armaments intended for the Afghan resistance into Pakistan.[6]

The Soviet invasion and the U.S. lead in giving aid also opened doors to other sources of support for Pakistan. Very soon negotiations with the World Bank and International Monetary Fund began to pour in, as did assistance from Japan and Western European countries. By 1981 Pakistan was receiving around $5 billion in foreign aid from all sources. In addition there was the direct relief aid to the Afghan refugees from international agencies.

For Pakistan the Soviet invasion was unsettling, potentially threatening the country's strategic posture and domestic stability. The country was more likely to be an innocent victim than the object of communist aggression. Unlike the United States, Pakistan felt no strong rivalry with the Soviet Union economically, militarily, or ideologically.[7] In the last analysis, whatever the sympathy for the invaded Afghans among Islamabad's policy makers, the war in Afghanistan never became for them Pakistan's prime arena of confrontation—that continued to be reserved for India.

In light of a previous history of U.S. failure to come to the aid of Pakistan in its conflicts with India, few Pakistanis expected, nor was any pledge made, that the United States would aid them militarily should they be attacked, most of all by India. Holding the United States in particular responsible for the loss of East Pakistan, Islamabad had reason to doubt the American resolve in South Asia. The risks to be taken in Pakistan's assuming a facilitating role in the war were also not minimal.

Zia thus expected to be amply rewarded with generous aid. The country had to have a credible defense if it were going to avoid being exposed to possible Soviet retaliation.

Of course, it was lost on no one that this same enhancement of the Pakistan military, replacing its outdated equipment, would also increase its defensive capability to deal with India. Whatever the suspicion of Washington's motives or reliability, as long as the Afghan war continued, it was felt that the close ties with the United States would help to deter Indian ambitions. For Pakistan's public, an aid agreement promised to relieve a growing sense of vulnerability with enemies at two borders. An opinion survey showed support for the military and economic aid agreements, with 60 percent in favor and only 10 percent expressing opposition.[8]

Pakistan still chose to portray its foreign policy on Afghanistan as entirely a principled stand, pointing out that it had indeed given some assistance to the mujahidin before any large scale foreign aid had begun to arrive. It was important to many in Pakistan's leadership that the country avoid being seen as merely doing Washington's bidding or engaging in a political quid pro quo. Pakistani foreign minister Agha Shahi led those insisting that no concessions be made on Pakistan's formally nonaligned status or nuclear policies. Pakistan's determination not to be dragged into the broader East-West conflict meant that there could be no visible U.S. military presence in the country. Nor were agreements with Pakistan expected to improve the U.S.'s position to project its power in the region, say against Iran, through Pakistan. Above all, Pakistan refused to be publicly identified as taking on Iran's old role as the leading instrument of U.S. policy in Southwest Asia.

Pakistan's President Zia managed to revive economic dependency on the United States and the West while avoiding giving offense to Iran's Islamic Revolutionary regime and also keeping open lines of communication to Moscow. Pakistan demonstrated throughout the 1980s the ability to talk to all the major players—Iran, Saudi Arabia, China, the Soviet Union, and the United States. Aside from providing a possible future bridge between the United States and Iran, Pakistan could potentially mediate differences between Iran and its nemesis, Saudi Arabia. Only with India was it difficult to hold any dialogue, including over Afghanistan.

Pakistan's ability to retain good relations with countries that were themselves so adversarial could be accomplished in part because its contacts with these countries were compartmentalized: different sectors of the Pakistan government were close to different countries with which Pakistan had to deal, and individuals in position of high authority in Islamabad often served as the "point men" for relations. In the case of

Iran, for example, General Aslam Beg, as army chief of staff, was known to have long played that role.

Pakistan's ability to "hang tough" against the Soviet Union depended to a large degree on Iran. Pressures on Islamabad to accommodate the Soviets would have increased had Iran's relations with the Soviet Union entirely normalized, possibly in an effort by Tehran's Islamic Republic to counter Western threats in the Persian Gulf. Despite Moscow's supplying of arms to Iraq, the Soviets continued to make progress in wooing Iran in the economic and commercial spheres. No doubt Moscow hoped to enlist the Iranian government to help end the war in Afghanistan on terms satisfactory to the Soviet Union.

Pakistan's relations with Iran might have been sorely complicated had discussions with the United States concluded with an agreement to provide early warning radar planes, especially were they manned by the U.S. military. Overall, it was remarkable how successful the Islamabad government had been in avoiding antagonizing Iran in the handling of Pakistan's increasingly militant Shi'ite community. Shi'ite-Sunni violence in Karachi, thought to have involved Iranians, had always loomed as a potential flashpoint in relations with the Khomeini regime. Pakistan's diplomatic skills were already strained in trying to avoid giving offense to the Tehran government while holding firm Islamabad's relations with those Arab states backing Iraq, most of all Saudi Arabia.

Saudi Arabia, long a friendly government, was pleased to be able to help in many fields and to use the opportunity to propagate Wahhabi Islam among the Afghan mujahidin. Early in the war, Pakistan was promised assistance with the refugees and received a commitment to help finance the modernization of its air force. Reciprocity was surely at work: Pakistan had already earned by 1981 a reported $1.2 billion from Saudi Arabia for stationing a 10,000 member military contingent in Saudi Arabia as a special security unit.[9] Somehow, Pakistan managed to support the Saudis' right to enforce their ban on demonstrations after the police actions against Iranian pilgrims in Mecca in August 1987, and yet refrain from denouncing Iranians for provoking the violence.

At least until 1988, when Iraq again took the offensive in the Iran-Iraq war, the possibility existed that the Gulf states, feeling threatened by Iran, might conclude that the Soviets were essential to the region's stability. Indeed, at one point in 1987, Kuwait apparently asked several Arab heads of state to convince Pakistan to ease its negotiating stand with Kabul as a way of assuring Soviet participation in securing open oil shipping lanes in the Persian Gulf and keeping the Iranians in check.

Although Pakistan's long-time ally, China, was still thought of as a valuable asset, the Chinese seemed unable to meet the expanded security needs brought on by the Afghan war. Pakistan even had reason to be apprehensive about future commitments. China had made a Soviet withdrawal from Afghanistan one of three conditions for improving ties with Moscow. Any convergence of Sino-Soviet differences on the other two issues, border troop concentrations and Vietnam, might lead, some feared, to a softening of Beijing's position on Afghanistan.

The Soviets as Antagonists

As a consequence of Pakistan's early lining up with the West, Moscow looked at Pakistan suspiciously. Even if a military attack on Pakistan was never contemplated in Moscow, throughout the decade the Soviets were ready to use their military power and that of their Afghan clients politically, that is, to influence decisions made in Islamabad. At times this led to badly strained relations. Yet both sides carefully avoided rupturing ties or giving the other great offense. Even while Pakistan was intimidated and bullied, left exposed to dissent and division, it was also promised economic rewards, regional security, and respect for its sovereignty.

The Soviets always left the door open for a negotiated, compromise settlement even as they remained steadfast in defending their Marxist allies in Kabul. A policy of negotiations through U.N. auspices was consistent with the Soviets' efforts to separate the Islamabad government from the mujahidin. The Soviets were determined that lines of communication be left open in order to allow for the possibility that the mujahidin could be defeated by inducing the Pakistanis to withdraw their support. By suggesting flexibility in its terms for peace, Moscow also courted international opinion in lobbying diplomatically with countries in the Third World and, most of all, in Muslim capitals.

The Islamabad government was on occasion openly courted by the Soviets, especially when relations with the United States soured during the Carter Administration. Much in Soviet policy involved generous application of the carrot and stick approach. Moscow never insisted upon directly linking Islamabad's foreign policy with trade and development assistance to Pakistan. Technical assistance continued on Soviet projects, and Moscow regularly proposed expanding commercial, economic, and scientific cooperation.[10] In 1981, a thermal power project built with Soviet aid was opened. In 1983, a steel mill was inaugurated with economic and technological assistance from the Soviets. The $5 million in commodities exchanged in 1987 represented the level of legal trade over the decade, although in December 1987, Pakistan and the Soviet Union signed a barter trade agreement worth $34 million for exchange of goods in

1988.[11] Within the Soviets' low profile during the 1980s, extensive propaganda and cultural and educational exchanges were also pursued.

On the coercive side, the Soviets employed steady diplomatic persuasion as well as military and even psychological pressure. Moscow had concluded that a less costly and earlier solution to the Afghan war lay with Pakistan. The resistance could be reduced to manageable proportions, essentially by isolating it. Without the sanctuary offered by the Islamabad government and the international assistance it received, there could be no effective resistance effort or viable refugee community. Wearing down the capacity of the mujahidin to fight also included ultimately denying them the support of the refugee population itself.

Needed was a Pakistan willing to serve as the anvil to the Soviet hammer. A fully cooperative Pakistan was one willing to interdict the flow of arms and other forms of assistance to the mujahidin and accept, more or less, Soviet terms for a Marxist-dominated coalition government in Kabul. It required convincing Pakistan's rulers that a more accommodating course served their country's national interests. There were in this historical parallels in the way the Soviets finally suppressed rebellious Muslims, called *basmachi*, in Uzbekistan, Tajikistan, and Kyrgyzstan in the mid-1930s. That post-revolutionary rebellion had collapsed when the Afghan rulers finally capitulated to the Soviet Union and even cooperated in pushing the fighters back across the border. Although Pakistan was not expected to become quite so cooperative, the outlines of a similar policy were clear in Moscow's maneuvering for a government in Islamabad likely to be less sympathetic to the resistance movement.

Soviet objectives aimed at simultaneously driving a wedge between Pakistan's people and the Afghans living among them and also at dividing the displaced Afghan masses from the mujahidin leadership. A principal feature of the Soviet strategy was a hard fist and an open hand that generously applied a combination of pressures and concessions, destruction and reconciliation. On one hand, the grass-roots refugee community was led to believe that peace was close at hand and an honorable return possible. The mujahidin leaders along with the Zia regime were alleged to be putting obstacles in the way of refugees wishing to be repatriated. On the other hand, Afghan refugees were subject to armed attacks, subversion, and propaganda, all designed to undermine their moral and material backing for the resistance.

Policies were also aimed at exacerbating popular domestic resentments among Pakistanis against the highly visible exiles and their cause. Doubts were planted about whether the mujahidin, in their factional disagreements, were sufficiently amenable to compromise with the Marxist regime and whether opportunities for peace were being lost.

In official propaganda, Kabul and Moscow generally portrayed the refugee masses as misguided and deceived by their leadership, while reserving for the resistance movement the characterization of irreconcilable bandits.

The Soviet Union toughened its strategy beginning sometime in 1986, playing strongly not only on popular Pakistani resentments against the refugees but also on the long-standing fears of political isolation within Pakistan's policy-making circles. Perhaps the origins of this policy go back to the previous year when Mikhail Gorbachev on assuming power attempted what can be interpreted as a last-ditch effort to defeat the mujahidin militarily. Having failed, the Soviets then opted for a hard-sell political approach that in the last analysis required the constant reminder that a powerful military force was close at hand.

Moscow used every opportunity to point out how support of the resistance was costly for Pakistan's security. Pakistan was repeatedly accused of "aiding and abetting Afghan insurgents at the behest of imperialist powers."[12] With Pakistan pinned between adversaries in the Northwest and East, the periodic military build-up by India along its border with Pakistan was thought to be part of the Soviets' double game. According to the popular view in Pakistan at the time, New Delhi provided the uncertainty and tensions along the eastern border that the Soviets needed in their campaign to "soften up" the country for a political agreement. Even if the border tensions were not directly instigated by the Soviets, Indian troop concentrations succeeded at critical times in diverting Pakistan's air defenses away from the Northwest frontier. The Soviet Union joined India in sharply attacking a request under consideration in Washington to supply AWACS to Pakistan. Using a more subtle approach than New Delhi, the Soviets gently reminded Pakistan's leaders that if an agreement with the United States were reached, there could be retaliation in the form of augmented arms deliveries to India, including advanced-warning aircraft and MIG 31s.

Repeated penetration of Pakistan's territory by Kabul government aircraft and sabotage within Pakistan's borders was meant to convey a clear message to authorities in Islamabad. The unprecedented, likely Soviet-approved air incursions were aimed at trying to seal the borders and stop the transport of men and weapons. The incursions by Kabul government jets, bombs planted in crowded urban places, and rockets fired from nearby tribal areas served as blatant attempts to force the Islamabad government to alter its stand on a settlement.

The deliberate, premeditated spreading of terror in the area served the purpose of increasing public uneasiness and raised questions about the wisdom of providing a safe haven for the mujahidin and meeting the material needs of the refugees. The strong intelligence network instituted by the Kabul government under Najibullah was extended to Pakistan. Infiltration by Afghan agents of Khah (*Khedamat-i-Dawlati*) into the camps and fighting units was responsible for the bombing and other disorders designed to harass and frighten. The attacks meanwhile provided ammunition to opposition politicians who argued for a more flexible approach in settling the war.

Supposedly, the cells established by Afghan and Soviet secret services for the organization of sabotage activities in the frontier and tribal areas spread across the country. Pakistan authorities claimed to have arrested more than 1,000 saboteurs said to be involved in terror campaigns and claimed that most were Pakistani citizens trained and directed by Khad.[13] Most of these acts of violence seemed timed to coincide with negotiations in progress in Geneva seeking a settlement. The purpose of the campaign of pressure was also to weaken public support for the resistance and tolerance of the refugees, who were to be seen as having added much to the breakdown of law and order in the country.

Efforts to destabilize the Pakistani frontier were particularly disturbing. Arms were provided to exacerbate local tribal and communal disputes. From the communist coup of April 1978 until the end of 1985, approximately 190 persons had been killed and hundreds more wounded by raids and shelling on Pakistan territory.[14] Helicopter gunships attacked Pakistan just over the Durand Line and struck at refugee camps in the NWFP. Over flights of Pakistan territory occurred repeatedly. Air attacks and bombings increased sharply in 1987.[15]

Politically, Soviet policy in Baluchistan was considerably more restrained, testimony of the modus operandi that prevailed. The province, beset with smoldering rebellion, was the most vulnerable target for any Soviet effort to destabilize and dismember Pakistan. While some government officials believe that Kabul and its benefactors in Moscow provide clandestine support for separatist tendencies in this province as well as in the Sindh, the Soviets were surprisingly cautious in their involvement in the province's long-standing rebellion against central government authority. Any attempt to break up Pakistan posed a risky course for Moscow; for one, it could backfire, uniting the other provinces. Dismemberment through ethnic separatism also left a precedent for the subcontinent that most officials in Soviet-aided India, beset with similar problems, found disturbing. In declining to arm the Baluch insurgents, the Soviets manifested their own time-honored policy of preferring to curry favor with established governments before taking their chances with revolutionary elements. By their restraint in face of the opportunities, the Soviets demonstrated their willingness to work with

Pakistan's leaders without precluding other options when those leaders proved uncooperative.

Pakistan's Tightrope

Pakistan, in its own way, adopted a dual strategy. President Zia was able to maintain a firm, principled stand on Afghanistan without giving provocation and entirely dampening hopes for a negotiated settlement. At times he seemed to enjoy brandishing a hard-line, portraying Pakistan as threatened by Soviet aggressive policies and worthy of international assistance. Simultaneously, even while refusing to negotiate directly with the Kabul government, the Zia government welcomed open diplomatic channels to the Soviets.

Zia's tightrope policies were well calculated.[16] Realism dictated that Pakistan recognize that it could not afford to live in hostility with the Soviets while they remained a power and influence in the region. Pakistan's leadership was convinced in the same vein that its ability to talk to the Soviet Union was essential if there were to be a Soviet withdrawal. Islamabad also welcomed Soviet initiatives to serve as mediators with India. Keeping diplomatic contacts correct meanwhile left open the possibility that Moscow might become more restrained in making commitments to the New Delhi government. Not unimportant, a dialogue with Moscow enabled Pakistan to maintain the pretense that it adhered to nonalignment and should not be taken entirely for granted in Washington.

Pakistan's leaders, then, showed themselves to be highly adept at playing off both sides and keeping their options open. They remained fairly assured that U.S. aid would continue to flow, whatever the critics said in Congress. As long as Washington's determination to keep the arms channels open held firm, Pakistan seemed in a good position to set most of the terms to Washington. At the same time, Pakistan increased strength militarily also increased the leverage of its officials in negotiating a compromise with Moscow—whenever the Soviets were ready.

Through most of the 1980s, Pakistan's leaders heard a steady stream of advice that the country should reach an understanding with the Soviets, in effect recognize their occupation of Afghanistan and their ascendance in the region. Advocates contended that Pakistan was in a potentially dangerous situation and that, based on earlier experiences, the United States could not be counted on.[17] The objective was to assure Pakistan's security by recognition of legitimate Soviet interests in

Afghanistan. Those who argued for such a course saw it as the only way that Pakistan could assure its national survival. Moscow was expected to guarantee Afghan acceptance of the Durand Line and to offer some insurance against an Indian attack. A deal with Moscow also carried promises of generous development assistance and military aid. If a pact also involved some loss of sovereignty, this was believed no worse than the loss of freedom implicit in Pakistan's dependence on the West.

Strongly represented among those who favored appeasing the Soviets were academics and journalists. For a variety of reasons, most were already avowedly anti-American. Critics on the left were allegedly behind the revelations in 1989 of dramatic progress in Pakistan's nuclear program. In a media interview, Dr. Abdul Qadeer Khan, director of the nuclear program, was allegedly set up to reveal Pakistan's gains in the hope that U.S. economic and military assistance would be broken-off if policy makers in Washington were upset. The opposition Pakistan People's Party under Benazir Bhutto, although avoiding a pro-Moscow policy, made clear its own preference for an early end to the conflict and a Pakistan less committed to the mujahidin. From the PPP's perspective, the United States had used Pakistan as an instrument to fight its battles against the Soviets, allowing the risks to fall to Pakistan while Washington limited its responsibility to merely supplying arms.

Critics of the military regime put most of the blame on the United States—supposed to be determined to keep the Soviets "tied down and bleeding"—for Pakistan's reluctance to make compromises, in effect, undermining a diplomatic solution. This argument rested on the assumption that a deal with the Soviets was in fact in the offing by 1982, and that a Soviet disengagement was possible that did not leave a Marxist regime, at least not without a major change in leadership, in power in Kabul. The resignation of Foreign Minister Agha Shahi from the government in February 1982 was over his efforts to press for a larger U.N. role in mediating a settlement. The call for a more conciliatory policy toward the Soviet Union produced the expected anxieties among the Americans and Saudis.[18]

Pakistan's military and foreign policy establishments doubted that any guarantees by the Soviets would work; in effect, Pakistan would be forced to give up much of its sovereignty. A policy of compromise with Moscow appeared to call for a Finlandization of Pakistan that they believed would leave it at the mercy of the Soviets and possibly India. At the very least it would create an Austrianization of Pakistan, a form of neutralization that entailed breaking military ties with the West in exchange for an understanding with Moscow. Surveys of Pakistani public opinion demonstrated that less than 10 percent would chose Soviet friendship over the United States.[19] The public was clearly not ready for an accommodation that required the denial of arms and the probable eviction of the Afghan resistance by Pakistan's military. The mujahidin would of course have resisted any such agreement. Policy makers would have had to contend, moreover, with the spirited defense of the Muslim cause by the several religious parties, one of which, Jama'at-i-Islami, General Zia had been cultivating.

In addition to paying a heavy domestic price, an accommodation with the Soviet Union would certainly have severed ties and forfeited the financial support not only of the United States but of China and very likely the Arab states. Worst of all, Moscow would still value its ties to India as more strategically important, meaning that Pakistan's interests would be subordinated to those of India. In any case, General Zia's determination ruled out consideration of a deal with the Soviet Union. Geostrategy aside, he felt deeply about Pakistan's responsibilities and, whatever the criticisms of his policies, was willing to stand up to the Soviets.

While Pakistan's policy makers were not prepared to disavow old alliances and enter the uncharted waters of a modus vivendi with the Soviet Union, Moscow's policies had brought home the fact that increasingly the social and economic costs of the war had to be weighed against political gains. Of course, Soviet and Afghan incursions into Pakistani airspace and acts of subversion made the arms obtained from the West and the political support attracted by Pakistan seem more essential than ever. But it was apparent that the external assistance had also intensified Pakistan's internal problems. To avoid unnecessary provocation to the Soviets and limit the war's domestic impact, Pakistan's strategic planners were determined to disguise the flow of support to the resistance and, as much as possible, control the conduct of the mujahidin leadership.

Notes

1. Riaz M. Khan, *Untying the Afghan Knot; Negotiating Soviet Withdrawal* (Duke University Press, Durham, and London, 1991), p. 11.

2. Robert G. Wirsing, "Pakistan and the War in Afghanistan,"*Asian Affairs*, Vol. 14, no. 2 (Summer 1987), p. 63.

3. Wirsing, *Pakistan's Security Under Zia, 1977–1988* (New York: St. Martin's Press, 1991), p. 40. The direct quote is from Charles Dunbar, "Afghanistan in 1986: the Balance Endures," *Asian Survey*, Vol. 27, no. 2 (February 1987), p. 136-137. See the Wirsing volume, especially pages 23–80, for a comprehensive and perceptive analysis of Afghan policy during the Zia years.

4. Through the late 1980s, by one estimate, 50,000 military personnel from Pakistan had served in the Gulf region. See Ahmed Rashid, "Pakistan, Afghanistan and the Gulf," in *MERIP*, no. 148 (September-October 1987), p. 36.

5. Norman Palmer, "The United States and Pakistan; a 'Tortured' Relationship," a paper read at the Bilateral Conference on Security in South Asian, Rosslyn, Virginia, June 8–10, 1981, pp. 2–3.

6. Tim Weiner, *Blank Check; the Pentagon's Black Budget* (New York, Warner Books, 1991), p. 147.

7. Wirsing, *"Pakistan and the War,"* p. 61.

8. Ijaz S. Gilani, "The Four 'R's of Afghanistan" (Islamabad: Pakistan Institute of Public Opinion, 1984), p. 23.

9. *Far Eastern Economic Review*, January 23, 1981, p. 28.

10. Yuri V. Gankovsky *et. al.*, "Soviet Relations with Pakistan," in Hafeez Malik (ed.), *Soviet-American Relations with Pakistan, Iran and Afghanistan* (New York: St. Martin's Press, 1987), pp. 197–198. Other assessments of Pakistan-Soviet relations include Wirsing, "The Soviet Role in South Asia: Potential for Change," in Leo E. Rose and Kamal Matinuddin (eds.), *Beyond Afghanistan: The Emerging U.S.-Pakistan Relations* (Berkeley: Institute of East Asian Studies, 1989), pp. 283–301; and Ali T. Sheikh, "Pakistan-Soviet Relations and the Afghan Crisis," in Noor A. Husain and Leo E. Rose (eds.), Pakistan-U.S. Relations: Social, Political, and Economic Factors (Berkeley: Institute of East Asian Studies, 1988), pp. 45–74.

11. Foreign Broadcast Information Service (FBIS), *Daily Report, Near East and South Asia*, December 30, 1987, p. 69, from Islamabad Domestic Service, December 29, 1987.

12. Interview with Soviet Deputy Foreign Minister Mikhail Kapitsa, *Muslim* (Islamabad), January 3, 1986.

13. U.S. Department of State, Special Report, no. 173 (December 1987), p. 20.

14. *Muslim*, January 3, 1986.

15. In just a two-day period in February, nearly 100 people were reportedly killed and 250 wounded in several populated areas close to the border. The victims included both Pakistanis and Afghan refugees. "Pakistan Affairs," Embassy of Pakistan, Washington, D.C., Vol. 40, no. 5 (March 1, 1987), p. 2.

16. A highly insightful commentary on Zia's strategies is that of Maleeha Lodhi, *Muslim*, May 4, 1987.

17. Leo Rose, "Pakistan's Role and Interests in South and Southwest Asia," a paper read at the Bilateral Conference on Security in South Asia, Rosslyn, Virginia, June 8–10, 1981, pp. 14–15.

18. Khan, *Untying the Afghan Knot*, pp. 52–53.

19. Gilani,"The Four R's," p. 37.

3

Orchestrating the War

Pakistan from the outset sought to orchestrate much of the conduct of the Afghan war and expected to shape an Afghan peace, were one to be found. Pakistani authorities worked to control virtually every aspect of the Afghan presence in Pakistan. The activities of resident Afghans as well as the armed efforts of their resistance fighters were expected to accord with the perceived interests of Pakistan; nothing was to occur without the knowledge and approval of Pakistani authorities. This regularly involved close management of refugees, and the direction and coordination of Afghan resistance parties based in Peshawar. The ISI's covert operations included intelligence gathering and training camps for mujahidin. More secret still was the dispatch by the ISI's Afghan Bureau of Pakistani military personnel to accompany resistance fighters as advisors, even as combatants, on special missions.[1] Above all, control over the supply of arms gave Pakistan its most direct opportunity to mastermind the course of the war. Throughout the conflict, Islamabad refused to admit to providing arms or military training to the resistance and denied that it was allowing other countries or organizations to do so. In one sense the Pakistan government was truthful: it provided none of its own military supplies to the Afghan mujahidin. More important, officials permitted the funneling of foreign arms to the fighters, an assistance that allowed Pakistan's military intelligence to exercise control over the nature of the weapons, their destination, and use.

Pakistan's direct involvement in the war began with the communist coup of April 1978, when the Zia regime, as already mentioned, allowed those opposing the Kabul government to escape to Pakistan and freely admitted large numbers of refugees. Arms reached Pakistan by both ship and aircraft, and were then trucked under military supervision to the border areas. At the frontier, weapons were recorded as they entered Afghanistan.[2] Yet during the first years of the conflict, Pakistan, while taking foreign aid to secure its borders and accepting international kudos for its principled stand, showed some restraint in its support of the resistance efforts. Efforts were made to have the arms carried by men and mules move quickly across the border. In these early years, Pakistan is also believed to have insisted that the quantity of weapons transferred through the country be limited to approximately two plane loads weekly.[3]

The ISI-distributed arms were not at this time the heavier weapons sought by the mujahidin, nor the intelligence guidance and logistical support requested.[4] Better equipped mujahidin, capable of escalating the level of fighting, were thought certain to greatly increase the number of refugees fleeing to Pakistan, adding to its economic burden. More effective mujahidin defenses against Soviet tanks and planes, as well as public acknowledgment of Islamabad's role in the arms supply network, would possibly antagonize Moscow and lead to retaliation. Pakistan's leaders feared air strikes against mujahidin staging areas in Pakistan as well as sophisticated Soviet arms reaching nationalist separatists in ethnically divided Pakistan. But despite a careful balancing of the amount and kinds of equipment to the mujahidin, Pakistani authorities never seriously inhibited the free movement of resistance forces across the border or the recruitment and training of fighters.

Arms for the resistance came from several sources. The cost of the operation as late as 1983 was no more than $50 million, with the United States financing about half and Saudi Arabia most of the rest.[5] By the late 1980s, Washington alone was providing as much as $600 million in support. Through the decade, more than $2.5 billion was set aside by Washington for the Afghan resistance. Chinese and Egyptian-supplied arms, much of them purchased by Washington, were placed in the hands of Pakistan's military for distribution. Iran's assistance went mainly to Shi'ite resistance groups while, with Pakistan's approval, supplies from several Arab countries were destined for selected Sunni parties. The level of Saudi funds for its friends among the resistance grew to an estimated $400 to $500 million by 1990.[6]

Over time, the weapons supplied through Pakistan increased in numbers and sophistication. In March 1985 the Reagan Administration reached a decision to sharply escalate U.S. covert action as a means of allowing the mujahidin to defeat the Soviets. The Islamabad government agreed to funnel subversive materials purchased by the U.S. Central Intelligence Agency (CIA) for distribution in the Muslim republics. But the United States soon backed off a policy, championed by CIA chief William Casey, to have Pakistan train and supply mujahidin for strikes inside Soviet territory. It left standing, however, the authorization to pass on to the resistance valuable detailed and extensive satellite reconnaissance data and approval of more sophisticated weapons. CIA specialists supplied and trained Pakistani officers in the use of secure communications equipment, use of explosives, psychological warfare, etc., all to be passed on to the Afghan mujahidin. The high technology and military expertise were accompanied by a marked increase in arms supplies.[7]

As the arms supplies became more massive, large depots were located in Pakistan, by far the largest at Ojhri Camp, a military installation on the outskirts of Rawalpindi. Zia had insisted that once the arms reached Pakistan they would come under Pakistan's control, specifically the ISI's. The mujahidin took direct delivery of weapons transfered by a fleet of trucks to small distribution centers around Peshawar—warehouses in the hands of individual resistance parties.[8] Weapons intended to be used by the mujahidin often found their way to the bazaars, however, sometimes with the connivance of the Afghan resistance groups. The Americans also tolerated the regular siphoning-off of aid passed across the border, the proceeds of which paid for a comfortable life for many resistance leaders in Peshawar. Resistance leaders are believed to have stolen and sold hundreds of millions of weapons from CIA arsenals.[9]

The United States also looked the other way when it received reports that elements of the Pakistani army and refugee administration were conniving with members of the Peshawar parties in the sale of weapons and relief supplies, as well as for other favors.[10] As a matter of policy, the Pakistan military laid claim to a share of the weapons' flow. Zia's armed forces saw it as their right to appropriate weapons from CIA shipments and the CIA, in effect, condoned the theft as a sort of commission, as the way one does business with the government in Pakistan. It is believed that at least 20 percent of the arms and perhaps more than 30 percent were siphoned off from the supply pipelines.[11]

Pakistani authorities, however, continued to deny active involvement in the fight. Early in the war, for example, the use of older Soviet-made weaponry, drawn largely from Egyptian and Chinese stocks, was supposed to disguise the source of arms and give credence to the explanation that the mujahidin's arms were all captured from the Afghan military. Repeatedly the Kabul regime charged the Islamabad government with employing regular Pakistani troops for logistical support to the resistance. While these accusations were largely false, the ISI did not feel restrained from offering training and tactical advice to the mujahidin and from sending "advisors" or "instructors" into combat zones, at times without the knowledge of high civilian officials.[12]

One of the better kept secrets of the war was the extent of ISI's involvement in training the mujahidin. Seven camps were operating simultaneously by 1987, four near Peshawar and three in the vicinity of Quetta, having trained up to that time some 80,000 Afghan fighters.[13] There were also normally two ISI teams operating inside Afghanistan at any time during the period from May through October. Pakistani officers and NCOs composing the teams were volunteers from all the branches of the Pakistan army. With the ISI selecting particular missions, determining the correct training, and providing the required arms, typically three ISI volunteers, disguised as mujahidin, accompanied forces under an Afghan commander across the border—mainly to strike at infrastructural targets. If necessary the Pakistanis also fought.[14]

To the extent that any cooperation was realized among the usually feuding resistance factions, the intelligence service could take much of the credit. From time to time, ISI officials were forced to intercede to stop attacks by one group on another. Not surprisingly, then, the United States deferred to Pakistan in its Afghan policies. CIA employees cooperated in the arms transfers determined by the ISI. U.S. operatives and others came to depend heavily on Pakistani military intelligence, not only for the delivery of supplies tactical advice to resistance groups but also for the ISI's strategic assessments.[15] Military intelligence provided the main source of information about the politics of the resistance groups. The ISI was assumed in Washington to have a good understanding of the Afghans and invaluable contacts among the resistance parties. As a result, the United States was misinformed about the popularity of former king Zahir Shah among the refugees as well as about rank and file support for some of the hard-line Islamic resistance groups. The CIA relied heavily on often less than reliable Pakistani sources for information about the reception and use of arms across the border, tending to undervalue the military effectiveness of the more moderate mujahidin parties.

The cooperation between some Pakistani military officials and mujahidin commanders in the drug trade has often been alleged. The clandestine traffic in arms offered a natural, lucrative pairing with drugs. With the patronage of high Pakistani officials, resistance commanders were supposedly afforded an alternative means of financing the war that also handsomely rewarded individual Afghans and Pakistanis. It is contended that the network that succeeded in smuggling drugs out of the North-West Frontier Province received the protection of the Pakistan military, specifically, the army's National Logistics Cell, the unit handling the shipment of arms to the border areas.[16] The same army vehicles that hauled weapons for resistance are believed to have transported drugs on their return trips. In all probability, the reluctance of the CIA to intervene in the cozy relationship involving the heroin trade was due to the belief that these were necessary costs in rewarding important army officials for their handling of the war. The United States cared little so long as the trade contributed in some way to putting pressure on the Soviets.[17]

Picking Favorites

To one extent or another, all of the resistance party leaders were cultivated by Pakistan and were propped up by either the government or an external power. Although previously there had been more than 40 resistance groups operating in Peshawar, by 1982 Pakistani authorities had forced them to coalesce into seven. Nearly all the party leaders had a following, often narrow, based on respect for their religious scholarship, religious status, and experience as dissidents. Yet, except for Yunis Khalis, leader of one of the hard-line Islamist parties in Peshawar, none of the party leaders had a territorial base inside Afghanistan, traditionally an important qualification for leadership. Permission to register refugees in the camps, an authorization given to the seven parties, was critical to their survival. Even so, Pakistani officials discriminated in their military and other forms of assistance in favor of the most radical Islamic resistance factions and cooperated in curtailing the activities of their more traditionalist, moderate competitors. Shi'ite parties and nonreligiously-oriented Afghan national parties were, in effect, excluded from the Peshawar alliance. Intelligence officials had concluded that the Shi'ite groups had too close ties with Iran to come under their wing; and for practical as well as ideological reasons, these officials were no more comfortable with secular groups and Afghan notables living in exile outside of Pakistan. Similarly, in an attempt to maintain fuller control, the ISI saw to it that the Peshawar parties rather than the commanders in the field distributed weapons.

Hezb-i-Islami, headed by Gulbuddin Hekmatyar, was clearly the most favored of the religious parties based in Peshawar. As already noted, Hekmatyar had been battling governments in Kabul since 1974, most of the time from exile in Pakistan. He received assistance first from Zulfikar Ali Bhutto and then from General Zia ul-Haq, who as army chief-of-staff ousted the prime minister in July 1987. Along with other hard-liners, Hekmatyar championed a monolithic theocratic state for Afghanistan that would be imposed on the traditional society, replacing the authority of pre-war tribal and ethnic leadership.

Aside from Hekmatyar's opposition to the idea of an ethnic, secular state—Pashtunistan, Pakistan had a number of practical reasons for the bias in his favor. After the communist coup and Soviet invasion, Zia and his military government found in Hekmatyar a handy and agreeable instrument with which to support an armed Afghan resistance. As a man of more than superficial Islamic piety, Zia saw in Hezb-i-Islami a group that, in its authoritarian, internationalist brand of Islam, shared with him an anti-communist zeal. There was admiration for its tightly knit organization, its dedicated to a cause. But the preference was on pragmatic grounds as well. Hekmatyar's Hezb-i-Islami was viewed as the best organized and most disciplined of the several Peshawar-based resistance parties. As such, it was thought to be in a strong position to contest the Soviets and the Kabul regime. Hekmatyar's party quickly developed what one observer referred to as "relations of trust and confidence with the military."[18]

Although a number of field commanders in Afghanistan were intensely loyal to Hezb-i-Islami, their forces were in fact neither the largest nor most effective. Oddly, ISI officials seemed more impressed with the frequent ruthlessness of Hekmatyar's leaders than with the scope of their fighting or accomplishments against Soviet and Kabul government troops. Given Hezb-i-Islami's limited popular base within Afghanistan, only with direct Pakistani support could it hope, after a resistance victory, to be a successful contender for power in Kabul.

Close ties with the conservative Jama'at-i-Islami of Pakistan, effectively a domestic political ally of General Zia, smoothed the way for assistance to the Hekmatyar group. From the outset of the conflict, Jama'at-i-Islami figured strongly in the government's efforts to mobilize public opinion, and had been made privy to the military's Afghan policy. In exchange for helping the government to rally Pakistanis and legitimize the call to jihad, Zia involved the party in managing refugee affairs, as well as in the planning and execution of the resistance fight.[19] In most of these activities, Jama'at-i-Islami was widely understood to be advancing the interests of Hekmatyar.

The bias in favor of Hezb-i-Islami and corresponding disregard, even the bullying, of other parties was nowhere better seen than in the allocation of weapons among the mujahidin. Although Hekmatyar espoused an anti-Western and, particularly, an increasingly shrill anti-American rhetoric, his party was said to have received 20 to 25 percent of U.S. arms during the late 1980s.[20] By one estimate, Hezb-i-Islami—also a beneficiary of money and weapons from Libya's Qaddafi and regularly accused of hijacking shipments of weapons, food and medicine destined for other groups—received a total of more than $500 million in U.S. support.[21] Few doubt that the weapons and communications systems received by Hekmatyar's forces were also of higher quality and sophistication than those furnished other parties.

The three more moderate or traditionalist parties (see note 8) claimed that the Peshawar alliance's four Islamist groups shared 75 percent of the mostly military aid received by resistance parties.[22] Periodically, the more moderate groups were cut off entirely in what they believed were attempts to weaken them in certain regions of Afghanistan. The best publicized of the resistance forces inside Afghanistan, the estimated 12,000 men under the command of Ahmad Shah Masoud, were not favored by either Pakistan or Saudi Arabia. Masoud, whose network of commanders covered six northern provinces (called the Council of the North), regularly criticized the Pakistanis and their U.S. suppliers for slighting his group in the arms transfers. The ISI refused to assist not only Masoud but also mujahidin leaders in Herat and Mazar-i-Sharif, a policy that was conspicuous for ignoring minorities in favor of Pushtun commanders.[23] Masoud, an ethnic Tajik, was unacceptable to the ISI higher command, who seemed devoted to the idea that only a member of the Pushtun majority could rule Afghanistan.[24]

Pakistan's less than friendly policy toward Masoud was also not unrelated to his refusing ISI dictates. Loosely allied with Rabbani's resistance forces and receiving some assistance from European sources, Masoud refused to have Pakistanis determine his military or political policies. Pakistan and, to some extent, the United States were leery of Masoud for his seeming willingness to strike his own deals with the enemy and his unwillingness to be pushed into attacking major cities after the Soviet pullout. Pakistanis, while admitting that Masoud had managed more than any other commander to create a regional government infrastructure in the country, argued that he had done so because his forces were less often militarily engaged.

Even the parties dominated by the radical Islamists were liable to have military supplies withheld for a time when they objected to ISI manipulation.[25] But unlike the traditionalist parties, the Islamist groups were more likely to find alternate backers among Arab private and governmental sources. Religious foundations and relief organizations provided a well-used means to disguise support. Varying amounts of arms, money, and other aid went to the hard-line groups, often bypassing official Pakistani channels.

Pakistani authorities meanwhile tolerated the free movement of jihad-seeking Arab volunteers, who began arriving after 1983, and for some years were able to keep a low profile. Large numbers came after mid-1988, during the tenure of Hamid Gul as ISI chief, after instructions were given that visas (usually tourist visas) be issued to anyone willing to fight with the mujahidin. Often using false names, most of these young, disaffected Arabs were affiliated with foreign governments and private, much of the time secretive, Islamic welfare organizations. At least 6,000 Muslim volunteers and perhaps as many as 20,000 (Pakistan did not keep records) during the course of the war came from Saudi Arabia, Egypt, Jordan, Kuwait, as well as Algeria, Sudan, Iraq, Libya, Yemen, and Tunisia. Others arrived from Burma, the Philippines, and Indonesia, as many as 20 countries in all. Their cordial relations with Pakistan officials, created in part by the money they spread around, protected those who stayed illegally from deportation. For the most part, volunteers had no interest in Afghan politics and were therefore not particularly concerned about which resistance party they served, so long as it agreed to train them.[26]

One sector to which Pakistan's military intelligence gave less heavy guidance and was more circumspect in showing favoritism involved the cross-border relief and reconstruction activities of Pakistan-based nongovernment organizations. To be sure, the ISI controlled authorization to operate in the sensitive border areas, and sometimes denied permission or delayed the entry of these groups. At least some organizations with direct USAID subcontracts for delivery of relief supplies also had their target areas and party quotas assigned in consultations between ISI and American aid officials. But for a number of activities, notably education, the Peshawar parties constituted as the interim government were given a direct role in the cross-border effort. Pakistani authorities also stood aside as the parties threatened to place obstacles before the relief organizations if they failed to recruit from their ranks. Although the foreign groups were not obliged to align with particular resistance parties, disporportionate numbers of employees were drawn from Hezb-i-Islami and Jamiat-i-Islami. These recruitment practices allowed the two parties to receive regular reports about the relief groups' activities. The presence of their followers in the nongovernment organizations also left radical Islamist elements in a position to intimidate more moderate employees and, should the parties choose, to cripple the operations of the private aid groups.

Many of these private aid organizations were subject to government regulations which, as in restrictions on purchases in the local market, impeded their delivery of food into Afghanistan. Also, in response to pressures from the more radical religious parties and Arab groups, Pakistani authorities refused to expedite the "No Objection Certificates" needed by the voluntary organizations in order to recruit their foreign employees legally. But despite these obstacles, the relief groups operated mainly without regular interference from Pakistan. Importantly, the ISI appears to have refrained from using the relief organizations for intelligence purposes. Pakistan's authorities were concerned that the private voluntary organizations as well as U.N. agencies and official foreign aid groups, many of whom also worked among the refugees in

Pakistan, not be scared off. Pakistan had no desire to be left without international good will.

Pakistan and Afghan Politics

The policies of Pakistan often seemed to play on the social changes and cleavages that had intensified during the long war. A disunified resistance gave comfort to those Pakistanis, mainly in the military, who wanted a future Afghanistan to pose no threat to Pakistan. These divisions lessened the possibility of parties coalescing in opposition to political figures favored by the military intelligence. Repeated attempts to create a common leadership structure produced just enough unity with an alliance of seven parties in May 1985 (called the Islamic Unity of Afghan Mujahidin) to ease the military's task of controlling the mujahidin while it facilitated military and economic assistance. It also helped Pakistan in its attempts to enhance the international reputation of the Afghan resistance.[27]

With the prospect of a Soviet withdrawal and the expectation of a mujahidin-led state, however, other considerations came into play. Until then Pakistan had even refrained from forming a government in exile. Aside from differences among the parties, such a government might have limited Pakistan's options in negotiating a Soviet withdrawal as well as increased the possibility of a direct confrontation with the Soviet Union.[28] Increasingly, however, it appeared that a highly fragmented resistance movement would be unable to approve the kind of peace that might permit the refugees to leave Pakistan any time soon. Later, a weak Afghanistan could become easy prey to outside influences, namely India, Iran, and the Soviet Union. Pakistan would be better served, authorities in Islamabad reasoned, by a more structured, cohesive alternative to the Kabul government, one that would improve chances for stability in a liberated Afghanistan and be pro-Pakistan.

A provisional government headed by Ahmad Shah, a little known member of one of the less powerful fundamentalist parties, was put together in 1988, with strong encouragement from the Pakistan intelligence service. Louis Dupree referred to it as the ISI's "shotgun marriage arrangement."[29] The new leadership structure was sought in anticipation of negotiations for an interim government in Kabul with a Soviet decision expected to begin a withdrawal. The choice of Ahmed Shah followed an Afghan tradition in which a member of the weakest element in an alliance, least threatening to the constituents of the coalition, is entrusted with titular leadership.[30] The same formula was again used in 1989 when Pakistan sought to create a more representative government, this time in expectation of a quick mujahidin victory in the wake of the Soviet pullout.

Priority was given to creating a broad-based Afghan Interim Government (AIG). Under the tutelage of the ISI's head, Hamid Gul, an assembly or *shura* was called in February 1989. Pressed by General Gul, the Peshawar party leaders agreed to a more articulated division of powers and a council-elected leadership, replacing the Seven-Party Alliance. Its rotating head assured that no Afghan leader, including Hekmatyar, could monopolize power, and that the movement would therefore continue to look to Pakistan for leadership. The ISI chief was also directly involved in the 1989 negotiations that now had an interest in bringing the Iranian-based resistance parties into the soon-to-be-formed interim government. It was in consultation with General Gul that increased representation was offered the Shi'ite parties in order to persuade them to participate in the shura (and presumably to mollify the Iranians). However, when Hekmatyar and several others in the Islamist camp refused to go along with the deal to provide additional seats for Shi'ites, questions were raised whether the initiative had been serious at all.

In other respects the shura—comprised of more than 500 party politicians, religious leaders, and a small number of commanders together with some intellectuals and technocrats—was hardly the widely representative group that Pakistan had supposedly sought. Aside from the absent Iranian-based parties, very few of the most powerful commanders from inside Afghanistan attended. And when the large body convened, party discipline was weak. In order for any decision to emerge from the meetings and to prevent the meeting from getting away from Pakistan's control, General Gul had again to take matters in hand. He dictated a process that led to the selection of an interim government by putting together a committee of 14 who were given the job of coming up with a formula that would lead to the shura's election of ministers and a president for the interim government. In the end, with each party given two votes, the election chose a moderate as president but gave the prime ministry and foreign affairs posts to hard-liners Rasul Sayyaf and Hekmatyar.

Involvement in resistance politics was also visible in the establishment of media services by the Peshawar parties. General Zia had no objection to low-keyed information services, and Hezb-i-Islami and Jamiat-i-Islami established their own news groups. But the Pakistani president was for some time reluctant to have an Afghan media center on Pakistan's soil, lest Islamabad cede too great autonomy to the resistance movement. When finally a center was created (after the United States argued that a more professional and coherent voice of the resistance was needed and, importantly, promised funds to back it), the government in Islamabad agreed to an informal arrangement, provided that a Pakistani be at its helm. Later, the center came into the hands of Afghans professionally trained. To please the parties, the print journalism division of the media center, called MEDIA, was placed under the AIG. Attempts by Pakistani authorities to have the organization carry its handouts were successfully resisted. But MEDIA, placed under the Ministry of Information of the interim government, became effectively the mouthpiece of the Afghan mujahidin party controlling the Ministry—the Jamiat-i-Islami.

Judging by the way Pakistani officials manipulated or sought to steer Afghan resistance politics, there is reason to question whether those concerned with Afghan policy fully understood the workings of Afghan institutions and resistance politics. The AIG was heavy with Ghilzay Pashtuns, under-representing the still important Durranis. Among other things, this assured that many field commanders would always feel somewhat estranged from the Peshawar parties that made up the interim government. Although the commitment by Pakistan to try to make the AIG work as an united front was probably sincere, there was only a belated realization that this government would always have an uphill struggle to prove its legitimacy. Limited understanding of Afghan traditions led Pakistan's policy makers to believe that a shura might serve as a decision making, conflict resolving body, when at best a shura allows for leaders' expression of views and ratifies decisions essentially already made.[31] Similar misperceptions allowed Pakistan's leaders to conclude that once they helped to install a friendly government in Kabul, those anointed to lead would feel beholden to Islamabad. In the years following the February 1989 shura, Afghan leaders complained about the difficulty in evolving a genuinely independent Afghan policy because of the close watch that the Pakistan government had maintained over the Afghan leadership while in Peshawar. Even then, the ISI, for all its influence in providing arms, training, and tactical advice, was far less successful in giving political direction, particularly in creating unity when most needed among the mujahidin.

Pakistan's Hand in the Jalalabad Fiasco

The grand finale or at least a watershed event of the Afghan war was supposed to have been a mujahidin victory at Jalalabad, a provincial capital 20 miles from the Pakistan frontier. Following the Soviet military withdrawal, the attack was expected to commence the rapid disintegration of the communist regime in Kabul. It also underscored the pivotal role of Pakistan's military in helping to effect a military victory over the Najibullah government.

During the period of Soviet withdrawal through the second half of 1988, Pakistan and the United States had cautioned the resistance against attacking Soviet forces and advised against a frontal assault on Kabul and other major strongholds. But with their final departure in February 1989, an early push by the mujahidin to capture key provincial cities, most of all Jalalabad, was deemed necessary by Pakistan's military planners and the newly elected Bhutto government if the resistance forces were not to lose their momentum. For the Foreign Office in Islamabad, the occupation of Jalalabad by the resistance forces was expected to give credibility to the interim government and hand it a base of operations within Afghanistan. At the same time, the proximity of the city together with the composition of the population of the area assured greater opportunity to exercise influence by the ISI and the Peshawar parties.[32] The transfer of the interim government to Jalalabad was also likely to blunt criticism that the Afghan government in exile could not stand except on Pakistani soil. The timing of the attack was probably intended to have the AIG in place in Jalalabad in time for a March 13–16 meeting in Riyadh of the Organization of Islamic Conference, during which the interim government would ask for recognition (which it received anyway).[33]

The campaign to capture Jalalabad went on for many weeks. When the mujahidin finally admitted their failure to oust Kabul's forces and no other cities fell, there was no shortage of recriminations and ample evidence of strategic miscalculations and tactical blunders. The ISI argued that the resistance had failed to carry through on a plan provided them. A lack of coordination surely existed among the mujahidin, and the refusal of key commanders to mount attacks elsewhere in the country enabled the regime to strengthen its garrisons in the Jalalabad area. At least some commanders seemed to be waiting until they were certain how well the Jalalabad campaign was going, but others were also reluctant to join in the attack because they were not anxious to see the Peshawar-based interim government, in which they had no representation, establish a strong foothold inside Afghanistan. Oliver Roy contends that the military failure was not unrelated to antagonism created among non-Ghilzay Pashtuns and the field commanders who, feeling excluded from the recently created AIG, halted their offensives on Jalalabad.[34] An incalculable mistake was the execution early in the Jalalabad operation of

Kabul troops who had surrendered, thus discouraging further desertions. The capability and motivation of the Kabul regime's troops, so generously supplied with arms by the Soviets, also led to gross miscalculations.

Although it had been the ISI objective for some time to have the resistance take Jalalabad and the broad operational plan for the offensive was formulated by the military intelligence, General Gul sought to pass the responsibility for the fiasco to the civilian leadership and the Americans. *The New York Times* was handed a story that the plan to attack the city was decided on March 5, two days before the operation was launched, at a meeting of foreign ministry officials and U.S. Ambassador Robert P. Oakley. The ISI claimed that it was forced to accede to the operation. The Foreign Office understandably retaliated by claiming that the idea for the attack came principally from military intelligence. (No one could blame the highest provincial officials in the Frontier and Baluchistan provinces since they had been kept entirely in the dark about the plan.)

Even before the fight for the city, resistance commanders in the area had complained that Pakistan's role had aggravated rivalries among the guerrilla forces. They claimed that the free-for-all character of the operation was a result of Pakistan's meddling. More specifically, at least several of the local commanders preferred to delay their attack in order to encourage defections by the communist garrison.[35] After the failed operation, the mujahidin blamed Pakistan and the United States for having rejected guerrilla warfare in favor of direct confrontation. Party leaders claimed that in meetings between the ISI and the Americans they were excluded. Yet neither Pakistan nor the United States would likely have counseled the attack, had the mujahidin themselves not been so confident about an easy victory at Jalalabad.

Whatever the full truth, the events at Jalalabad again demonstrated that wishful thinking and faulty information guided much of Pakistan's Afghan policy. The involvement of Pakistani, U.S, and Saudi intelligence groups in the defeat gave Kabul propagandists a powerful piece of ammunition. Aside from being able to make the claim that the regime forces fought better without the Soviets, they could argue that the only foreign interference in Afghan affairs came on the other side. They dwelled on the participation of Wahabi Arab mercenaries and charged that regular Pakistani army units fought alongside the mujahidin. With the Jalalabad campaign carried out under the authority of the interim Afghan government, the Kabul regime's pointed reference to it as the "Rawalpindi government" carried a new sting.

Post-Soviet Withdrawal

In the year following the February 1989 Soviet withdrawal from Afghanistan, there were strong indications of basic changes in Pakistan's Afghan policy. Any immediate threat to Pakistan's political integrity through military means became remote. Only two months prior to the Soviet pullout, a democratically elected government headed by Benazir Bhutto was formed. Although during the election campaign her People's Party's long-term criticism of General Zia's unwavering support of the Afghan resistance was somewhat muted, Ms. Bhutto was widely expected to put her own stamp on Afghan policy, moving toward an early political solution and clipping the wings of the military. The military and civilian hierarchies would then be brought into a near uniformity of views on the Afghan issue.

President Najibullah in Kabul even entertained the idea, in view of the Bhutto family's past subversive activities against the Zia government, that a Benazir-led Pakistan might soon turn its back on the mujahidin. The Al-Zulfikar group headed by the sons of Zulfikar Ali Bhutto had some years earlier based its operations in Kabul, and Najibullah was believed to have personally given it support while he headed Khad, the communist government's secret police.[36] Certainly, a government by the People's Party, traditional adversary of Pakistan's religious parties, was expected to find the possibility of a fundamentalist government in Kabul distasteful. Once Soviet troops left Afghanistan, the government of Pakistan would probably face the prospect of the Americans, or for that matter other international supporters of the resistance cause, losing interest in financing the resistance and Pakistan itself. This would argue for Pakistan's seeking an early resolution, lest it find itself nearly alone in backing the resistance and caring for the refugees.

The mujahidin leadership clearly had reason to worry. President Zia, so long steadfast in his support and a valued spokesman to the international community, was dead, killed in the August 1988 plane crash in which many believed his Afghan enemies had a hand in. Also killed was Lt. General Mian Muhammad Afzal, head of the military intelligence's cross-border operations, and General Akhtar Abdul Rehman Khan, Zia's intelligence chief and an ardent advocate of continued military pressure on the Kabul government. Furthermore, the likelihood of some revision in arms policy seemed in the offing as a result of increasing complaints by U.S. officials over the special treatment accorded Hekmatyar's Hezb-i-Islami.

Washington had begun to look beyond the Soviets and a resistance victory to the kind of regime Pakistan had in mind for Kabul. The new government in Islamabad was expected to go along with the Americans in their insistence that in the future arms be put, where possible, directly into the hands of those commanders doing the fighting inside Afghanistan. The approach, not entirely new—Islamabad had begun before Zia's death to channel weapons and money where the Peshawar parties had little following—represented a more serious attempt to establish a contract method of arms transfer. Although it did not begin in earnest until August 1989, weapons deliveries were to be more individually "packaged," that is, more specifically subcontracted to particular commanders based on what was determined be to their need, effectiveness, and absorptive capability. Because the United States strengthened criteria linked to military effectiveness inside Afghanistan, more moderate elements in the resistance hoped to receive increased aid. If the approach to directly place arms in the hands of commanders worked, commanders would be held on a tighter string. Those who supplied them might be expected to gain greater influence with forces inside Afghanistan who were expected to carry the war to its conclusion. However, the ISI had always opposed a direct line to the commanders, who, it felt, could be more accurately monitored for their needs and their arms more efficiently supplied by the Peshawar parties to which they were affiliated.

As prime minister, Ms. Bhutto, at the urging of Washington, was expected to crack down on drug involvement by the military in the border areas. More control was also sought over the illegal sale of arms. Greater inclination in the Bhutto government for distancing Pakistan from the more radical Afghan leaders was expected to give the government a freer hand to explore peace formulas considered unacceptable to the four Islamist parties, including a political role for former Afghan king Zahir Shah.

The reality of Pakistan's post-withdrawal policy was far different from that anticipated. For some months after her election, Prime Minister Bhutto approved arrests in what promised to be a far-reaching campaign against official involvement in the drug trade. But the effort to expand the investigation ended abruptly when the trail led to additional major figures in the military and to individuals with strong ties to her own People's Party.[37] More than anything else, the tenuous parliamentary control by the Bhutto forces during the prime minister's 20-month tenure in office (to August 1990), and the very fragility of Pakistan's democracy help explain the absence of early, substantial policy changes.

In the wake of defeat in the spring 1989 campaign for Jalalabad, the embarrassment of Pakistani military planners had allowed Bhutto to dismiss the ISI's head, Hamid Gul, once a close confidant to Zia. This decision, taken in May 1989, was hailed by many as a highly important move, both in terms of signaling change in Pakistani foreign policy toward Afghanistan and in leading to a reduced Pakistani presence in Afghanistan.[38] Gul's firing by Bhutto was thought to be critical to the prime minister's efforts to consolidate her power domestically.

The personnel change did not, in fact, lead to the anticipated modifications of Pakistan's Afghan policies. The military strongly resisted any diminution of the ISI's power. Although the rhetoric supporting a negotiated solution increased, Pakistan failed to devise any fresh approaches toward a political solution. Rather than exert her will over the military, the prime minister found it necessary to conciliate the generals to try to gain their neutrality in her battles with the aggressive opposition party alliance. The military and Pakistan's president, Ghulam Ishaq Khan, often its spokesman, exacted a price, however. Bhutto's choice as ISI chief, General Shamsur Rahman Kallu, never amounted to much more than a figurehead. In effect, control of the ISI and Afghan policy was assumed directly by Pakistan's army chief of staff, General Aslam Beg. Mujahidin leaders in Peshawar, including Hekmatyar, were assured that there would be no important changes in policy. Indeed, General Gul, having been reassigned to a key army command post in Multan, continued to be consulted by the intelligence service on important decisions.

The program designed to channel military assistance more directly to the commanders got off to a slow start, largely because of weather conditions and unavoidable delays in importing arms. Of greater significance, however, was Washington's decision to withhold new equipment beginning in December 1988 in anticipation of the war's early end. While overall the distribution of arms among factions was supposed to become more equitable when it resumed in July 1989, no major changes in the transfer of weapons occurred. (Several commanders with more moderate resistance groups insisted that arms deliveries for them were never revived.) American intelligence officials involved with arms shipments together with those aid officials responsible for cross-border humanitarian aid claimed to be carefully monitoring deliveries, adhering to the package approach; in fact, even late in the conflict, they had few sources of information outside of the ISI. It is difficult to ascertain whether they knew that they were being misled as to who was receiving arms or in fact did not care.

Predictably, attempts to arm the commanders directly drew complaints from the AIG. Being bypassed reduced the already tenuous hold of most Peshawar parties on their nominally allied commanders. It was in an important sense a contradictory policy. For while the contract approach with commanders was bound to undermine the authority of the interim government, the United States and Pakistan were pressing the AIG to unify its military command. Moreover, rather than the redirected arms allocations serving to create friends for Pakistan and the

United States among groups fighting inside Afghanistan, additional resentments emerged, either because their suppliers failed to deliver promptly on promised weapons or because some commanders claimed that they were being ignored. In any case, there was general condemnation when U.S. arms were cut off without warning or even admission.

The decision to deprive the mujahidin of a new stock of weapons had at the time seemed entirely rational, even to some a humanitarian policy. In the belief that the war with the communists would soon be over, fewer weapons in Afghan hands meant that in the event of a subsequent factional war the conflict among mujahidin would be less lethal. The CIA was also anxious to collect more sophisticated arms, a task made less complicated by ending their flow.[39] The Soviets had meanwhile greatly increased arms to their Kabul friends. The arms stoppage alone could not explain the poor military performance by the mujahidin, but it gave resistance leaders an excuse for their failures.

With a quick victory unlikely, Pakistan's civilian government appeared increasingly impatient with the mujahidin and seemed prepared to get tough with the parties of Hekmatyar and Sayyaf. When the Americans finally insisted that they wanted to distance themselves from Hezb-i-Islami, Pakistan's policy makers, including some in the military, indicated a similarity of views. As expected, in the diversion of weapons directly to the commanders, Hezb-i-Islami received fewer arms. The diminished access to weapons and food did not, however, disadvantage Hekmatyar disproportionately to the others. For whatever the feelings at higher civilian and military ranks, at the operational level, the ISI was as wedded as ever in its loyalties to the Hezb-i-Islami and, to a lesser extent, the other fundamentalist parties. Not only was Hezb-i-Islami still being treated well in the distribution of arms, it was permitted to augment its stocks. By early 1990, the failure of the contract method to show positive results prompted a partial return to the more familiar modes of arms delivery through the parties. Plainly, the hard-line parties had become so much a part of Pakistan's security establishment that, whatever Washington's demands, they were almost impossible for Pakistan to disown.

ISI officials answered their critics that it was far better to have Hekmatyar supported than to have him alienated, "outside the tent," and thus more likely to be disruptive. An unwillingness to cut Hezb-i-Islami out was, however, better explained by the continued presence of ISI officials who in effect were repositories of the Zia legacy on policy toward Afghanistan. Built up over many years, these personal relationships with Hezb-i-Islami could not be easily severed. ISI officials and Hekmatyar's followers were widely acknowledged to have worked together in questionable, sometimes unauthorized activities, notably arms and drug smuggling. Any decision by the intelligence service to desert their former friends might have invited Hezb-i-Islami to expose ISI misbehavior .

In any case, even with fewer supplies from Western sources, Hekmatyar could still count on private and government channels in the Islamic countries. He could even boast of an independence from Pakistan in arms and money. In late 1989, to demonstrate this independence, the Hezb-i-Islami leader resigned as foreign minister in the AIG and removed his party headquarters to his principal base in Afghanistan. Still, when he met soon after with an aide to Soviet leader Gorbachev, it was with the consent of Pakistan's Foreign Ministry.

The Afghan Interim Government was a particular disappointment to its Pakistani handlers and had become increasingly irrelevant to the war. Virtually no party leader was willing to meld his organization entirely into the cooperative structure necessary for it to be effective. Increased fighting between the parties, particularly between commanders of the Jamiat-i-Islami and Hezb-i-Islami, had contributed to the latter party's leaving the AIG. For all of Islamabad's efforts to have the AIG assume the responsibilities of a government-in-exile, it was unable to create the administrative apparatus that gave anyone confidence that it could become a successor government to the Kabul regime. Without the inclusion of the Iranian-based Shi'ite resistance parties based in Iran and the major field commanders inside Afghanistan, the interim government had little claim to being representative. It also failed to conform to the realities of the larger refugee community with respect to giving a fuller voice to the supporters of Zahir Shah and the ethnic minorities.

The basic difficulty was that the AIG was never meant to be a government-in-exile, a bureaucratic entity that would take root in Pakistan. It was a jerry-built structure designed by Pakistan and its allies to be available to rush into Afghanistan when, as expected, the Kabul government fell after the Soviet military departure, and to last only until a power-sharing arrangement could be devised. When events did not occur as predicted, the AIG's sponsors were saddled with a body of officials who wanted to behave like a legitimate government. By funding the ministerial trappings for the AIG, the United States supported, and appeared to believe, the fiction that it was a viable entity. Pakistan also persisted in the illusion that the Afghan leadership it installed could serve as the starting point for a more broad-based government in the future.

Pakistanis charged with Afghan affairs were involved in late 1989 and early 1990 with the business of reconstituting the AIG with elements left out in February 1989. Afghan resistance leaders and their Pakistan patrons realized the need to have an elected body in order to establish the credibility of a government, though the mode of selecting representatives remained in dispute. In an elaborate plan involving representation of Afghans from 217 constituencies in Afghanistan, General Aslam Beg assumed direct involvement in a fashion not unlike former ISI head Hamid Gul. Yet there existed a wide consensus that a new shura must contrast with the last in giving less of the appearance of outside interference. The United States was particularly determined that the assembly not be another "shura made in Pindi," referring to Rawalpindi, the Pakistani city neighboring Islamabad. Washington was reported to have allocated several million from its covert budget to help organize elections to a shura.[40] With the inability of the Peshawar leaders to agree on the details, a second shura was never called.

That the ISI expected to play an active role in the end-game and that its links with the Hezb-i-Islami remained firm was demonstrated by events surrounding the failed coup attempt in Kabul of March 6 and 7, 1990. Afghan interior minister, General Shahnawaz Tanai, and fellow members of the Khalq faction of Afghanistan's People's Democratic Party, launched a poorly executed attempt to oust President Najibullah. At one level the coup resulted from a long festering intra-party struggle among party factions. The available evidence also suggests that it involved planning on the part of Pakistani intelligence, although the timing caught them by surprise. For some time it had been known that Hezb-i-Islami had succeeded in penetrating the Kabul government's military and had spread money generously. Whatever the extent of their involvement, within hours of the beginning of the fighting (after having failed in an air strike to kill Najibullah), the dissidents in the Afghan military found common cause with Hezb-i-Islami and its partners in the ISI. General Tanai and his confederates were associated with the most hard-line of the communists, those who had been in favor of a more vigorous pursuit of the war against the mujahidin. Although it was difficult to imagine how, in so opportunistic an alliance, the communists and Islamists could be reconciled should the coup succeed, each side was hopeful of prevailing in an almost certain power struggle to follow.

For their part, the Pakistanis and Hekmatyar's partisans grasped at what appeared to be a golden opportunity. Aside from their common desire to oust the Najibullah government, the Khalqis and Hezb-i-Islami leaders appeared to share a similar fate in their almost certainly being left out of any internationally sponsored political compromise that would favor more moderate elements. For Pakistan's military and civilian authorities, the coup offered a possible chance to short-circuit the war. It was a return to a military solution made attractive by the lack of progress in finding a negotiated political settlement. Prime Minister Bhutto gave her endorsement. Badly informed herself of the progress of the fighting, she approved a media campaign intended to give momentum to, and try to save, the coup attempt. Pakistani government-controlled television and radio participated along with ministry officials in the false reporting of events in Afghanistan, lending additional credence to accusations from Kabul that Pakistan had directed the entire affair. The deep involvement of Pakistan was impossible to disguise, however, after it became widely known that Pakistani jets had escorted an Afghan helicopter carrying the coup leaders across the border to Pakistan—where Afghan military officers including General Tanai were met secretly by Generals Beg and Kallu—and the ISI had facilitated meetings between Tanai and representatives from Hezb-i-Islami.

While the coup attempt was in progress, the Pakistani chief of staff and ISI head also met with AIG party leaders in an unsuccessful effort to line up their endorsement for the Hekmatyar-Tanai-ISI front. The AIG refused to accept the Afghan general's sincerity in his conversion to the Islamic cause or join in creating a revolutionary council against Najibullah—seen as nothing more than an attempt by Pakistan to spread the responsibility for the coup's failure. For the parties of the AIG, the coup was merely an internal struggle between communists and a stunning example of an unscrupulous Hezb-i-Islami.

ISI preparations for a new offensive, to be spearheaded by Hekmatyar's forces, were reportedly already in progress within weeks following Bhutto's removal from office by President Ishaq Khan in August 1990.[41] An assault aimed at penetrating Kabul's defenses began mid-October and was preceded by new arms shipments to Hezb-i-Islami and revived attempts at internal subversion to depose the Afghan government. But the campaign was doomed to failure without other mujahidin field commanders joining in. Meeting inside Afghanistan, some 40 of them settled on a competing strategy that avoided a conventional assault on the capital, especially the expected heavy civilian casualties, and concentrated on increasing coordinated attacks against provincial centers. Impressed with the commanders' meeting, Masoud was invited to Pakistan in late October 1990. Notwithstanding Masoud's visit—he met with Ghulam Ishaq Khan, Aslam Beg and ISI head Asad Durrani, as well as resistance leaders, including Hekmatyar—the ISI found its immediate plans to end the war effectively vetoed by the unified, independent commanders' council. For the time being at least, the military intelligence could deliver neither reconciliation among traditional and Islamist elements nor a joint operation by the mujahidin.

Questions were again raised about the competence of the ISI and gullibility of Pakistan's civilian leadership. Both had misread the strength of Najibullah and his domestic adversaries. The ISI excused its failure to devise a well-coordinated policy as owing to the differences among the mujahidin. Indeed, the parties of the AIG had once again demonstrated that they could unite only when they chose to take no decisive action. Events had in any case reconfirmed the presence in the ISI of officials who, in their unbroken partnership with Hekmatyar, were, in effect, repositories of Zia's visions for Afghanistan. With the sweeping defeat of Benazir Bhutto's party in the October 1990 National Assembly elections by a broad alliance of parties, the military had seemed destined to strengthen its legitimacy in national politics and gain freer rein. Bhutto held the military intelligence directly responsible for her ouster. The supposed close links of a government coalition headed by Nawaz Sharif to Pakistan's army and the country's Islamists were expected to result in a more rigorous Afghan policy.

Notes

1. Confirmation of this direct assignment of volunteers from military intelligence, disguised as Afghan mujahidin, was not available until Brigadier Mohammad Yousaf, head of the ISI's Afghan Bureau from October 1984 to August 1987, revealed the full extent of Pakistan's involvement militarily inside Afghanistan in his book, co-written with Major Mark Adkin, *The Bear Trap; Afghanistan's Untold Story* (London: Leo Cooper, 1992); see especially pp. 113–127.

2. Edward Girardet, *Afghanistan: The Soviet War* (New York: St. Martin's Press, 1983), p. 67.

3. Carl Bernstein, "Arms for Afghanistan," *The New Republic*, July 18, 1981, pp. 8-10.

4. Robert G. Wirsing, "Repatriation of Afghan Refugees," *Journal of South Asian and Middle East Studies*, Vol. 12, no. 1 (fall 1988), p. 35.

5. *The New York Times*, May 4, 1983.

6. Ahmed Rashid, *The Herald* (Karachi), March 1990, p. 18.

7. Yousaf and Adkin, *The Bear Trap*, pp. 93-94, and pp. 189-194.

8. The Peshawar-based parties have included four Islamist groups: Gulbuddin Hekmatyar's Islamic Party (Hezb-i-Islami), Yunis Khalis' Islamic Party (Hezb-i-Islami), Burhanuddin Rabbani's Islamic Society (Jamiat-i-Islami), and Rasul Sayyaf's Islamic Union (Ittihad-i-Islami). The three considered traditionalist are Sayyed Ahmad Gaylani's National Islamic Front Mahaz-i-Melli), Sibghattullah Mojadeddi's Afghanistan National Liberation Front (Jebh-i-Nejat-i-Milli), and Muhammad Nabi Muhammadi's Islamic Revolutionary Movement Harakat-i-Inquilab-i-Islami). For more description see Robert Canfield, "Afghanistan; The Trajectory of Internal Alignments," *The Middle East Journal*,Vol. 43, no. 2 (Autumn 1989), pp. 642-643.

9. Tim Weiner, *Blank Check; The Pentagon's Black Budget* (New York: Warner Books, 1991), p.150.

10. Edward Girardet, *The Christian Science Monitor*, September 7, 1988. The U.S. supply network of arms to the Afghan resistance was also alleged to have been used, with the cooperation of the Zia government, as a back door operation to provide weapons to Iran during the 1980s. Washington's planned diversion of weapons would explain complaints that only $390 million of the $1.09 billion appropriated by Congress for CIA operations area from 1980 to 1986 had actually reached the mujahidin. The same Israeli and Pakistani intelligence sources responsible for the allegations assert that between 1983 and 1986 an Israeli military advisory group also helped to train mujahidin, including Hekmatyar's forces, in military tactics and in the use of sophisticated weapons such as Stinger anti-aircraft missiles. Lawrence Lifschutz, *Far Eastern Economic Review*, December 19, 1991, pp. 14–15. Also, Ahmed Rashid, *The Independent* (London) November 7, 1991, p. 14, quoting the Lahore weekly *The Friday Times*.

11. Weiner, *Blank Check*, p.153. The higher figure is offered by Robert G. Wirsing, *Pakistan's Security Under Zia, 1977–88* (New York: St. Martin's Press, 1991), based on personal interviews. There were also rumors of fraud and corruption at the beginning of the pipeline in Karachi. Brigadier Yousaf claims that there was indeed ineptitude and probably dishonesty, but that the CIA was in charge at this section of the supply channel. He insists that the middle section of the pipeline, was "virtually corruption-free." He argues that the only instance when the Pakistan army was given arms from shipments to the mujahidin involved 200 machine guns given explicitly in order to provide additional security after increased Soviet and Afghan border violations. Yousef and Adkin, *The Bear Trap*, p. 102.

12. See, for example, Foreign Broadcast Information Service (FBIS), *Daily Report*, Near East and South Asia, Washington D.C., February 2, 1989, p. 70.

13. Yousaf and Adkin, *The Bear Trap*, p. 117.

14. Ibid., p.113.

15. Pressure by the CIA for a larger role was more visible by 1988, but Brigadier Yousaf takes a different view: he claims that from the very start the ISI had to resist the Americans' desire for a direct hand in the distribution of weapons, operational planning, and the training of fighters. Ibid., p. 115.

16. Lifshutz, from interview reported in *The Nation* (Lahore), February 15, 1990. James Rupert and Steve Coll contend in *The Washington Post*, May 13, 1990, that drug corruption could not have occurred without the awareness of the ISI and, indeed, its protection and participation in the trafficking.

17. Ibid.

18. Mushahid Hussain, quoted in *The Christian Science Monitor*, October 3, 1989.

19. Seyyed Vali Reza Nasr, "Islamic Opposition to the Islamic State: The Jama'at-i-Islami, 1977–88," *International Journal of Middle East Studies*, Vol. 25 (1993), p. 268–269. Nasr observers that in the process the Jama'at developed close ties with the Saudi Arabian as well as Pakistani security forces.

20. Sheila Tefft, *The Christian Science Monitor*, October 3, 1989. Also see Steve Coll, *Washington Post*, July 20, 1992.

21. Weiner, *Blank Check*, p. 149.

22. Foreign Broadcast Information Service (FBIS), March 9, 1988, p. 53, from *Frontier Post* (Peshawar), March 8, 1988, interview with resistance leader Sibghattullah Mojadeddi.

23. Ahmed Rashid, *The Herald*, May 1992, p. 26.

24. There were reports that Pakistan's military intelligence at one point cooperated with resistance fighters loyal to Hekmatyar in organizing a 2,000-man force for the purpose of attacking Massud's army. *The Washington Times,* April 11, 1990.

25. *The Guardian* (Manchester), March 12, 1989.

26. *The Friday Times* (Lahore), March 19–25, 1992. The largest number of fighters joined Rasul Sayaff's Ittehad or Gulbuddin's Hezb-i-Islami. It was General Gul who estimated that as many as 25,000 Arabs came during the course of the war. Ahmed Rashid, *The Herald*, May 1993, reprinted in *Afghan Forum*, Vol. 21, no. 4 (July 1993): 18–19. Sheila Tefft in the *The Christian Science Monitor*, June 20, 1990, claimed the presence in the war zone of 4,000 volunteers during mid-1990. Salamat Ali put the number of Arabs fighters in Pakistan in spring 1991 at 5,000. *Far Eastern Economic Review*, May 23, 1991, p. 24. One of the largest of the Arab revolutionary groups operated on both sides of the Pakistan-Afghanistan border and was run by a Saudi Arabian national. It is reported to have spent about $100,000 a month on its military instruction and paid its recruits during their instruction. Ibid. Other sponsorship is traced to the Cairo-based Islamic Brotherhood.

27. Riaz M. Khan, *Untying the Afghan Knot; Negotiating Soviet Withdrawal* (Durham, N. C.: Duke University Press, 1991), pp. 79–81.

28. Ibid. p. 73.

29. Louis Dupree, "Post Withdrawal Afghanistan: Light at the End of the Tunnel," in Amin Saikal and William Maley (eds.), *The Soviet Withdrawal from Afghanistan* (London: Cambridge University Press, 1989), p. 33.

30. See Barnett R. Rubin, "Rebuilding the Afghan State: From Above and From Below," a paper presented at meetings of the Middle East Studies Association, Los Angeles, November 3, 1989, p. 16.

31. Stereotypes affect expectations about Afghan political behavior. Many Pakistanis in decision making positions tend to view Afghans the way they see Pakistan's own tribal Pathans, as untrustworthy and a "swaggering, armed aggressive lot." Akbar S. Ahmed in a 1984 ms. cited by Nancy Dupree, "Demographic Reporting on Afghan Refugees in Pakistan," *Modern Asian Studies*, Vol. 25, no. 2 (1988): 243.

32. Rubin, "Rebuilding the Afghan State," p. 15.

33. Ibid., p. 16.

34. Oliver Roy, *Adelphi Papers* #259 "The Lessons of the Soviet/Afghan War," Summer 1991: 41. According to one report, the ISI offered large stocks of weapons to the commanders in the Qandahar area in southern Afghanistan if they would agree to attack this large city; but they felt alienated from the shura-created government in Pakistan and hesitant to cause the deaths of a large number of fellow tribesmen, so they refused the Pakistani offer. Rubin, "Rebuilding the Afghan State," p. 19.

35. Ibid., p. 16.

36. Raja Anwar, *The Nation* (Lahore), May 21, 1989.

37. Lifshutz, ibid. , February 15, 1990.

38. FBIS, October 3, 1989, p. 64, Benazir Bhutto interview with BBC World Service, October 2, 1989.

39. The United States was particularly interested in retrieving from the Afghans the effective hand-held Stinger anti-aircraft weapons which the Pakistanis had received in 1985 and the mujahidin in late 1986. Along with Sidewider air-to-air missiles, they had been supplied after much hesitation in Washington in response to Pakistan's request for defensive systems to counter repeated air violations of its territory by Kabul government and Soviet aircraft.

40. *The Washington Post*, March 9, 1990.

41. Steve Coll and James Rupert, ibid.,November 4, 1990.

4

The Refugees

Throughout the Afghan conflict, Pakistanis shared a sense of concern about the threat posed by refugees to their country's political stability and economic well-being. In a Pakistan already beset with serious cleavages between secular westernizers and Islamic radicals, political conservatives and left-oriented populists, many voiced fears about the implications of an Afghan refugee population, some 80 percent of it ethnic Pashtuns, on the regional politics of Pakistan, especially on the continued political dominance of the country's Punjabis. The refugees, a large, heavily armed population, were already held as responsible for many of the country's social ills, above all, contributing to the breakdown in law and order. There were frequent references to Pakistan's "Kalashnikov culture," an intensification of violence in the society imported by the Afghans. The country's economy was also seen as being adversely affected, especially should the refugees have to be permanently absorbed. To many Pakistanis, the socio-economic impact of the displaced Afghans was thought to be greater, or likely more durable, than the domestic political effects.

Notwithstanding this, the hospitality or at least toleration shown by Pakistan toward the Afghans has been, by all measures, quite extraordinary.[1] Throughout most of the war the number of Afghan refugees sheltered in Pakistan exceeded 3.2 million. The overwhelming number of them were ethnic cousins of Pakistan's Pathans, with whom they share linguistic, cultural, and religious ties. Moreover, taking responsibility for Afghans fleeing to Pakistan to find security and take up arms followed Muslim and tribal traditions of giving protection to those asking for it. Even while hoping for the early repatriation of the refugees, most Pakistanis accepted that the Afghans should not be forced to return until they could do so in peace and honor—to an independent country that would eventually be rehabilitated. In general, the Pakistanis took

pride in having borne the political and economic burdens in the true
spirit of Islamic brotherhood. In this spirit, the Afghan cause evoked
sympathy as a "holy war" against the communists.

The Camps

Afghan migration into Pakistan was not entirely a new phenomenon
or one necessarily related to the fighting. Even before the Soviet invasion,
it is estimated that normally about 75,000 Afghans crossed the border
yearly.[2] Plainly, when Afghans were faced with an unpopular, repressive
regime and the invasion of their country by Soviet troops, Pakistan
would be a convenient and logical place of refuge. In a practical sense,
the porous border made it nearly impossible to block their entry into
Pakistan. The flow of political refugees across the border had actually
begun on a small scale before Moscow's armed intervention. As
mentioned in Chapter 1, having failed in a 1974 insurgency against the
Afghan Republic's president Mohammad Daoud, Muslim
fundamentalist insurgents escaped to Pakistan. They were welcomed by
Pakistan's prime minister, Zulfikar Ali Bhutto, who had given support to
the rebellion in the hopes of discouraging Daoud's expected pressing of
the Pashtunistan issue.[3]

The massive exodus to Pakistan began soon following the
communist coup of April 1978, and the flow followed the intensity of the
conflict inside Afghanistan. Now a more diverse group of refugees, they
were fleeing from the armed struggle that had begun in the countryside
by the summer of 1978, after the communists had tried to impose their
ideologically inspired reform program. Conformity was also imposed on
the cities, and large numbers of government officials and intellectuals
departed. There occurred a steadily increasing flow of refugees to
Pakistan from the end of November 1979, just before the Soviet invasion,
when there were approximately 315 thousand registered refugees, to the
end of March 1981 when the number had jumped to 1.8 million.[4] In
summer 1984, the number had reached 2.86 million. No figures were
very accurate, however, given the difficulty in registering refugees once
they had crossed the border and the limited personnel available to the
Pakistan refugee administration to enumerate the population. Some
arrivals failed to register with Pakistani authorities; but according to
U.N. sources, there were more cases of over-enumeration resulting from
bogus or multiple registration by those claiming dependents eligible for
rations. Just as it served the Afghans' interest to exaggerate their
numbers, Pakistani authorities were motivated to raise the figures on

which foreign aid was based.[5] Larger numbers also helped to dramatize the acuteness of the refugee problem.

Very clearly, Pakistan was not prepared for the massive movement of Afghans across the border. The long-term problem of settling the refugees received little thought in Islamabad, and haphazard policies prevailed, initially giving district administrators considerable discretion.[6] Prior to the post-Soviet invasion influx, there had been few official camps, and the refugees settled as best they could in the border, tribal areas. It was on the advice of the U.N. High Commission for Refugees (UNHCR), which Pakistan had turned to in April 1979 for help in caring for the refugees, that camps were gradually established and moved farther from the border in the two eastern provinces, North-West Frontier (NWFP) and Baluchistan.[7] Attempts to coordinate relief efforts with the UNHCR and others led in 1981 to overall supervision of the refugees being given to a Pakistani Chief Commissionerate for Afghan Refugees (CCAR), with its main office in Islamabad and sub-offices in Peshawar and Quetta. The commissioner was charged with implementing the policy set by various cabinet ministries and President Zia, and administered Pakistan's policies through civil servants at the provincial level.

The refugee camps, more than 350 in Pakistan, were typically set up with about 10,000 inhabitants and divided into refugee villages, each serving 1,200 to 1,300 families. One of the largest, however, had a population of 120,000 that covered five square miles. Every settlement was assigned several officials who helped administer the available services, maintained order, and occasionally helped settle disputes among the refugees. In all, by the time that the bulk of refugees had arrived in the mid-1980s, somewhere between 10,000 and 12,000 people, mostly local Pakistanis, were involved in the governmental and non-governmental administrative infrastructure.[8]

Until January 1979, the Islamabad government allocated its own resources to care for the refugees, paying a subsistence allowance for the hundreds of thousands. At this time, about $12 per head was the official monthly payment to the refugees. The designated subsidy was lowered by more than half when the UNHCR, World Food Program, and others joined the relief effort, as commodity aid (e.g., wheat, edible oil, powdered milk, sugar) was introduced to supplement the cash allowance. The assistance also provided limited vocational training as well as a primary and middle school in each tent village. Official government figures listed three high schools, 125 middle schools, and 571 primary schools, with 2,877 teachers, two-thirds of whom were from among the refugees. Refugees could also receive free medical services at government health units run by the government and private voluntary agencies. In all, Pakistan claimed that there were 186 Basic Health Units and 66 satellite units staffed by 295 doctors and 2,000 paramedical personnel.[9] Pakistan transported and distributed the basic foodstuffs supplied by relief agencies. Dependence for regular assistance was made unavoidable by Pakistan's regulations preventing the Afghans from cultivating the land.

In Iran, with more than two million Afghans (by some estimates almost three million), little or no financial support was given to individual refugees; and only a small number of aid agencies were permitted to operate. Eighty refugee camps, or "guest cities" as they were called, were built, but less than 10 percent of the refugees lived in them since most chose to settle in Iran's eastern border towns and Tehran. Afghans found work in a number of occupations, most of all the building trades and, as in Pakistan, their competition was resented. Overall, Afghans in Iran were offered greater independence than refugees in Pakistan; yet despite their fuller integration into Iranian society, they also suffered more hardship.

By the mid-1980s, the Government of Pakistan had taken official responsibility for 45 percent of the costs of maintaining the refugees, the UNHCR, 25 percent; the World Food Program, 25 percent; and others, including Saudi Arabia and Kuwait as well as the Red Cross, the additional 5 percent.[10] Pakistan assumed the costs of the internal transport of refugee aid, a figure estimated at $70 million yearly in the mid-1980s, along with its responsibility for the administration and security of commodities.[11] In all, Pakistan's share was supposedly in excess of $1 million daily and considered a considerable drain on the national budget. The figure given was in fact misleading; it did not take into consideration other monies that were brought into the Pakistan's North-West Frontier Province and Baluchistan by virtue of the Afghans' presence and the stimulus of the refugees on local economies. The size of the government's contribution may itself have been grossly inflated. By most reports, refugee families seldom in fact received their rupee cash allowance, which made up much of Pakistan's publicized expenditure for the Afghans.[12]

Arriving refugees from Afghanistan were expected to become affiliated with one of the Afghan political groups in order to be certified as refugees. To qualify for rations from the Pakistan government, they had also to settle in a government-designated camp area. In effect, the procedures served as an endorsement of the mujahidin groups by the Pakistan government and, more accurately, allowed a bias in favor of those that could best organize the camps. By carrying out relief work of various kinds, these parties could cultivate support among the refugees. Especially in the early years, Pakistan's fundamentalist party Jama'at-i-

Islami also had good access to the camps. The party's presence facilitated the operations of strongly Islamist groups among the Afghans.

Hezb-i-Islami was particularly favored by the Pakistani refugee administration. Many camp officials provided easier registration and earlier assistance if individuals identified with Hekmatyar's party. Licenses for trucks owned by Afghan refugees were facilitated for those who joined the Hezb-i-Islami. U.N.-monitored funds were regularly diverted to the Hezb-i-Islami, enabling it to gain more than its fair share of rations, tents, and other relief aid.[13] To please the Hezb-i-Islami and the other hard-line parties, and also to assure that any Afghan nationalist ideas were kept to a minimum, the Pakistanis gave the Islamists a stronger voice in the educational programs in the camps and, later, in the cross-border transfer of educational materials and establishment of schools inside the war zone.

Overall control in each camp was put in the hands of a Pakistani official whose legitimacy was gained not only from his government appointment but from the approval of the dominant political group in the camp as well as the camp's elders. The Pakistani camp managers dealt, then, with a camp leadership who were often not part of the traditional elite. The Afghan camp heads, or *maliks*, were frequently called "ration maliks" for their ability to get people on the ration list and to offer other favors. Expected to get along with the authorities, the maliks were more the choice of Pakistani officials than the refugees.[14] Under Pakistani administration, *jirgas* (councils) were also formed to deal with problems facing the refugees. Although attempts were made to organize these meetings in a traditional manner, they were often politicized by those Afghan parties favored by the authorities.

Diffusion in lines of authority in the camps was understandable. The long exile found many of the traditional village and family heads incompetent to deal with Pakistani authorities and relief organizations. Individual loyalties to clan and tribe have naturally suffered as an alternative body of leaders, most of them young and educated, emerged to fill the vacuum. To survive, traditional status groups were often forced to take on new or revised roles. For example, members of the *ulema*, the clerics, gained increased respect in their role as deputies to the mujahidin leadership. Often serving as intermediaries, they participated in carrying the unifying message of Islam, inspiring and consoling refugees and resistance fighters. Rather than necessarily competing for influence, functional distinctions developed among leaders in the refugee community, reflecting different layers of competence and authority over different matters.

Private Voluntary Organizations

Critical components in the relief operation were the private voluntary organizations, or PVOs (more inclusively known as NGOs—nongovernmental organizations together with international agencies), that were given permission by Pakistan to work among the refugees. Very early in the war, Pakistan authorities sought to minimize the importance of the arrival of refugees in the NWFP and Baluchistan. No official policy in Islamabad was in effect, and provincial governments regulated the activities of relief organizations. In June 1980, however, the Zia government issued policies on the PVOs that sharply restricted their activities, especially in the border tribal areas. Even then, exceptions were made: the federal and provincial governments, as well as refugee leaders, encouraged one PVO, the International Rescue Committee, to set up a medical program in the camps.

In the early period, most of the PVO officials and U.N. experts sent to administer the aid programs displayed little understanding of the social structure and organization, or even the needs, of the Afghans.[15] Allowing foreigners more first-hand experience in the tribal areas where most of the camps had been located carried drawbacks, however: freer access could allow the Kabul government and their Soviet allies to claim that foreign advisors were training Afghan guerrillas, thus conceivably giving the communists a possible pretext for expanding the war into Pakistan.[16] Pakistani officials did authorize a number of countries' humanitarian aid organizations, such as those from Sweden and Austria, to open offices in Peshawar. However, the Islamabad government was more cautious, as was the U.S. government, about the involvement of private groups, fearing that their presence would draw charges that they were CIA front operations.[17] For several years, then, nearly all U.S. relief assistance was channeled through the United Nations.

The resentment that could be detected among Pakistani authorities toward the PVOs—that is, against the foreign relief workers—was particularly evident in the early years when these personnel had difficulty receiving clearances for travel and were beset with bureaucratic delays and "obfuscation."[18] Religious parties and Arab associations in Pakistan tried to convince government officials that Western volunteer organizations were engaged in Christian missionary activities or that they were communists. Foreigners faced long delays in obtaining official permission from Pakistani authorities to work for PVOs, and many did so illegally on tourist visas. While the NWFP government was often more cooperative, authorities in Islamabad were especially slow to give clearance to foreigners employed by PVOs engaged in cross-border operations, most of which had been operating successfully if modestly since 1988. There is evidence of bribery and extortion in the form of "transit fees" being imposed on foreign aid officials by Pakistani border police as well as certain mujahidin groups. The Pakistan army, police, and refugee administration, often in connivance with members of Afghan resistance parties, operated scams to sell relief supplies, weapons, and favors.[19]

The prime figure in suppressing PVO activities between 1980 and mid-1983 was the Pakistani appointed as commissioner for the refugees, Sheikh Abdullah Khan. A deeply committed Muslim, he made little effort to disguise his suspicion of the Western relief groups, and he managed to discourage several. It was through Abdullah's efforts that the Afghan hard-line Islamic parties gained ready access to the refugee camps; he was especially partial toward the resistance's Hezb-i-Islami. Only after considerable foreign pressure on Islamabad was Abdullah finally removed. Subsequent commissioners were far less ideological and were not viewed as obstacles to foreign relief work.

As the burden of administering to the refugees grew and international interest in the needs of Afghan civilians both in the camps and across the border increased, Pakistani authorities admitted larger numbers of relief organizations to set up shop in Peshawar. In 1983, 17 PVOs were registered. The only identifiable U.S. group among those operating in 1983 was the International Rescue Committee. By the end of the decade, 75 foreign organizations, 43 of them from Europe and 14 from North America, maintained offices in Pakistan, many with operations among the refugees while also engaged in cross-border activities. Approximately 6,000 local people were employed in nongovernmental relief organizations, including U.N.-related projects.[20] In 1990, 22 of the private voluntary organizations were receiving financial support from the UNHCR for assistance programs.[21]

Afghan resistance parties in Peshawar, despite their suspicions, placed many of their own followers in the employ of the PVOs on whose activities they were expected to report. The relief organizations accepted this infiltration as a necessary price to pay for carrying out their mission. There existed a loose quota in hiring, although followers of Hezb-i-Islami were best represented, a token of the party's influence and of the fact that its members often made the most qualified employees. Because at least some PVOs, working as subcontractors to international or foreign country projects, were obliged to work directly with the AIG, they also came under the watchful eye of Pakistan's military intelligence. Many PVOs felt obliged to hire Pakistani administrators to help them cut red tape in dealing with the Islamabad government.

Concern that the PVOs in their aid activities would become politicized and competitive was felt even within the international community. Donors worried that they could get caught up in inter-party struggles or in the rivalries between regional commanders and Peshawar party leaders. Quarrels had already begun with individual parties leaders over who should control the aid and where resources were to be distributed, especially across the border. Aid resources were, after all, an important means by which these leaders expected to insure the loyalty of groups and individuals. Although PVOs professed no interest in trying to influence political structure, the aiming of most activities in Afghanistan at the local level no doubt helped to enhance the status and consolidate the positions of local commanders and notables. PVOs have also showed a preference for popular participation in assistance programs and encouraged the involvement of village councils, where they exist.

Cooperation among PVOs in assessing the needs of the refugees and in determining priorities was critical to efficient and effective programs. While still only a relatively few groups, largely engaged in independent operations, they had succeeded in avoiding serious overlapping of activities and disagreements. But as many more groups appeared and far more financial resources became available, the potential for overlapping and even conflictive relations among the private and governmental groups greatly increased. Their ability to divide up aid responsibilities functionally and geographically and avoid working at cross purposes was questionable, given their sometimes different development strategies and organizational goals. There was an obvious need for an expanded and more formal effort to coordinate and assist refugee repatriation and rehabilitation projects in order to assure a maximum use of resources and a minimum of friction.

In mid-1988, some 40 PVOs in Peshawar, both those with cross-border activities in place and those planning to enter with new programs, formed the Agency Coordinating Body for Afghan Relief (ACBAR). A similar umbrella organization was formed in Baluchistan. ACBAR's organizers were particularly anxious to avoid a competition for expected U.N. funding. A U.N. coordinator for refugee resettlement, Prince Sadruddin Aga Khan, had been appointed to coordinate all the public and private Afghan relief activities. As an "aid czar," he was designated to bring together the efforts of the several U.N. agencies, the PVOs, and those donor governments likely to participate in resettlement and rehabilitation. Prince Sadruddin announced his intention to raise more than $2 billion from U.N. member states for a three-to-four year program.

Demands were frequently heard that more PVOs be located under direct Afghan supervision. Western expatriate mangers and directors usually expressed sympathy with the need to hire Afghans or turn activities over to Afghan organizations but insisted that not enough qualified Afghans were available. In any case, Pakistani authorities were not helpful. The several Afghan PVOs that managed to form found it difficult to obtain the "no objection certificates" from the government necessary to hire a staff. The Pakistanis, in fact, preferred the Western organizations that brought their own funds and that were more successful than Afghan PVOs in remaining independent of particular mujahidin groups.

Even though the presence of PVOs also meant that the local administration was obliged to share control over the refugees, many in the Pakistani bureaucracy were also appreciative of the efforts of foreign groups and, in general, did not interfere in their activities, whether in Pakistan or across the border. Humanitarian aid in commodities and services inside Afghanistan begun in 1985 by USAID—distributed through local resistance commanders and their shuras—required transport through Pakistan with government approval. In cooperation with Pakistani authorities, USAID in 1988 established the Afghan Construction and Logistic Unit that in addition to the transport of goods also improved and constructed necessary roads and bridges. The unit, employing 200 Afghan drivers, maintained a facility on the outskirts of Peshawar. U.S. Air Force planes also landed goods in Pakistan donated by American private organizations for use across the border.[22]

Yet the Islamabad government was at times inconsistent and self-defeating by applying restrictions on those PVOs engaged in cross-border relief efforts. Some of these restrictions, including those on the transfer of wheat, edible oil, sugar, and other commodities to Afghanistan and on the number of border crossing points, were justified by concerns that the transfers to Afghanistan had raised prices in nearby Pakistani markets and spurred the smuggling of essential commodities. At other times, policies that made the work of these PVO programs more difficult appeared to result from normal bureaucratic confusion in ad hoc policies, or was a reflection of the frustrations over the failure of PVOs to induce more refugees to return.

Anxious to have the refugees leave at the earliest possible time, the Pakistan government was prepared to facilitate the international relief groups and PVOs in activities that might hasten resettlement. Islamabad was particularly supportive of de-mining operations—essential if refugees were to find it safe to return—and allowed them to be run out of military camps in Pakistan. By the end of the 1980s, however, humanitarian aid offered by Western relief groups was at times also criticized in Pakistan as offering an incentive for refugees to delay or refuse repatriation.

Refugees as an Issue

Pakistani authorities tried for many years to give the impression that there were no serious domestic political, social, or economic problems associated with the settlement of refugees. They were proud to point out that the Afghan refugees were normally free to move about throughout Pakistan; nowhere were there restricting checkpoints or fences around villages. But Pakistanis were quick to acknowledge the impact of the refugees on their economy and society. Overall the refugees came to represent about 20 percent of the population in the two most affected provinces, the North-West Frontier and Baluchistan. In some areas, however, the ratio of refugees to local population was one-to-one and in a few areas they outnumbered the local population. The refugees thus upset a balance of population among tribes and sects in certain tribal districts. The influx of Afghans into Baluchistan tipped the ethnic balance in favor of the ethnic Pathans over the Baluch. Sectarian tensions were also heightened as the balance in the Kurram Agency of the NWFP was altered with the influx of thousands of Sunni Afghans into the homelands of a traditional majority of Shi'ites. At the same time, Persian speaking Hazaras arriving from central Afghanistan, mostly Shi'ite, affected the ratio in some areas between this group and Sunni Pashtuns.[23]

The decision to settle the overwhelming number of Afghans in the two provinces and border areas served both mujahidin interests and those of the Islamabad government. Afghans were not anxious to settle down in camps distant from the war zone or far from the population centers of Peshawar and Quetta where they were among their ethno-linguistic relatives and closer to the center of international relief groups. (Almost four-fifths of the camps were located in NWFP, and roughly 61—almost 20 percent of the refugee population—were placed around the city and district of Peshawar.) For a time, the Pakistani authorities had thought it wise to move refugee camps farther from the border, mainly in order to relieve the pressure on resources and improve the law-and-order situation. In 1987, they succeeded in establishing refugee villages in the Mianwali District in the Punjab, bordering the NWFP. But ethno-linguistic differences and the extreme heat made these camps highly unpopular among the Afghans.[24] More important, many Pakistanis argued that large refugee settlements should be kept out of the country's largest province—the Punjab. It was seen as symbolically unwise to transfer the refugee settlements into the heartland of Pakistan, among the Punjabis with their history of antagonism with Pathans. By keeping the camps at a safe distance from the dominant, sensitive

Punjabi population, authorities expected to better sustain national acceptance of the Afghan refugees.

Evidence of widespread ill feeling toward the Afghans in exile is lacking for the first few years following their arrival. At most, a few petty lawsuits occurred, mostly over land appropriated for refugee camps.[25] Pakistanis from South Waziristan and other tribal areas were among the first to complain about privileges accorded the refugees that, they claimed, enabled the Afghans to live better than they did. They criticized the wide array of services available in the camps as compared with far less access to education, housing, and health-related services available to border-area Pakistanis. Locals especially resented cash payments to the refugees. The food commodities supplied the Afghans assured that there was no starvation in the camps and few cases of severe malnutrition, while no parallel programs existed among Pakistan's tribal population. Locals believed, with some reason, that domestic expenditures on the refugees meant that assistance came at the expense of development efforts for their impoverished areas. Disputes also erupted in time over control and use of grazing fields and limited water resources, the consumption of forest wood, and the employment competition in agriculture and construction.[26] The refugees brought with them as many as three million head of livestock—detrimental to the environment because of their grazing on scarce pasture land and the fragile soil. Serious deforestation in Pakistan's Chitral, Dir, and Hazara border districts could be easily traced to refugees seeking firewood for cooking and heating.

The competition of refugees in trade and the crafts and their alleged displacement of local Pakistanis made resentments inevitable in the cities. An adult male wage earner could be found in the great majority of refugee families. Desperate for work, the poorer Afghans were hired by Pakistani traders and builders. They were often transported long distances and paid very modest salaries. Because the Afghans in the labor force usually worked for less money (possible in part because of their camp welfare programs), they depressed wages and put thousands of local workers, those at the bottom of the pay scale, out of work. Better-off Afghans, sometimes with Pakistani partners, opened restaurants, hotels, and retail shops, usually displaying more enterprise than their local counterparts. The competition for jobs even extended to doctors in Peshawar where there was an oversupply. Refugees who had brought trucks and buses with them quickly took up transport activities. Afghan trucks generally have a greater load capacity to transport goods than Pakistani trucks, giving them a particular advantage on longer haul transportation. Also the Afghans were successfully able to compete in providing the public with private bus service in Peshawar and

Islamabad.[27] Importantly, Afghan entrepreneurs employed their brethren Afghan refugees rather than local lower class Pakistanis. Better-off Afghans were accused, moreover, of not paying taxes.[28]

Many refugees are said to have secured "unjust and illegal benefits" from the relief program as a result of connections and corrupt practices, and through manipulation of the relief system with and without the knowledge of Pakistani officials at the district level and below. Some refugees accused of settling on private property refused to move or give compensation to the landowner. Although non-Pakistanis were prohibited from purchasing immovable property, some better-off refugees in fact managed to get around the restrictions through legal means and purchased real estate. As a result, prices, in particular house rents, were inflated, adding to the resentments of middle- and lower-class Pakistani residents of Peshawar and Quetta. In general, Afghans were accused of pushing up the prices of consumer goods.[29] Shortages of wheat and rice in Pakistani markets were blamed on the smuggling of commodities into Afghanistan. Despite Pakistan's bumper wheat crop in 1989, for example, the country was forced to import 1.8 million tons of wheat, a result, it was widely believed, of grains being smuggled to higher priced markets in Afghanistan as well as India. At the same time, some refugees were making a living selling carpets and other goods smuggled from Afghanistan. When Pakistani authorities early in 1990 succeeded in closing a major smuggling route across the Pakistan-Afghanistan border, this aroused the anger not only of the Afghans but of many Pakistani tribal traders, who were themselves selling illegally imported good from the Soviet Union, Japan, and the West.

The refugees stood accused of contributing to a serious breakdown in law-and-order in host provinces and throughout Pakistan. There was greater lawlessness in the schools and on the roads. Afghans were held responsible for an increase in armed robberies. At least some attacks were aimed at Peshawar-based foreign relief agencies, in a number of instances by people incited by their leaders into believing that the groups were engaged in Christian missionary activities. (In one instance, in April 1990 between 5,000 and 6,000 people plundered the facilities of Shelter Now International, a U.S.-funded agency.) The Pakistani police accused the refugees of involvement in 75 percent of the crimes committed in the NWFP during 1991.[30]

The illegal sale and spread of weapons throughout Pakistan was also linked to the Afghans. By some estimates, about a quarter of the arms from the United States, Saudi Arabia, and China were thought to have been diverted for use by Pakistani secessionists, bandits, and others.[31] More than ever, with more small arms in circulation, Pakistanis were using weapons to settle differences. Violent ethnic conflicts in the metropolitan areas of the Sindh were blamed on the refugees, if only indirectly.[32]

Involvement by Kabul's agents in the ethnic riots that flared up in Karachi in 1986 and 1987 is often alleged. Many observers believe that with the Soviets and Kabul government acting as paymasters, money in the right hands—those of drug-dealing gangs of Afghan exiles—helped to instigate communal conflict between economically hard-pressed Pathans and Mohajirs (earlier refugees and their descendants from India). The Karachi ethnic riots seemed to be linked to the Geneva-based talks going on between Pakistan and Afghanistan. Officials in the Pakistan government were convinced that the violence was designed to weaken Islamabad's bargaining position at the negotiations.

Refugees were accused of deep involvement in international drug trafficking. To be sure, Afghans had long been active in the heroin trade which escalated during the war. Opium grown in Afghanistan was typically brought into Pakistan by trucks and mules returning from trips carrying CIA-purchased arms into Afghanistan. Incentives increased for Pakistani farmers in border areas to grow more poppies and, together with resistance-controlled areas of Afghanistan, the larger region became one of the world's major suppliers to the West.[33] Heroin addiction for the first time also became a serious problem within Pakistan; for prior to the war, very little heroin was refined in Pakistan and the number of addicts numbered only a few thousand. By the end of the 1980s, Pakistan was thought to have more than a million drug addicts, and the number may have risen to 1.7 million by 1993.[34] Income from the production and purification of heroin and hashish—reportedly in about 100 labs in the tribal areas southwest of Peshawar—understandably had a major, distorting impact on Pakistan's economy. The illegitimate money, moving in covert channels, could not enter the formal sectors of the economy. Instead it flowed into a gray market that influenced the country's internal commerce in the form of conspicuous consumption and speculative investment, particularly in real estate in all of Pakistan's major cities.[35] The guns and corruption that accompanied the explosion of drugs meanwhile added to the social destabilization of Pakistan.

The presence of the exiled Afghans, it was often charged, had attracted foreign saboteurs and infiltrators who were seen as posing a threat to Pakistan's security. Soviet and Kabul government agents were held directly and indirectly responsible for sabotage efforts, and cross-border penetrations of Pakistani airspace and territory sought to exploit local feelings. It was widely believed that individuals in the pay of the Kabul regime infiltrated the camps with the intention of creating antagonisms and fomenting riots among the Afghans and with Pakistanis. The subversion which began in earnest in 1984 had changed in character by late 1986; the bombings became more costly in lives and were designed to attract attention by targeting hotels, hospitals, and other public places. At the same time, the popular perception among Pakistanis was that the government had not cracked down hard enough on the refugees in their illegal activities.

Opposition to the Zia regime in the press as elsewhere probably intentionally exaggerated the refugees' disruptive effects. The refugees served as a lightening rod for the opposition, a convenient scapegoat for many of Pakistan's problems. Politically, the terrorist acts were tests of the commitment of the Pakistan government toward helping the resistance and larger refugee community. Whatever groups were actually responsible, the readiness of officials and many in the public to associate urban terrorism with the Afghan conflict rather than with internal problems alone contributed to the uneasiness of the Afghan refugees.

Thus the explosions that occurred in Karachi on July 14, 1987, and claimed the lives of 80 people were predictably blamed by Pakistani officials as well as U.S. government spokesmen on Afghan government or Soviet agents, with the aim of forcing Pakistan to change its Afghanistan policy. However, it is also plausible that in collusion or on their own, the bombings were politically motivated acts by leftist dissidents in Pakistan against the Zia regime that only a week earlier had marked ten years in power. Some also suggested that the explosions in a busy market and crowded residential area were associated with the upcoming trials of five Palestinians accused of hijacking an American airliner at Karachi Airport in September 1986. Other bombings in the NWFP in August 1978 seemed clearly designed to shake Pakistan's support for the mujahidin.[36]

The refugees had their explanations and their own complaints. A widespread view existed that refugees were not being treated equally under the laws; if there were a dispute with a local Pakistani, the Afghan was held to blame. In general, the refugees saw themselves as scapegoats for many of Pakistan's social problems and as exploited when convenient. Refugees were forced to accept lower wages: an Afghan hired as a construction worker earned 15 rupees to 20 earned by a Pakistani.[37] Afghan leaders have insisted that drug offenses were neither inspired nor condoned by the refugee community. The offenses alleged had been only minor incidents involving truck drivers motivated by greed, who denied that Afghan parties had been involved.[38]

Refugee leaders regularly complained about CCAR's provincial administration of relief efforts. There is widespread belief in the camps that officials in charge of ration distribution were able to appropriate much of the aid for themselves. Cash subsidies and provisions intended for the refugees were often delayed and fees exacted for the registration of refugees. Normally, the system of contracting allows for bribes or skimming off of 10 percent. But when Pakistani officials went beyond these culturally allowable bounds, demanding 20 or 30 percent, complaints increased and pressures mounted for a crackdown. The authorities were forced to admit to lapses by ill-trained and hastily recruited officials and were obliged from time to time to punish employees with transfers, demotions, and even dismissals.[39] As early as 1981, 225 persons assigned to administrative duties had punitive action taken against them.[40] More typically, the Pakistan government denied leaks in the humanitarian aid pipeline and refuted allegations of corruption among high CCAR officials.

The health clinics and schools, although appreciated by the refugees, seldom had enough doctors and nurses, and teachers and books were in short supply. The level of education was generally below standard; the curriculum was usually poorly designed; and teachers frequently unqualified. The Pakistanis also attempted to control the curriculum, at least to the extent of discouraging the teaching of materials stressing Afghan nationalism. They also vetoed some teaching programs, such as those that taught vocational skills applicable in the local economy, for fear that those less dependent on charity might have more incentive to remain in Pakistan. Thus, the ministries in Islamabad held up releasing funds for a World-Bank-sponsored income-generating project for refugees.[41] Government officials tried to limit the refugees to self-contained projects such as truck farming or to involvement with camp-related infrastructural construction, where they would be less able to put down economic roots. Carpet-weaving projects sponsored by the government did take hold among certain ethnic groups but not among the Pashtuns who have no tradition in the carpet trade.

Despite these services, most unavailable in rural Afghanistan and certain to raise popular expectations in the future, the camps were hardly desirable places to live on a long-term basis. Women, in particular, were obliged to remain cooped up in the camps and missed the freedom of movement that they had once had in Afghanistan; they were anxious to return to more productive lives.[42] Afghan urban, middle-class women suffered in particular from ultra-conservative attitudes in Pakistan society that sought to limit or deny them education or career opportunities. Tradition-minded Afghans lamented the deterioration in the Afghan social structure and the emergence of new social groups and individuals disrespectful of previous authority figures. Pakistani authorities were not entirely apologetic about physical and social conditions. The lives of the refugees were, after all, not supposed to be so comfortable that most would not want to return once the fighting had ceased.

Many Afghans also expressed the existence of a climate of fear in Peshawar for those who might express themselves in a fashion critical of Pakistan. They claimed that they could not speak freely. These Afghans, mainly outside the favored parties, were bitter about the local authorities' inability to halt assassinations and apparent lack of interest in pursuing the killers of well-known Afghan personalities among the refugee community. The PVOs often expressed similar concerns about the need for better protection by Pakistani authorities for their foreign and Afghan personnel.

The inability of the Afghan resistance parties in Peshawar to mount an effective united front against the Kabul government no doubt contributed to the erosion of public sympathy in Pakistan. But in the changing opinion climate, refugees were never denied the freedom of travel and employment within Pakistan and, indeed, many were permitted, even encouraged, to pursue vocations outside the camps in order to supplement their relief payments. To be sure, had the Pakistani authorities ever attempted to restrict the movement of the refugees, forcing them to remain or return to camps, the possibility of armed clashes might have occurred. And whatever friction emerged between the refugees and local Pakistanis, government officials normally tried to minimize their importance. (Pakistani police also frequently avoided intervention in clashes between rival groups of refugees.) Still, given the increased animosities and opportunities for friction between the refugees and their hosts in the NWFP and Baluchistan, there were remarkably few incidents of violence between the two communities in the cities or countryside.

Delayed Repatriation

With the withdrawal of Soviet forces throughout the second half of 1988, Afghan refugees in Pakistan did not stream back to their villages and cities. Their desire for an early repatriation notwithstanding, most refugees insisted that they would return only after an Islamic government had been installed in Kabul. Political leaders of the seven-party alliance of resistance fighters, to whom most refugees in Pakistan owed at least nominal allegiance, admonished their followers not to leave. They argued that the communist regime would like nothing more than to attract large number of refugees, giving the impression that the returnees had opted for joining a government of national reconciliation.

In fact, the refugees' behavior was more practical than political, based on concerns for personal security, economic as well as physical.

The Soviet-backed communist government did not crumble, after all, as the Soviets withdrew their forces. However anxious most refugees were to escape the hardships and boredom of the camps in Pakistan, they were unwilling to get caught in the crossfire in Afghanistan or to forfeit the basic material support provided by international donors and Pakistan for uncertainties across the border. Most resistance commanders inside Afghanistan in fact cautioned against a too early return, envisioning the refugees competing in the short run for scarce food and fuel and otherwise complicating the military effort. An estimated half million farm animals had been killed during the war, and 100,00 acres of scarce forest had disappeared. The presence of thousands of uncleared land mines, seeded by both sides in the conflict, was by itself sufficient to disrupt agriculture and delay the refugees' return. Chances of massive resettlement in 1989 were also influenced by the weather, the timing for planting of a wheat crop, and the availability of adequate transportation across the border. After as much as 14 years in exile, many who would return to the provinces had forgotten or had never learned how to farm. Most important, the international relief effort was not in place in 1989 (or in subsequent years) to assure returning refugees of sufficient food, agricultural inputs, and the likelihood of physical reconstruction— especially irrigation systems, roads, and shelter—required for the rural masses to manage a successful resettlement. The additional time needed to oust the Kabul regime was as not altogether unwelcome by international agencies in need of more time to organize and finance their programs.

The concern in Islamabad had been that if the war with the Najibullah regime had dragged on indefinitely, international humanitarian aid would be reduced substantially or ended. To avoid severely aggravating the hardship among the refugees, Pakistan would have had to bear more of the burden. For a while there seemed little to worry about. In the expectation of an early repatriation of the refugees following the Soviet withdrawal, the United Nations had announced its "Operation Salam" in order to raise money to implement programs for the reconstruction and rehabilitation inside Afghanistan. Offices were established in Islamabad, Peshawar, and Quetta as well as in Kabul. But with the war's prolongation—with increased fighting an additional 70,000 refugees entered and were registered in Pakistan in early 1989— pledges of international support for "Salam" fell far short of the anticipated $1.16 billion target.

The Soviet Union promised $600 million for the fund. By early 1992 Moscow's commitments had become meaningless. The mujahidin insistence on billions of dollars in war reparations for Afghanistan from the Soviet Union remained a realistic demand until that country's breakup in late 1991. Whatever the good intentions of the leaders in Moscow to work in a common effort to help rebuild the devastated country, it became soon apparent that an economically prostrate Russia would have little to offer financially. In any case, despite an announced willingness of Russia to inherit the obligations of the former Soviet Union, the prevailing view in Moscow is that for past mistakes by communist party leaders, notably cases like Afghanistan, the successor states of the Soviet Union should not be held responsible.

Most of the international community hesitated to make large commitments until the conditions for return of the refugees seemed more favorable. Such potential donor countries as Japan made it clear that their contributions would be delayed until the fighting and divisions among the resistance groups ended. By 1991 the entire program had been sharply scaled down and many of its projects canceled; its budget was cut by $31 million. Operation Salam lacked almost $95 million and 61,000 tons of wheat for needs that had been allocated in a projected 1992 budget for returning refugees.[43]

Continuing corruption and conflict among the resistance elements and Pakistanis also affected cross-border relief operations. Less than half of the overall assistance designated for Afghanistan is believed to have gotten through to the intended recipients. The rest is thought to have been siphoned off by strategically placed groups and individuals in Pakistan, including some government officials. One of the more serious problems was the extensive corruption among Pakistan's border police and resistance leaders in Peshawar. Typically, in order to secure safe passage for supplies and aid workers, bribes were paid. Relief groups frequently kept quiet about abuses, fearing a backlash from donor governments and individuals.

After evidence that wheat deliveries were siphoned off by ISI officials for private gain, the U.S. program worth $30 million in food aid to the mujahidin was temporarily suspended in early 1990.[44] The Peshawar-based Agency Coordinating Body for Afghan Relief (ACBAR), which by mid-1991 represented 58 foreign and Afghan non-governmental relief organizations, was forced to suspend activities in the provinces after intense mujahidin in-fighting and the looting of ACBAR's offices. The work of PVOs was further handicapped when the Pakistani government in early September 1991, following several kidnappings, announced that expatriate aid personnel other than those from the United Nations would be prevented from crossing into Afghanistan.

Assistance to Afghan refugees in Pakistan was also curtailed. About $400 million in U.N. and bilateral aid had been spent in 1988; the amount expended in 1990 was one-third less.[45] By the end of 1989 there had been a 25 percent cut in assistance provided the UNHCR. Correspondingly, during the following year most PVOs (whose combined annual budgets had been $107 million) cut back their programs at least 25 to 30 percent as a result of a drying up of private donations and U.N. and national funds that had been put into their programs.[46] Wheat supplies in 1991 were reported to have been reduced by 25 percent.[47] By some accounts UNHCR-furnished relief supplies had been diverted by the agency to other countries, including Iraq for the Kurdish refugees. Anti-American and anti-Western sentiment, including street demonstrations, forced the temporary departure from Pakistan in early 1991 of aid officials of donor governments and PVOs.

Also as a consequence of the Persian Gulf war, twelve Islamic relief associations grouped as the Islamic Coordination Council and heavily supported by Saudi Arabia and Kuwait saw a reduction of funds and closing of relief centers. Finally, by late 1991, UNHCR financial assistance for the refugees, which had been over $200 million annually, was reduced to about $20 million.[48] The reductions affected not only refugee aid in Pakistan but UNHCR-funded projects for reconstruction and rehabilitation inside Afghanistan. With the sharp reductions of U.N. and other organizations' aid to the refugee camps, many more refugees had shifted to the cities, forcing wage labor rates down still further.[49]

The shortfall in wheat and other commodities as a result of declining deliveries from foreign donors such as the EEC and Japan through the World Food Program had forced Islamabad to draw from its own stocks—with hope of replenishment later. Rations had been reduced from 500 grams per refugee to 400 grams. Malnutrition, which had never been a problem in the refugee camps, was a distinct possibility. Declining food aid to the refugees was said to have prompted thousands of people to flee the camps and, in exchange for modest loans, to enter bonded labor contracts with unscrupulous Pakistani traders.[50] Dependence on scarce forest wood for fuel increased as the supply of kerosene oil was reduced in half. Yet the hardships from a slowdown of relief aid deliveries were also seen as serving Pakistan's interest in encouraging refugees to seek earlier repatriation.

At least through 1991, most resistance groups in Pakistan had sought to discourage, even prevent, repatriation, declaring it a betrayal of the jihad. However, in mid-1990 Pakistan cooperated in devising with the UNHCR and the U.N.-backed Operation Salam a three-month pilot project designed to voluntarily return roughly 250,000 Afghans. A year later only about 60,000 Afghans had in fact been repatriated—most to those border provinces in Afghanistan already secure from Kabul government control.[51] When the UNHCR suggested in November 1991 that Pakistan consider granting citizenship to Afghan refugees who would not or could not return, the Islamabad government flatly rejected the idea of legal integration.[52]

The government of Pakistan had always conceived of the refugee problem as a temporary one. As a consequence, no long-term plans were considered for the integration or assimilation of the Afghans into the socio-economic fabric of Pakistani society.[53] Many policies adopted toward the refugees, not entirely popular in Pakistan, were probably tolerated because they could be viewed as only applicable for a time. The distortions that the refugees brought to Pakistan's development priorities and plans, it was plausible to argue, would be sooner or later corrected.

Many had predicted that the influx of refugees would intensify local Pathan nationalist feelings. Since it was relatively easy for Afghans to illegally obtain a National Identity Card or demonstrate a domicile, sooner or later the Afghan refugee population might be drawn into political campaigns and elections.[54] The exiled Afghans could enter coalitions with other political groups, or, worst of all, evolve into a state within a state, able to defy the central government.[55] By gaining political autonomy on Pakistan's soil, the Afghans and their ethnic brethren would then have then succeeded in creating a de facto Pashtunistan.[56]

The failure in fact of refugee Afghans to stir more nationalist consciousness among Pakistan's Pathans was to an extent a result of their somewhat differing history and customs. Relatively speaking, the Pathans were a favored group in Pakistan, unlikely to take their cues from their impoverished Pashtun cousins. Nor had the refugees by themselves been numerous enough to create a major impact on the NWFP—with its upwards of 15 million citizens. But if large numbers of refugees are to become permanent residents of Pakistan, and the focus of their attention to shift away from the possibility of returning, the stake they feel in Pakistan's national politics will become less distinguishable from that of local Pathans. Avoiding the long feared major confrontation between Afghan exiles and elements in the larger Pakistani population will then be more problematic. More certain, had Kabul's communist regime not collapsed, the Pakistan government would before very long have been forced to reconcile its adherence to the principle of voluntary repatriation with domestic demands that the refugees leave.

Notes

1. This was despite the fact that Pakistan was not a signatory to the 1951 Convention on the Status of Refugees and the Protocol of 1967. Strong language and cultural ties with the refugees are explained by the fact that much of the Pashtun population of the NWFP and northern Baluchistan traces its ancestry to

Afghanistan. Also, some 62 percent of the refugees fled from the ten provinces of
Afghanistan bordering Pakistan. Richard English, "Preliminary Report on
Conditions Affecting the Repatriation of Afghan Refugees," prepared for the
United Nations High Commissioner for Refugees, Geneva, June 20, 1988, p. 13.

2. Grant M. Farr, "The Impact of the Afghan Refugees on Pakistan," in Craig
Baxter (ed.), *Zia's Pakistan; Politics and Stability in a Frontline State* (Boulder:
Westview, 1985), p. 94.

3. Tahir Amin, "Afghan Resistance: Past, Present and Future," *Asian Survey*,
Vol. 24, no. 4 (April 1984): 378.

4. Hafeez Malik, "The Afghan Crisis and its Impact on Pakistan," *Journal of
South Asian and Middle Eastern Studies*, Vol. 5, no. 3 (spring 1982): 43. Also see the
discussion by Mohammed Ayoob, "Dateline Pakistan: A Passage to Anarchy, "
Foreign Policy, no. 59 (summer 1985): 164.

5. Farr, "The Impact of the Afghan Refugees," p. 95.

6. Akbar S. Ahmed, "Afghan Refugees, Aid, and Anthropologists,"
Internationales Asienforum, Vol. 12, no. 1 (1981): 83.

7. Farr, "The Impact of the Afghan Refugees," p. 161.

8. Edward Girardet, *Afghanistan; the Soviet War* (New York: St. Martin's
Press, 1985), p. 205, reports a figure of 7,000 in the administrative infrastructure
mid-decade.

9. A Pakistan government advertisement, *The New York Times*, September 21,
1987, p. 19.

10. Askari Rizvi, "Afghan Refugees in Pakistan: Influx, Humanitarian
Assistance and Implications," *Pakistan Horizon*, Vol. 36, no. 1: 49. Riaz M. Khan,
Untying the Afghan Knot; Negotiating Soviet Withdrawal (Durham, N.C.: Duke
University Press, 1991), p. 173, note 15, estimates that an average of nearly $200
was spent annually on all foreign relief assistance to the refugees. The United
States was contributing in the early 1990s, $5 million in aid to the U.N. refugee
assistance program and $10 million for food and medicine. *The Wall Street Journal*,
June 29, 1992.

11. Nancy Dupree, "Demographic Reporting on Afghan Refugees in
Pakistan," *Modern Asian Studies*, Vol. 25, no. 2 (1988): 244.

12. Ibid., p. 243. Also, Robert Wirsing, "Pakistan and the War in
Afghanistan," in *Asian Affairs*, Vol. 14, no. 2 (Summer 1987): 74, note 14.

13. John Fullerton, "A Rift Among Rebels," *Far Eastern Economic Review*,
October 29, 1982, p. 20.

14. A. Lynn Carter and Kerry Connor, "A Preliminary Investigation of
Contemporary Afghan Councils," unpublished report to the Agency
Coordinating Body for Afghan Relief (ACBAR), Peshawar, April 1989, pp. 18–19.

15. Ahmed, "Afghan Refugees," pp. 86–87.

16. Henry Hamman, "The Afghan Refugee Crisis," unpublished paper, 1980,
pp. 47–48.

17. Ralph H. Magnus, "Afghanistan: Humanitarian Response to the Inhuman
Strategy, " in Grant M. Farr, and John G. Merriam (eds.) *Afghan Resistance: The
Politics of Survival* (Boulder: Westview Press, 1987), pp. 204–205.

18. Hamman, "The Afghan Refugee Crisis," pp. 47–48.

19. Edward Girardet, "Corrupt Officials Reap Spoils of Afghan War," *Christian Science Monitor*, September 7, 1988.

20. Jon Bennett, Executive Director of ACBAR, at an address at the Afghanistan Relief Committee Conference of Afghanistan Humanitarian Support Organizations, held February 8–10 in New York City on February 10, 1991, reported in *Afghanistan Forum,* March 1991, p. 23. Also see Louis and Nancy Dupree, "Afghan Refugees in Pakistan," *World Refugee Survey: 1987 in Review*, U.S. Committee for Refugees, March 15, 1988, p. 18; Also, Dawn (Karachi) May 13, 1989. *The Herald* (March 1993), p. 84, claims that with 51 unregistered PVOs counted, many of them Arab, there were as many as 136 groups working in Peshawar by early 1993.

21. *Frontier Post* (Peshawar), February 17, 1990.

22. *Pakistan Times* (Islamabad), May 27, 1990. Initially, humanitarian aid inside Afghanistan was funded by AID's Office of Foreign Disaster Assistance, then by the Office of the AID Representative for Afghanistan. The International Rescue Committee was a prime grantee, and it subcontracted to other PVOs, including several European ones. In 1988, the humanitarian aid program became the Rural Assistance Program. Other cross-border programs for education and health received separate AID grants. From information provided by Louis Wiesner, a former foreign service officer.

23. Kamal Matinuddin, "Afghanistan Refugees: the Geostrategic Context," in Ewan Anderson and Nancy Hatch Dupree (eds.), *The Cultural Basis of Afghan Nationalism* (London and New York: Pinter Publishers, 1990), p. 223.

24. Louis and Nancy Dupree, "Afghan Refugees in Pakistan," pp. 17–18. The authors also note that a refugee village was established outside of Karachi for 18,500 unregistered non-Pashtun refugees, most of whom had their quarters in the city destroyed by authorities during a search for smugglers and drug dealers.

25. Alfred Janata, "Afghanistan: the Ethnic Dimension" in Anderson and Dupree, p. 68.

26. Rizvi, "Afghan Refugees in Pakistan," pp. 51, 53.

27. *Frontier Post*, November 11, 1991.

28. Janata, "Afghanistan: the Ethnic Dimension," p. 68. Also see Hafeez Malik, *Journal of Middle East and South Asian Studies* , Vol. 5, no. 3 (spring 1982): 45–56. Officials in the NWFP, in a brief effort during 1984 to reduce the number of Afghans entering the job market in the cities, imposed half-hearted measures to confine the refugees to their camps. *The New York Times*, November 25, 1984. Concern about the disparity in treatment of refugees and Pakistanis in the refugee-affected areas led to a program under a cooperative arrangement in 1990 between the government of Pakistan, the UNHCR, and the World Bank. That program was designed to create employment opportunities for Pakistani citizens as well as Afghan refugees. *Frontier Post*, February 17, 1990.

29. Azmat H. Khan, "The Afghanistan Problem: Its Impact and Pakistan," *Central Asian Studies* (Peshawar), no. 24 (Summer 1989): 142.

30. Aziz Siddiqui, *The Herald*, May 1992, p. 40a.

31. "Silent Voices #1," a report by the Refugee Council in association with the British Agencies Afghan Groups, reprinted in *Afghanistan Forum,* Vol. 19, no. 2 (March 1991): 14.

32. Aftab A. Kazi, "Ethnic Nationalism and Super-Powers in South Asia: Sindhis and Baluchis, in the *Journal of Asian and African Affairs*, Vol. 1, no.1 (July 1989): 7.

33. Weiner, *Blank Check*, p. 151. The United Nations ranked Afghanistan, with an estimated 2,000 tons in 1992, as the No. 1 supplier of opium. U.S. government, using satellite photographs, found 670 tons produced, making it second to the Myanmar and the golden Triangle region of Southeast Asia. Bob Drogin, *Los Angeles Times*, April 26.

34. *The New York Times*, July 30, 1989. Also, John Ward Anderson and Molly Moore, *The Washington Post*, April 29, 1993, and Bob Drogin, *Los Angeles Times*, April 26, 1993. Other sources insist that the country has between 2 and 3 million addicts. *Newsday*, February 23, 1992.

35. Shavid Javed Burki, *Muslim* (Islamabad), February 14, 1989.

36. *The New York Times*, July 14, 1987. It had become convenient to accuse the Soviets or Kabul leaders of responsibility for anything that tended to discredit Pakistan. This was plainly evident when, in denying involvement in an attempt to export a steel alloy from the United States for possible nuclear weapons, Islamabad authorities suggested that the charges were part of the campaign to discredit them and force Pakistan to give up support of the resistance. Ibid., July 17, 1987.

37. UNHCR report, February 1986, cited in Hafizullah Emadi, "Resettlement Pattern: The Afghan Refugees in Pakistan," *Cultural Survival Quarterly*, Vol. 12, no. 4 (1988): 22.

38. A summary of proceeding from the International Symposium "The Crisis of Migration from Afghanistan: Domestic and Foreign Implications," co-sponsored by the Refugee Studies Program. Oxford University, March 29–April 2, 1987, p. 12. Arab volunteers were probably responsible for many of the crimes blamed on Afghan refugees, including the smuggling of military equipment. Salamat Ali, *Far Eastern Economic Review*, May 23, 1991, pp. 23–24. There were also reports that Pakistani officials were ignoring charges that the Arab volunteers were keeping Afghan women as slaves as well as buying Soviet POWs from mujahidin and killing them. *The Friday Times*, Lahore, March 19–25, 1992 and *The Herald (March 1993)*, pp. 54–55.

39. Said Azar, "Refugees in Pakistan: The Pakistani View," in Anderson and Dupree, p. 112.

40. *Muslim*, October 19, 1981.

41. Ibid., June 14, 1989.

42. Louis Dupree, "Post-Withdrawal Afghanistan: Light at the End of the Tunnel," in Saikal and Maley, *The Soviet Withdrawal from Afghanistan*, p. 36.

43. FBIS, November 29, 1991, p. 42, from a statement by U.N. representative Benon Sevan, reported by AFP, November 27, 1991.

44. *The New York Times*, February 2, 1990. Direct U.S. humanitarian aid for the Afghans, including the refugees, amounted to about $70 million, not counting the aid contributed to international agencies. Ibid., April 26, 1992.

45. Address by Jon Bennett, Executive Director of ACBAR on February 10, 1991, reported in *Afghanistan Forum*, Vol. 19, no. 2 (March 1991):23.

46. Ibid., p. 16.

47. BBC Foreign Service reported in *Afghan Jehad*, Vol. 4, no. 4 (July-September 1991): 312.

48. *Frontier Post*, November 2, 1991. There were some new commitments of assistance during the period. The Saudi Ambassador to Pakistan pledged $7.5 million for education programs sponsored by the AIG in both Pakistan and Afghanistan; the existing schools had been closed for a lack of funds. *AFGHANews* November 15, 1991. A year later the United Nations appealed to the international community for $17.6 to help returning refugees to survive the first winter in Afghanistan. *The New York Times*, November 8, 1992.

49. *Frontier Post*, November, 2, 1991.

50. Tim Kelsey, in *The Independent* (Islamabad), August 14, 1991. Over the period of April and May 1992, and despite the major reductions in the quantity of rations provided, the nutritional status of Afghan refugee children had not in fact changed significantly. Bob Pond, Debroah Glass, and Elsie Pamuk, "Survey of Nutritional Status and Infant Mortality of Afghan Refugee Children in Pakistan, April-May 1992, a report of the Division of Nutrition, Centers for Disease Control, Atlanta, Georgia, 1992.

51. Nasim Zehra, "Afghan Refugee Repatriation: A Pakistani Perspective," in Soroosh Irfani and Fazul-ur-Rahman (eds.), *Afghanistan; Looking to the Future* (Islamabad: Institute of Strategic Studies, 1992), p. 49.

52. *Frontier Post*, November 2, 1991.

53. Azar, "Refugees in Pakistan," p. 109.

54. Rizvi, "Afghan Refugees in Pakistan," p. 57. It was often noted that once armed with a fake identity card, Afghan refugees were able to obtain Pakistani passports for working in the Gulf. Many of the drug carriers caught in Saudi Arabia and the Gulf States with Pakistani passports were believed to be Afghans. Rahimullah Yusufzai, *The News*, (Islamabad) August 5, 1993.

55. See Malik, "The Afghan Crisis," p. 46.

56. Baluchistan offered a harbinger of possible domestic political conflict with an ethnic base. The arrival of the refugees in the province during the war had tipped the balance to a Pashtun majority. Tensions ran especially high, and a domestic political fallout was often imminent. The presence of Afghan refugees was undoubtedly a contributing factor in the armed strife between Baluchis and Pathans that occurred in Quetta in 1992. Farr "The Impact of the Afghan Refugees" (p. 99) notes that the Zia regime, realizing the explosiveness of the ethnic tensions in Baluchistan, tried to buy off the traditional Baluch leaders with promises of development projects.

5

The War and the Politics of Pakistan

The years of conflict in Afghanistan left a visible and deep social, economic, and environmental imprint on neighboring Pakistan, the country that more than any other sustained the armed resistance and embraced the war's refugees. The absorption of exiled Afghans, mostly in Pakistan's North-West Frontier and Baluchistan provinces, created economic disruptions and social dislocations, and strained the country's scarce natural resources. As already described, rising prices, unemployment, growing drug trafficking and addiction, and violent crimes traceable to the influx of weapons into Pakistani society stirred public consciousness. Less examined and understood are the war's mixed effects on the politics of Pakistan.

Predictions were that the massive refugee influx would swamp and distort provincial politics. Resident, armed Afghan resistance groups were expected in time to be drawn to political alliances with Pakistani parties, influencing local control and even national power. Many observers anticipated that the refugees' continuing presence would increase ethnic, linguistic, and sectarian mistrust and suspicions in a country already beset with regional tensions. In Baluchistan, the settlement of Afghan refugees upset a delicate population balance that had existed between Pathan and Baluch ethnic groups and threatened for a time to aggravate conditions in the already troubled, rebellious province. Still more, the refugees in the NWFP were thought likely to embolden demands for provincial autonomy among Pakistanis and possibly breathe new life into the irredentist cause of an independent Pashtun state that would encompass much of eastern Afghanistan as well. The largely Sunni Pashtuns could also exacerbate sectarian religious antagonisms.

Most of all, with the Afghan resistance supplied weapons and given sanctuary inside Pakistan, many worried that Pakistan's very territorial integrity would be threatened. If Moscow and Kabul decided to retaliate, there were believed to be in Afghanistan some 10,000 Pakistani political exiles, among them 8,500 seasoned Baluch and Pashtun fighters.[1] As noted in Chapter 2, strategists also confronted the prospect of Pakistan's being drawn into a conflict against armed forces of the Soviet Union and the Afghan communists and, in the worst case, into an attack coordinated with Pakistan's traditional adversary, India. As it happened, most of these concerns were exaggerated or poorly founded. Other outcomes were unanticipated.

Afghans settled in Pakistan did not have the massive influence on the country's electoral politics that many predicted. Pakistan's parties never succeeded in mobilizing Afghans to influence local contests, and Afghan demands for an independent voice in provincial policy making failed to materialize. Pashtun nationalism, instead of awakening, virtually disappeared as an issue during the 1980s, and Baluch secessionist activity, so threatening during the 1970s, lost most of its steam. Tensions between Shi'ites and Sunnis in Pakistan's northern areas—that may have intensified because of the refugee camps—were contained, at least until outbreaks in 1992. And, despite the war's spill-over in the form of cross-border shelling and repeated violations of Pakistan's air space, at no time was Pakistan security seriously threatened by invasion from Soviet/Afghan forces or a two-front war that included India. Nor did the concentration of a body of armed, displaced people assume the features of a state within a state, as so many in Pakistan had feared. To be sure, domestically, the level of violence in Pakistan intensified and its modes changed markedly during the 1980s. Yet the often-cited breakdown in law and order occurred mainly as the result of factional rivalries within the same national communities rather than the pitting of Afghans against Pakistanis.

This chapter seeks to explain why much of the expected political fallout on Pakistan never materialized, especially how, to a remarkable degree, Afghan refugees and armed resistance fighters developed stable, even if not always harmonious, relations with indigenous authority and communities. Just the same, these discussions reveal that the war and its refugees became politicized issues within Pakistan, affecting the country's political dialogue and, to some extent, the competition for power among its elites. Although the chapter details the built-up resentments against the refugees, it also finds somewhat remarkable the fact that there was not more disorder and instability given their numbers and the length of their stay in Pakistan. There remained throughout the conflict a reservoir of good feeling, a sympathy for Muslims fighting for their freedom. If the sense of obligation to protect and assist the Afghans was also dissolving, the change occurred only gradually.

The Zia Regime and Its Critics

If asked what the single most important political consequence of the war was for Pakistan, few Pakistanis would fail to mention the perpetuation of General Zia ul-Haq's military rule. The influx of hundreds of thousands of refugees and the adoption of the Afghan cause of national liberation against the Soviet-backed communists gave a boost to the Zia regime. Afghanistan provided Pakistan with a self-congratulatory opportunity. Under Zia it had stood beside a brave and valiant people. As chief Martial Law Administrator, General Zia had come to power in a military takeover from the civilian government of Zulfikar Ali Bhutto in July 1977 and, despite promises, refused to hold elections for a new civilian government. Zia's rule seemed destined to be short-lived. Doubts were expressed about whether he had the skills and stature for the job. His promises of creating an Islamic state had aroused considerable controversy. Despite good harvests and the return of investment capital under the martial law regime, the government's development and rearmament plans were set back as a consequence of the alienation of U.S. aid following the Islamabad government's refusal to give up its nuclear program and its handling of the mob attack on the American Embassy in Islamabad in November 1979. The Soviets' December 1979 intervention in Afghanistan's civil war changed all this.

At least for a time, attention in Pakistan was diverted from domestic to international issues. As described earlier, the United States revived its aid program and, joining with other Western and Middle East countries, provided generous assistance to Pakistan's military and its economy. Pakistan also profited materially from allowing arms and other supplies to be passed to the Afghan resistance through its military channels. Zia meanwhile gained international stature as a courageous and principled leader. While the General's political resourcefulness should not be minimized, the war helped to justify Zia's repeated delay in holding elections and gave him valued time to consolidate his position. The foreign largesse provided a stimulus to Pakistan's economy and became an important means by which Zia neutralized his critics.

If Pashtun nationalism became largely moribund as a result of the war, Baluch nationalism inside Pakistan, if not entirely dead, was certainly handed a major setback. Baluch leaders who had hoped to obtain material support from Afghanistan to oppose the Islamabad government were disappointed and discredited. Surprisingly, as mentioned earlier, the Soviets in their desire to avoid further commitments in the Afghan conflict refrained from instigating the Baluch rebels, including those waiting inside Afghanistan. It also proved difficult for Baluch nationalists to rally nationalist feelings in a Pakistani province that had become host to hundreds of thousands of Afghan refugees. A revival of secessionist activities against Islamabad would have called for a close alignment with a Kabul regime at war with fellow Muslims.

The conflict in Afghanistan nicely reinforced General Zia's efforts to institutionalize a state governed by Islamic law—a major policy used to legitimize his rule. The struggle against the communists was depicted by the Zia regime as well as the Afghan resistance as a holy war to rid Afghanistan of its infidels, both Afghan and Soviet. Adamant support for the mujahidin became concrete evidence of the sincerity of Zia's commitment to Islam in both foreign and domestic policy. The opposition to Zia instead stressed what they believed was his insincerity, his use of the Afghan and refugee cause for political rather than humanitarian or Islamic purposes.

While outside of the two border provinces the war failed to rivet popular attention or greatly affect people's lives, the country's Afghan policies did become a matter of controversy. With the frustration and fatigue of a long war in which Pakistan could ultimately be saddled with refugees unable or unwilling to return home, it was inevitable that domestic opponents of the regime would try to exploit the issue. The deep commitment to the resistance and dependent alliances, particularly with the United States, led to disagreement over where Pakistan's national interests lay. Policies on Afghanistan fashioned in Islamabad also subjected decision makers to threats and intimidation by external forces that tested the political resolve and sagacity of Pakistan's leaders.

The Islamabad government's stifling of all political expression largely precluded the war from becoming a widely debated issue in Pakistan's politics. Without legal parties and in the absence of even quasi-parliamentary politics until 1985, the opposition had difficulty amplifying its views. Opposition groups were severely curtailed in their activities, including access to the press. As with many other party chiefs, Benazir Bhutto, successor to her father as leader of the Pakistan People's Party (PPP), spent almost a decade in detention or exile. Only the government-allied, conservative Jama'at-i-Islami firmly backed Pakistan's handling of the war.

Most feared of the opposition parties, the PPP repeatedly made the case that Zia had seized upon the war as a means of getting the West to help prop up his unpopular regime. In this view, Pakistan, rather than pursing its own interests, was being used by Washington as an instrument of its Cold War strategy of containing Soviet ambitions. Unless the United States reduced its aid to Pakistan, most of all its military support, Zia would be able to resist ending martial law and conducting elections, which the PPP felt confident of winning. Enemies of the regime were convinced that with Zia's major concern the rebuilding of Pakistan's military, the government wanted to keep the war going, even passing up chances of a settlement mainly out of fear of losing international aid.

Although foreign aid continued unabated through the war, the price of harboring the refugees and giving a sanctuary to fighters in fact carried increased liabilities over time. Political gains for the Zia regime began to be attenuated by the impact of refugees on local economies and an intensifying of the country's social problems. Complaints focused on the unrestricted freedom enjoyed by the Afghans and on evidence of a breakdown of law and order. Semi-automatic and heavy weapons had increased the lethal character of fighting among groups. It was widely acknowledged that black markets for weapons and heroin flourished. Afghans were thought to be active in illegal arms transactions and drug smuggling. Many weapons intended for battle in Afghanistan were sold and resold in the bazaars in Pakistan and ended up being used in Pakistan's cities and towns. Resettled Afghan businessmen were believed to be involved in the opium trade, buying it across the border and reselling it in Pakistan. The border tribal areas, traditionally outside of direct government authority but the site of many refugee camps, had become especially lawless. Assassinations and kidnapping of well-known Afghans, including mujahidin commanders, were repeated occurrences.

Any outbreak of disorder allowed political opponents of the regime to exploit resentments among Pakistanis. Some Pakistani politicians were ever ready to exaggerate the problems, and an otherwise docile press helped to fan the accusations against the Afghans. It became convenient to blame all of Pakistan's ills on the refugees. Refugees were not infrequently accused by authorities of crimes in fact committed by Arab volunteers. Left-wing groups were quick to implicate the refugees in ethnic riots in Karachi despite the evidence, and to hold rivalries between various mujahidin groups responsible for bombings in Peshawar. Even when agents of the Kabul government secret police, Khad, were implicated in the violence, often through infiltration in the camps, or when the local left-wing parties had instigated violence, most Pakistanis accepted the conclusion that refugees attracted the troubles. Because no one ever took credit for the incidents, anyone could be blamed.[2]

In Pakistan's cities, opposition elements complained that while they were prohibited from operating a free press and their political parties suppressed, Afghan parties were free to organize, publish their own organs of opinion, and hold political meetings inside Pakistan. Afghan parties were allowed to address student gatherings in the universities at the same time that most of Pakistan's own parties were barred from the campuses. Whereas the authorities required that Pakistani publications obtain a special license, foreign-financed organizations, such as a Saudi-funded welfare organization in Peshawar, were able to publish newspaper and journals unimpeded. The exemption was supposedly because most of these publications, in Arabic and English, circulated outside of Pakistan. But since they focused on Muslim sectarian issues, they helped fan the expanding sectarian strife within Pakistan.[3]

The mujahidin of Hezb-i-Islami were also allowed to run their own security service, presumably to watch for infiltrators and leftists but actually more to crush competing Afghan resistance groups. Although the parties were intended to assume security arrangements in the camps, their apparatus carried over into urban areas as well. Beginning early in the war, Afghans arrested by Pakistan's law-enforcement agencies were often interrogated in the presence of Hezb-i-Islami security personnel. Hekmatyar's followers were also widely believed to maintain their own jails, incarcerating and badly treating not only suspected communists but followers of other parties.[4]

By the mid-1980s, a number of opposition groups were arguing publicly for a mutually acceptable agreement with the Soviet Union to end the war. They expressed fear that with hot pursuit of the resistance and violations of air space by Afghan government warplanes, the epicenter of the conflict was shifting from Afghan territory to Pakistan. In 1987, raids were occurring daily, with hundreds in mujahidin camps and border villages killed or wounded. The raids, intended before 1987 to reduce Islamabad's support for the mujahidin and after to gain political concessions for a settlement, left the impression that the government possessed only limited ability to protect those people living along the frontier, including its own citizens.

The Zia regime's opponents found that their views most resonated in expressions of concern about the unraveling socio-economic fabric, manifested in rising prices, unemployment, drug trafficking and addiction, crime rate and terrorism. They asserted the possibility of armed clashes between Pakistanis and Afghan refugees increasing.[5] Confrontations of this sort remained relatively isolated, however.[6] In general, there appeared to be an unwritten rule that so long as the Afghan rivalries did not spill over in any large way into the Pakistani community, Pakistani authorities would tolerate them.[7] Attempts, successful and failed, made on the lives of Afghans from competing parties and working for relief groups increased in Peshawar and elsewhere in 1991. But without the factional bloodletting reaching wide proportions, endangering large number of Pakistanis or foreigners, the government refrained from taking firmer measures, such as a crackdown on the illegal trade in arms. As a result, Afghans could expect little protection from the police, and perpetrators of killings and kidnapping were almost never apprehended or even seriously pursued. Indeed, Afghan exile leaders were ignored when they took problems of security in the camps and towns to high Pakistani officials and the military.[8]

Many unfavorable, often inaccurate perceptions of the Afghans persisted. To be sure, there was a remarkable degree of tolerance among Pakistanis toward the refugees and the mujahidin. The Afghans were widely admired for their resiliency and motivation, growing out of their national values and Islamic beliefs. The sense of religious obligation toward fellow Muslims suffering at the hands of the communists won the Afghans broad support. Additionally, among their ethnic cousins in Pakistan, tribal codes commanded that hospitality be offered. But the view spread widely that the refugees had taken Pakistan's generosity for granted and failed to appreciate the sacrifices that their hosts had incurred. It did not take long for stereotypes to emerge portraying the Afghans as untrustworthy and unruly. Many better educated Pakistanis were deeply suspicious of what they considered the feudal thinking of nearly all the Afghan parties. They also found objectionable among Afghans a kind of rigid Islamic political ideology that, however deeply ingrained in Pakistan as well, had never succeeded in winning many elections in that country.[9] Should it prevail ultimately in Afghanistan, the danger of contagion in Pakistan seemed very real.

The lack of resolution of the Afghan conflict made it prudent for the Zia regime to take precautions that Afghan exiles never be permitted to take the law into their own hands. Zia's experiences serving as a military advisor in Jordan during Black September, the crushing of the independent-minded, armed Palestinians, no doubt made a impression, leaving him particularly sensitive to the possibility of a challenge to state authority. To minimize this possible outcome in Pakistan, Zia chose to work with Afghan factions that he and his military intelligence trusted. The backing of the more fundamentalist religious parties, as previously mentioned, gave some assurance that the dominant forces in the resistance would have their sights set on winning the conflict in Afghanistan and creating an Islamic state there, and have no designs on Pakistan, particularly an interest in carving out a Pashtun state. The regime could take some comfort in knowing that fundamentalist Afghan parties in fact had long been in the forefront in opposing the secular, nationalist idea of Pashtunistan. In return for equipment and political support, the parties were expected, especially in the event that the refugees remained indefinitely in Pakistan, to minimize their involvement in domestic politics and cooperate with the military intelligence. Or, in the event of a mujahidin victory, Pakistan would hope to assure warm ties with an Islamic-oriented government in Kabul, if necessary, having its cooperation in pressing for the return of refugees.

Pakistan's Security

Pakistan's becoming a front-line state by adopting the Afghans' effort naturally carried implications for the country's security. General Zia appears to have concluded, however, that he had more to be concerned about from efforts by his enemies to destabilize the country than he did from direct attack by the Soviets or the Afghan army. Had General Zia failed to develop a consistent and generally acceptable policy toward the mujahidin and Pakistan's role in the conflict, domestic instability would undoubtedly have been far more of a problem than it was for the regime. It is probably true that the foreign military assistance the government attracted favored the Punjabis among the ethnic groups, if only because they have long dominated the military. By this reasoning, any strengthening of the federal government enhanced the power of the Punjabi majority and served to increase ethnic resentment. At the same time, the resources provided by the war probably improved the position of the central government in its ability to deal with the centrifugal forces besetting Pakistan. What the regime failed to do was to use its enhanced security to satisfy the aspirations of the constituent ethnic groups by allowing their increased sense of control over provincial affairs.

The Soviets and their Kabul allies were prepared to test Islamabad's commitment to the Afghan resistance and to discover where they could strengthen internal Pakistani opposition to Zia's policies. The pressures they mounted were expected to influence Pakistan's decision makers, above all, by building public resentment against the war. Government calculations had also to deal with the possibility that there would be, sooner or later, direct efforts from Soviet-occupied Afghanistan to promote Pakistan's fragmentation.

The Soviet Union's persuasive methods included diplomatic initiatives and economic and technical aid. Bilateral economic cooperation, although reduced, continued throughout the 1980s. But beginning in 1986, coercive means, involving intimidation and overt pressures, was more apparent. Strafing of border areas, rocket attacks, bombs planted in crowded streets, assassinations as well as radio broadcasts beamed at Pakistan were intended to raise the costs of the war for Pakistan. Communist propagandists were particularly active in targeting Gulbuddin Hekmatyar and Saudi-backed Wahabi religious influences among the Afghans in an effort to drive a wedge between the refugees and the local populations. There was good evidence that communist agents had infiltrated Afghan refugee camps, supplying lethal arms and explosives.

The Afghan communists also played on tribal and sectarian rivalries in the border areas of Pakistan. Early in the conflict and again after late 1986, the Kabul government's Khad agents successfully infiltrated the Turi in Pakistan's tribal Kurram Agency, a Shi'ite group, creating problems for the Pakistani authorities as well as the mujahidin passing through the area. They also instigated conflict between the Kukikhel Afridi tribes in the Khyber Agency in November 1985. Kabul was said to have been less successful in stirring up the Marris of Baluchistan.[10]

During 1978 and 1988, the government in Islamabad regularly announced the smashing of rings of saboteurs and offered evidence that subversives had entered the country. Many among Pakistani leaders were concerned that over time a failure to respond to the pressures would leave the impression that the regime was ineffectual and weak. Yet the campaign to convince Islamabad to reduce its support for the mujahidin or, barring that, to agree to easier terms in the on-going peace talks in Geneva by and large failed. General Zia stubbornly refused to make any concessions to those employing bombs and assassinations. He remained confident that his security forces could cope with the pressures. In fact, the targeting of bazaars in villages in cross-border air raids, rather than shaking the leaderships' determination, probably succeeded more in wedding Pakistanis to the country's Afghan policy. Repeated violations of Pakistan's territory gave some ammunition to critics of the war who warned of the country's deep involvement, but it served more effectively to discredit long-time supporters of the Kabul regime. Because of the way it was played in Islamabad, the potential military threat to Pakistan from abroad helped the regime by shifting attention away from domestic problems.

Significantly, both the Soviet and Pakistani militaries sought to minimize occasions when their forces came into direct confrontation. The Soviets also saw limits to the degree to which they were willing to try to destabilize Pakistan. Moscow never gave up on the idea of keeping the diplomatic channels open for a settlement. As such, the Soviets, probably to India's disappointment, avoided striking at Pakistan where it was most vulnerable. Although Moscow allegedly approved the infiltration of Afghan agents among dissident Pakistani tribes, as already mentioned, it avoided the diplomatic break with Pakistan that would have come had Afghan-based Baluch tribesmen been incited to stir up trouble inside Pakistan.

The War and Party Politics

The war that added to the strains already present in Pakistan's society unavoidably carried into the arena of Pakistan's partisan politics. Despite this, the Afghan conflict and its refugees never emerged as issues around which large numbers of Pakistanis could be mobilized to support one set of policies or another. In the country's most populous provinces, the Punjab and Sindh, the war and its fallout failed to impact strongly on the lives of most citizens, despite admiration for the mujahidin and sympathy for the war's victims. All but a few refugee settlements were located in the NWFP, Baluchistan, and the autonomous tribal areas; elsewhere the refugees were more or less absorbed into the commercial life of the cities. Even in the areas where the Afghans' presence in fact created ethnic imbalances, tribal and religious traditions blunted the issue. Unlike Kashmir, also involving Muslim self-determination, the Afghans' struggle failed to ignite emotions and encourage Pakistan's politicians to either advocate direct military involvement in the fighting or demand the outright expulsion of refugees.

The presence on Pakistan's soil of large numbers of refugees, most of them cut off from their traditional leadership, economically dependent, and united in belief of the righteousness of their resistance cause, benefited most the highly conservative domestic religious parties. As already mentioned, it was Pakistan's Jama'at-i-Islami that took the lead in assisting displaced Afghans and promoting their cause. The party built quickly on already established ties to Afghan fundamentalists, especially to Hezb-i-Islami. Although formally banned with other Pakistani parties under the martial law government, Jama'at-i-Islami was in fact allowed to carry on its activities relatively unimpeded. Zia had counted on party members to help legitimize his Islamization program and give cover to the collaboration between Pakistan's military intelligence and favored mujahidin groups.

The refugees became, in fact, an important domestic political resource for Jama'at-i-Islami. Initially, it was the only party allowed to enter the camps. With the party's closeness to the aid pipeline destined for the refugees, it had access to enormous patronage made possible by the 6,000 Pakistanis on the payroll of the Commissionerate for Afghan Refugees.[11] While serving as commissioner, Sheikh Abdullah Khan, the convinced advocate of trying to instill Islamic values within the camps, allowed the party's supporters not only to insulate the camps from leftist influences but also to cleanse them of secular Afghan nationalistic and more moderate Islamic elements. Moreover, Afghan assistance programs funded with generous international aid naturally multiplied the opportunities for corruption in a government where officials customarily take a percentage cut of a contract for themselves.

As a consequence of Pakistan's poorly disguised bias in favor of the Islamic parties, little room was left for organized appeals to the exiled Afghans on the basis of ethnic group, tribe, or region. The once potent nationalist, political left and, in particular, the Awami National Party (ANP), had already forfeited its potential role. The ANP of Wali Khan, veteran leader and long the champion of Pakistan's Pathans, should logically have become the vehicle for mobilizing refugees in the Frontier Province. Instead, the cause of displaced Afghans was ignored, even belittled. The ANP soon earned the deep enmity of many former Afghan friends, earlier brothers in the Pashtunistan movement, as it broke a basic precept of Pashtunwali or tribal law—the obligation to extend protection to those cut off from traditional sources of security.

Despite the arrival of so many ethnic brothers, Wali Khan chose to follow his leftist inclinations, honoring his established links with Moscow rather than group affinities. He and his followers threw in their lot with the communist government in Kabul and, in particular, the pro-Moscow faction, the Parchamis. ANP loyalists were suspected of working together with the Kabul security service to terrorize the refugees and resistance leadership. Anxious to undermine public support for the resistance, the party was believed involved in many of the bombings and assassinations that occurred with increased frequency beginning in 1987.

The involvement of the ANP was suggested in the events that followed a truck bomb that killed 14 people and injured 70, detonated in Peshawar on February 19, 1987. Because the bomb went off near a school, several of the victims were children. Within a short time after the attack, slogan-yelling armed men arrived at the scene and, in what appeared to be a spontaneous outpouring of anti-Afghan sentiment, burned mujahidin-owned vehicles, set ablaze several shops, and opened fire on refugees. In subsequent days, violent anti-resistance and anti-refugee demonstrations occurred in the city. Many believed that the reaction occurred too quickly and was too well organized not to have been planned in advance by those who planted the bomb.[12]

The ANP demanded that the Islamabad government end its backing of the resistance, recognize the Kabul regime, and facilitate early repatriation of the refugees. Pakistan's leaders were accused of trying to serve imperialist masters.[13] Followers of the ANP were well rewarded by their paymaster in Moscow with trips, scholarships, party subsidies, and arms. Wali Khan made periodic trips to Kabul and the Soviet Union. On returning with his supporters in buses from Kabul he is believed to have brought back numerous weapons, encountering no interference from Pakistani border officials.

From the outset there were other political elements in Pakistan prepared to appease the Soviet Union. Nusrat Bhutto, widow of the late prime minister, although probably not speaking for a majority of her People's Party, advocated a deal by which the Soviets would guarantee Pakistan sovereignty in exchange for the Islamabad government's recognition of the communist Babrak Karmal regime in Kabul.[14] More generally, the opposition parties to Zia, the 11 parties in the Movement for the Restoration of Democracy (MRD), did not press very hard on the Afghan issue. They took a position in favor of direct negotiations with the Kabul regime, justifying their policy of peace as necessary because so many of the ills of Pakistan were seen as caused by the Afghan refugees.

More broadly, the left's sympathy with Kabul, or at least its arguments for a conciliatory approach, was its way of opposing a Zia government intent on pursuing the war.[15] Leftist intellectuals in Pakistan's major cities, most of them journalists, academics, and labor leaders, constituted one of the more vocal groups in opposing the military regime's policy. Few went so far as to demand that the refugees be denied humanitarian assistance or be rounded up and deported. Yet most favored having the mujahidin's economic and political freedoms curtailed. These elements regularly attacked the government for ignoring the desperation of the citizens of the NWFP and Baluchistan and for indifference to the bombings and killings, while it soft peddled the repressive actions of the Kabul government. The left became increasingly strident in calling for a more sympathetic attitude toward the Kabul government. With the lifting of martial law and the coming to office of the Benazir Bhutto government, their views gained easier access to the media.

The anti-refugee stand of leftist politicians and intellectuals also resulted directly from their long-standing antagonism to Pakistan's militant religious parties. Once strong ties had been forged between Jama'at-i-Islami and radical Islamists among the mujahidin, the Afghan exiles were bound to become targets as well. Should the Afghan resistance prevail in the war, leaders on the left reasoned that Pakistan's religious parties would be strengthened, together with the military, at their expense.

In other ways the Afghan war proved to be the left's undoing. As a direct result of the conflict, parties of the left were subjected to internal strains, resulting in splits over the extent of support for the April 1978 Revolution in Afghanistan and then over which communist faction in Kabul deserved their support. The division of Wali Khan's followers on the Afghan issue produced defections and small splinter parties. The Afghan issue also complicated attempts to forge an united front with other groups in opposition to the Zia regime. Few of the parties that made up the Movement for the Restoration of Democracy were ready to join Wali Khan in championing the Kabul regime against the resistance and calling for the refugees' expulsion. Eventually this stand, particularly the suggestion that the ANP was effectively pro-Indian, would also lose the party electoral support within its traditional stronghold in the NWFP.

The deep involvement by Pakistan's Jama'at-i-Islami in Afghan politics notwithstanding, there was little to support the left's contention that the Afghan mujahidin were joined with the Jama'at-i-Islami in violence against the ANP and other leftist groups or were covertly aiding the religious party at the polls.[16] The potential for a partnership to strengthen the militant Islamic party's hand at the federal level no doubt existed, but the Islamabad government, ever sensitive to the danger of allowing Afghan involvement in Pakistan politics, discouraged the use of the exiled population in domestic political wars.[17] This was clearly demonstrated when post-Zia Pakistani authorities acted to assure that Afghans would not be exploited by any of the parties during the period leading up the 1988 parliamentary elections. Some feared that Afghans near polling places could set off anti-Afghan demonstrations and that refugees might be involved in vote-rigging schemes. Particularly likely targets were anti-government candidates, most of all PPP followers known to be lukewarm to the mujahidin.[18] Despite this, provincial governments, under federal direction, ordered refugees in the cities to stay indoors and those in the rural camps to remain there until after the national and provincial elections were conducted.

The military was less cautious in allowing the mujahidin to become a resource for the Jama'at-i-Islami in the party's efforts to assist the Muslims in Indian Kashmir. Events in Kashmir and the Afghan war were not unrelated. The steadfastness of the Afghan fighters was believed to have provided a model as well as inspiration for Kashmiris in their goal of self-determination. In 1990, Hezb-i-Islami claimed, like Pakistan, to be offering only moral and political support and vowed to fight alongside their Islamic brothers only if India attacked Pakistan. But by mid-1991, Hekmatyar was publicly willing to call for the participation of Afghan mujahidin in the jihad in Kashmir and to boast that Kashmir would be his fighters' next destination after Kabul was liberated.[19] Other Afghan resistance leaders, including officials of the interim government, had for some time been hinting at a readiness to give direct military assistance to an armed struggle inside Kashmir.[20]

While there is no conclusive evidence of mujahidin fighters' direct involvement in the Kashmir fighting, arms available in the bazaars or directly from tribal and Afghan sources ended up in the hands of young men carrying on raids against Indian forces.[21] Still more, many claimed that, facilitated by Pakistan's Jama'at-i-Islami, young Kashmiris trained

with the Afghan refugees and went on "training missions" with them
inside Afghanistan. The ample supplies of weapons from private sources
well suited the Islamabad government, which was relieved from
pressures of having to offer arms and ammunition from regular army
stocks. Pakistan could also claim that it had given no official sanction to
preparing Kashmiris for battle.

Democratic Government, the Opposition, and the Military

The Afghan conflict brought to the surface the tensions between
Pakistan's civilian and military authorities. Because the conduct of the
war was from the outset considered as a national security issue, it was
left to the military rather than the diplomats. While General Zia ruled he
made certain that those responsible for carrying out policy shared his
views of the conflict as akin to a holy war, to be supported whatever the
domestic costs to Pakistan. Not only did the ISI share Zia's policy
preference, the intelligence service was a critical part of his political
control. Pakistan's leaders had traditionally used the military to run
surveillance on domestic opposition groups and undermine them by
giving support to politicians deemed more friendly. In many of these
operations, it was often charged that the military intelligence had in fact
become a government unto itself.[22] Because of the ISI's often influential
role in foreign policy and involvement in domestic politics, it came as no
surprise that the agency was allowed to exercise far-reaching discretion
in formulating and implementing Pakistan's Afghan policy (see
discussion in chapter 3).

It was only in 1985 when President Zia decided to allow a nonparty
civilian government, in effect to share some of his powers, that the
Afghan issue first became openly divisive within the government. Much
of it focused on the estrangement of Zia from his hand-picked prime
minister, Muhammad Junejo. By the end of 1987, Pakistani policy on
Afghanistan had become badly polarized. Its incoherence was sharply
felt following the October 1987 ousting of Foreign Minister Sahabzada
Yaqub Khan by Prime Minister Junejo. Yaqub Khan, who had given
strong direction to policy making on Afghanistan and had shared with
the prime minister a desire to reach a negotiated settlement, was forced
from office by Junejo largely because the foreign minister was seen as
upstaging him, bypassing him to work out a settlement plan. The result
was, as described by Riaz Khan, then a senior official in the foreign
ministry, "a complete breakdown between the prime minister and the

Foreign Office, on the one hand, and the president and the ISI on the other.[23]

Prime Minister Junejo would soon be forced out of office himself. High on the list of disagreements between Junejo and Zia was the prime minister's effort to build a national consensus on ending the war. Junejo was determined to realize an early settlement and diverged from Zia on the need for compromise in order to reach agreement with the Soviets in the Geneva talks on troop withdrawals (see chapter 6). In March 1988, Junejo called a two day All Parties Conference on Afghanistan, signaling that under his leadership Pakistani politics was about to take off in new democratic directions. No doubt the prime minister expected to gain politically.

President Zia had become apprehensive of a prime minister who took increasingly independent actions and who threatened to alter the system that Zia had created.[24] The President did little to hide his resentment of Junejo's efforts to build his own popular constituency. On May 29, 1988, taking advantage of the government's embarrassment weeks earlier over the Ojri ammunition camp explosion near Islamabad that destroyed tens of million of dollars in CIA-supplied weapons, Zia ridded himself of his prime minister by dissolving the national and provincial assemblies, but only after he had reluctantly gone along with the Geneva accord on Afghanistan and had eliminated, for the time being, chances that Pakistan could install a interim mujahidin government to its liking in Kabul.

While the People's Party remained in opposition, Pakistan's role in the Afghan war was offered as evidence of General Zia's undemocratic and cynical policies. All the same, Benazir Bhutto repeatedly rejected confrontational politics over the issue and disavowed the terrorist actions of Al-Zulfikar, an anti-regime group led by her two brothers and based for a time in Kabul. Ms. Benazir and her followers did not object to humanitarian assistance being given refugees. But they insisted that the number of refugees was being inflated by the government to attract more international aid. It was thought likely that should the PPP succeed in winning office, it would more tightly control the activities of the refugees and adhere to stricter interpretation of the Geneva accord—meaning reduced aid to the resistance. Understandably, the mujahidin leadership was apprehensive about a Bhutto victory in the elections of November 1988.

Once in power, however, the PPP gave little priority to Afghanistan. The Prime Minister's rhetoric suggested the expected impatience with the war, but her policies differed little from those staked out earlier by President Zia. Islamabad did nothing to break the resistance parties' special relationship with Pakistan's fundamentalists and persisted, despite the evidence, in the belief that the (Pakistan-created) Afghan interim government might in time acquire the ability to bring together disparate elements, sufficient either to preside over a military victory or force the enemy to terms. Government officials also kept faith with the mujahidin in insisting that Afghan communist leader Najibullah be required to step down as a precondition for elections and a negotiated settlement. As such, the Bhutto government remained largely faithful to its predecessor's legacy on Afghanistan.

The Afghan issue was not a particularly divisive one within the PPP ranks or a matter of deep conscience for its leaders. Few holding seats in the federal assembly felt that their election mandated their bringing the conflict to an early end. Above all, they were preoccupied with what it took to satisfy their constituents and assure that they could enjoy the perquisites that come with office. PPP strategists concluded that to push the peace issue, to take the lead in offering new initiatives, could only complicate the government's already precarious political situation and might even precipitate its downfall. At the same time, the Bhutto government did not allow the Afghan issue to get in the way of its other foreign and domestic policy goals. Thus when French President Francoise Mitterrand visited Pakistan in March 1990 to discuss his government's assistance to Islamabad in building a nuclear facility, Islamabad conveniently ignored an announcement from Paris just weeks earlier that France planned to reopen its embassy in Kabul.

In broader elite circles the Afghan issue carried greater salience and tended toward polarity. The failure of Afghan mujahidin to win a victory on the battlefield played into the hands of the opponents of the PPP government. Benazir's combined opposition eulogized Zia's policies, most of all those on Afghanistan. These parties, strongest in the Punjab, largely agreed that Pakistan should stand firm. Were the government in Islamabad to question older commitments or push hard for a political compromise, its critics, especially in the press, were certain to say that the government had sold out the resistance and, worse still, turned its back on Islam.

For the opposition to Bhutto in the National Assembly, the war become a convenient way to attack the government for its U.S. connection. Anxious to insure the continued flow of economic and military assistance and keep her restive military content, Benazir had indeed cultivated friends in the U.S. Congress and Bush Administration with her promised market-oriented policies and commitment to non-nuclearization. The Prime Minister was seen as more inclined than her predecessor to be subservient to Washington's global strategy. Where doing the bidding of the United States in its efforts to contain or punish the Soviet Union was once said to be required for foreign aid,

Washington was now accused of seeking a premature disengagement—before Pakistan's interests in the region had been secured. With the Soviet withdrawal, a conspiracy was suspected. As conceived, Pakistani-supported mujahidin were to be denied claim to the final fruits of their long efforts, part of a joint endeavor by Washington and Moscow to thwart an Islamic victory that would threaten Soviet control over its Muslim republics and undermine Western influence in the Middle East. Aside from undermining Pakistan's independence, economic and military dependence on the United States was believed intended to discourage the country's contribution to the emergence of Islam as a regional and global force.

Benazir Bhutto still hoped to keep the religious parties, especially the Jama'at-i-Islami, from firming up their alliances with the parliamentary opposition. The Jama'at-i-Islami expected that the government would leave intact the cozy relations among the fundamentalists and the military, and refrain from any settlement not having the assent of the Afghan parties. Bhutto was expected to avoid appearing to pit the resistance parties against one another or maligning their leaders. In return, the Hezb-i-Islami and other more hard-line Afghan Islamic groups were careful not to alienate the Bhutto government by siding openly with the Prime Minister's opposition, with whom the mujahidin in fact felt closer in their views.

From the left, Bhutto's softened criticism of the war was interpreted as evidence of the insidious influence exercised by the resistance parties on Pakistan's politics. Wali Khan's Awami National Party had joined in the coalition that enabled the PPP to form a government in December 1988. Initially, the Prime Minister had hoped to use Wali Khan to find a solution to Afghanistan, perhaps by persuading Najibullah to step down. Later when the ANP broke with the government at the national level, Wali Khan questioned the government's sincerity in resolving the conflict, claiming that like their predecessors, Bhutto and her backers were in the service of imperialist masters.[25]

In fact, the ANP's position on the Afghan issue was also more expedient than principled. Wali Khan had no trouble taking his party into the parliamentary opposition. But for the Islamic Democratic Alliance led by Ghulam Mustafa Jatoi and Nawaz Sharif, the war was portrayed as nothing less than a jihad or holy struggle, a cornerstone of the Alliance's policies. The Bhutto government was repeatedly accused of having betrayed the mujahidin. Sitting with the opposition, the ANP could agree that the government polices on Afghanistan served the interests of the United States. Yet, while the left thought of the United States as prolonging the war, its legislative partners complained bitterly that Washington was willing to cheat the resistance of its well deserved triumph and was ignoring Pakistan's national interests.

During its 20-month life, the Benazir Bhutto government showed considerable deference to the military. Despite occasional attempts to reign in the ISI, she allowed the military leadership to assume nearly exclusive responsibility in setting the course of Afghan policy.[26] The Prime Minister's reluctance to interfere with the military reflected, above all, her political weakness. Specifically she feared the military's openly favoring her opposition or, worse still, directly intervening to undo democratic government. The military intelligence was credited by some with having worked initially against the consolidation of the major opposition.[27] But there was a steep price to pay for military support: a largely free hand in those areas of policy, notably including Afghanistan, that they considered their own. With so compliant a government, the military high command was thought to have little incentive to side with Bhutto's political opposition who, while closer in their views on many issues, also promised to be more difficult to control once in power.

Afghanistan opened other cleavages within the Bhutto administration. Resentments were to be expected from a foreign policy establishment that had been elbowed out by the army in policy setting for Afghanistan. The Foreign Office had doubts about the belief that a military victory was possible following the Soviet withdrawal. Together with Pakistan's representatives in Washington, ministry officials were also less inclined to insist on a political settlement aimed at installing a pliant regime in Kabul. Few civilians shared with the military Zia's dream that, together with Islamic allies Iran and Turkey, Pakistan could gain the kind of strategic depth that would counterbalance India's military advantages.

Not given an opportunity to participate in the formation of an Afghan interim government, ministry officials also doubted the exile government's viability and succeeded in withholding Pakistan's formal diplomatic recognition. Initially, recognition seemed unnecessary since Pakistani authorities and others expected that a mujahidin government would soon be installed in office in Kabul. Later, when the interim government officials were left waiting indefinitely in Peshawar, Islamabad refrained from giving the Afghan Interim Government formal status, in no small part because of criticism that it was little more than the handiwork of military intelligence. The government promised diplomatic recognition once the AIG was successful in establishing at least some territorial authority that included a major city within Afghanistan. Notwithstanding the army's objection, the Foreign Ministry prevailed in this instance, claiming that with any other policy Pakistan could be accused of a clear breach of the Geneva agreement on neutrality—which it had been already accused of violating.[28]

The Foreign Office was also less adamant in its opposition to the return of the deposed Afghan monarch, Zahir Shah. As part of a political solution, civilian offfials in Pakistan were not nearly so concerned as the military with the former king's allegedly pro-Indian past. For the Interior Ministry, a fresh look at Afghanistan was thought imperative in the belief that the continued deterioration of law and order in Pakistan was linked to its prevailing Afghan policies. Yet whatever the misgivings among the civilian bureaucrats, their input on Afghanistan was negligible, and they were reduced to carrying out policies set at the highest military echelons, particularly after May 1989 when the head of military intelligence was replaced and greater authority for decisions involving Afghanistan was transferred to army chief of staff General Aslam Beg.

The competition between civilian and military policy makers was sharply etched in postmortems over the premature attack on the Afghan city of Jalalabad following the Soviet pullout (see chapter 3). For the failure of the resistance to dislodge Kabul regime troops from the near border city, the ISI held the Foreign Office responsible, claiming the civilians too impatient to see an interim government strengthen its legitimacy. Simultaneously, the Foreign Office turned on the military intelligence for its planning and direction of the operation. In any case, both had given the green light.

By contrast, civilian and military quarters avoided public recriminations over the other major failed policy to end the war quickly, the Islamabad-supported aborted coup attempt in Kabul on March 6–7, 1990, by Afghan General Shahnawaz Tanai. Yet, privately, government officials again felt used by the military in what appeared to be a botched operation that counted on the coordinated attacks together with the resistance's Hezb-i-Islami. The refusal of other mujahidin parties in Peshawar to join what they viewed as Hekmatyar's cynical bid for power in alliance with hard-line communist coup leader General Tanai gave lie to claims that the ISI's close collaboration with the radical Islamists of Hezb-i-Islami had ended. The Prime Minister's distrust of military intelligence also deepened in the belief that it had misled her and her advisers about the coup's progress—this just months before she would finally split with the military over its role in containing civil strife in the Sindh.

The Bhutto government might have given greater urgency to a political settlement and tried to cultivate a popular support were it convinced that the public could be mobilized around the issue sufficiently to override resistance to change among politicians and

military officers. Repeated surveys had shown that substantial if
somewhat declining majorities of Pakistanis supported continued
government assistance to the refugees.[29] The quest for a negotiated peace
in Afghanistan and the early return of refugees also won broad national
approval. Even so, and notwithstanding rising complaints about the
refugees, the issue still lacked the intensity that would have led the
public to place the Afghan issue ahead of other concerns and enable the
prime minister to build new partisan loyalties. So long as Muslims are
not forced to live under communist dominance, few Pakistanis,
particularly outside of the NWFP, care what kind of government
eventually assumes power in Afghanistan. Thus, as Prime Minister, Ms.
Bhutto had concluded after a short time in office that little was to be
gained politically and much to be risked by defying her opposition and
the Afghan resistance leadership.[30]

Implications for a Peace Settlement

Not only day-to day-decisions but the larger policy choices regarding
Afghanistan remained mainly the preserve of elites in Pakistan,
essentially outside the wider political process.[31] At the same time,
domestic politics could at critical times hamstring the government in
reformulating policies. The inhibitions were especially obvious in efforts
during 1990 to reach a political solution to the war. Policy makers were
unable to reassess their support for the mujahidin or seriously debate
Pakistan's national interests in a postwar Afghanistan. Internal pressures
conspired with foreign influences to limit the options available to
Pakistan in trying to conclude the conflict and bring about the early
return of the refugees.

The government of Benazir Bhutto was ever fearful that it would be
accused of turning its back on the brave resistance. Sniping domestic
parties and their Afghan allies insisted that repatriation could occur only
with the consent of the refugees and cooperation of the Afghan resistance
leaders. It was impossible to advocate dislodging large numbers of
Afghans and driving them across the border into an environment that
they still considered hostile or that was unready to receive them. Political
costs were also bound to be heavy were an attempt made to bypass or
squeeze the mujahidin leadership in the pursuit of a compromise
settlement. A policy that tried to impose a wide sharing of power among
the disparate resistance groups and also include individuals associated
with Kabul's communist regime was certain to be attacked by the
religious parties.

Meanwhile, public opinion among Pakistanis never succeeded in forcing the Afghan issue to the top of the parliamentary or electoral agenda. Without popular pressures, the country's leaders were denied the kind of ground swell they would need to feel confident enough to defy the Afghan mujahidin and their domestic allies. In place of democratic pressures or a national consensus, domestic instability in Pakistan helped to accelerate a political solution. An acute law and order situation, as was occurring in Karachi and Hyderabad in May and June 1990, gave a sense of new urgency in dealing with the Afghan issue. Because the civil strife was conceived as broadly linked to the Afghan presence in the country, the government in Islamabad found it easier to justify a reassessment. Whatever the pro-mujahidin biases remaining inside the military, many in its command were willing to countenance new policies once they had concluded that Pakistan's security problems were essentially home grown and the unresolved Afghanistan war had badly complicated the job of domestic control.

The Kashmir crisis that erupted in early 1990 had at least for a while a different effect. Although it succeeded in diverting attention from Afghanistan at a time when the press and others were actively criticizing the government's lack of policy initiative, Indian repression in Kashmir strengthened the hand of those elements in Pakistan that argued that Islamabad carried heavy responsibilities for realizing Muslim self-determination. The Afghan cause was again—as it had been while the Soviets occupied the country—part of the liberation struggle of all oppressed Muslims, Afghans along with Kashmiris and Palestinians.

Chances that Prime Minister Benazir Bhutto would be in a position to subscribe to a peace plan seemed most likely if Pakistan were carried along by an international initiative. Essential to any solution was an agreement between the United States and Soviet Union restricting the flow of new weapons to belligerents, almost certainly linked to a role for the United Nations (and possibly one for the Organization of the Islamic Conference). A projected internationally-sanctioned election-centered peace plan would presumably include the active or tacit approval of Saudi Arabia and Iran. Pakistan's role in this consensus would not be a passive one; it had the rather unique position of being perhaps the only country that could simultaneously talk to the Americans, Iranians, Saudis, and Chinese, as well as the Soviets.

In the end, the key to any plan lay with Pakistan's capacity and determination to halt the flow of weapons, from whatever source. Chances that the military would go along counted on the willingness of the United States, commanding the major arms supply network, to limit the ISI in its ability to undermine a policy agreed to in Islamabad. Then, with all the pieces in place, Afghan resistance leaders and their domestic backers were expected to go along reluctantly with the plan. But the scenario's designers had not counted on the distraction of the designated players by a Persian Gulf crisis or the dismissal of Ms. Bhutto.

Without a solution orchestrated from the outside, the Afghan struggle was thought likely to continue and dissolve into a low intensity conflict, without end. Whatever happened, U.S. economic as well as military assistance was expected to peter out, probably gradually. So was aid from other outside sources. Less foreign assistance would leave the Pakistan government with fewer external resources with which to keep in line domestic political forces whose support had, in effect, been bought previously. Faced with reduced U.S. arms, Pakistan's rulers could also be expected to be more likely to bow to popular domestic demands that the country throw off its Washington-imposed restraint and proceed full throttle on a nuclear weapons program. By stubbornly clinging to its nuclear option, a government in Islamabad would be able to demonstrate the kind of determination that wins approval from most Pakistanis and denies the issue to the opposition.

While most political figures in Pakistan supported Islamabad on the war for reasons of principle or because they derived support for their stance, this backing was expected to be put to the test if international relief money dried up and Pakistan were left with the burden of the refugees. In the event that foreign relief operations became the regular target of anti-Western mujahidin parties or the resistance leaders were viewed as intransigent in peace negotiations, an early loss of Western interest in the war and its victims was believed probable. Pakistan was then likely to be saddled with large numbers of Afghan refugees prevented by resistance parties from returning and angered at the sharp decline in food and other services. In that event, only Saudi Arabia had the capacity and possibly the will to be a reliable financial source. Whether the Saudi government, preoccupied with its own national problems, would have increased or even continued an indefinite commitment to the Afghans is uncertain. Saudi competition with Iran, which underlay much of its involvement, was also subject to change. In any case, many Pakistanis questioned whether their country had not already become too beholden to the Saudis and if these ties would not eventually lead to a souring of relations with Iran.

Until a resolution of the Afghan war occurred, there was increased possibility that Pakistan's differences with Iran, kept to a minimum during the course of the conflict, could become more prominent. The regime in Tehran, more concerned with the outcome in Afghanistan while its western front with Iraq remained quiet, had after 1988 established strong commercial links with Moscow and had become more sensitive to Soviet concerns in the region. The revolutionary Islamic government had begun, moreover, to play a larger supporting role with Afghan Shi'ite resistance parties based on Iran. Aside from Tehran's desire to assure that the largely Shi'ite minority of central Afghanistan and elsewhere received a better deal in a postwar state, Iran had remained ever vigilant that Sunni fundamentalism be restrained, particularly where it was bankrolled by Saudi Arabia.

The Afghanistan issue still carried the potential to impact on Pakistan's political processes in a basic way. On more than one occasion Benazir Bhutto had asserted that the Afghan war could threaten not only her government but the democratic system itself.[32] No doubt, those who preferred not to see democracy succeed were content to allow the war to continue.[33] The war was not directly responsible for Ms. Bhutto's downfall, but her inability to confront it was symptomatic of her problems in trying to govern. An Afghan conflict that strengthened one Pakistani regime for nearly a decade and weakened confidence in another, if left unresolved, threatened to be a catalyst in destabilizing future governments of Pakistan.[34]

Notes

1. Eqbal Ahmad, "If Pakistan Slides Into Civil War," *The New York Times*, November 18, 1983.

2. Louis and Nancy Hatch Dupree, "Afghan Refugees in Pakistan," *World Refugee Survey: 1987 in Review*, U.S. Committee for Refugees, March 15, 1988, p. 20.

3. Salamat Ali, *Far Eastern Economic Review*, May 23, 1991, pp. 23–24.

4. John Fullerton, "A Rift Among Rebels," *Far Eastern Economic Review*, October 29, 1982, p. 20.

5. Foreign Broadcast Information Services (FIBIS), South Asia, February 23, 1988, p. 71.

6. One occasion of violence took place in July 1982, when Afghans attacked a Pakistani village, burning houses and killing one person. Edward Girardat, *Afghanistan; the Soviet War* (New York, St. Martin's Press, 1985), p. 206. An armed attacks on Afghan refugees by Pakistani leftists occurred in early April 1987 when an angry mob indiscriminately attacked Afghans in the streets following a bomb blast in which 16 persons were killed, many of them children. *Dawn Overseas Weekly* (Karachi), March 5, 1987.

7. When Pakistanis were placed in jeopardy, the authorities were prepared to act. In the fall of 1986, after largely indiscriminate bomb blasts in the Quetta and Peshawar areas, police rounded up some 50,000 Afghans, moving them temporarily back to their respective camps. The fighting that took place in Karachi in the late 1980s was between citizens of Pakistan, although it pitted Pathans having settled from the north against Urdu-speakers who immigrated to

Pakistan from India. Afghan refugees in the vicinity of mob violence were believe marginal to the disorder.

8. Expressed in an interview with Afghan Interim Government President Sighbatullah Mojadeddi with *WUFA*, Writers Union of Free Afghanistan, Peshawar, Vol. 5, no. 2 (April–June 1990): 9–10. Mujaddidi claimed that the Pakistani authorities knew the identity of the terrorists very well.

9. From a summary of the proceedings of an international symposium on "The Crisis of Migration from Afghanistan: Domestic and Foreign Implications," co-sponsored by the Refugee Studies Program, Oxford University, March 29–April 2, 1987, pp. 9–10.

10. For the activities of communist agents in the tribal areas see Riaz M. Khan, *Untying the Afghan Knot; Negotiating Soviet Withdrawal* (Durham, N.C.: Duke University Press, 1991), pp. 79, 173, and 174. Also see Oliver Roy, "The Lessons of the Soviet/Afghan War," Adelphi Papers, Brassey, Summer 1991, p. 22.

11. Robert G. Wirsing, "Repatriation of Afghan Refugees," *Journal of South and West Asian Studies*, Vol. 12, no. 1 (fall 1988): 32–33. The UNHCR, the United Nations High Commissioner for Refugees, was the coordinating agency for relief to the camps.

12. Afghan Information Center (AIC), *Monthly Bulletin*, nos. 71-72 (February and March, 1987), p. 4.

13. *Frontier Post* (Peshawar), January 31, 1990.

14. *The Economist*, June 6, 1981, p. 11.

15. The parties urging nationalist and progressive forces to cooperate with the Kabul government also included the Pashtuoonkhwa Milli Awami Party (PMAP) and the National Democratic Party, a leftist party headed by Farooq Qureshi. Another pro-Najibullah party without parliamentary membership was the traditionally more moderate Tekhrik-i-Estiqlal of Retired Air Marshall Asghar Khan.

16. See John Fullerton, *The Soviet Occupation of Afghanistan* (Hong Kong: Far Eastern Economic Review, Ltd., 1983), p. 70, note 10.

17. The Jama'at-i-Islami gained considerable respect among all the Islamic parties for the role that the party was allowed to play in the March 1990 Kunar elections. In this liberated Afghan province bordering Pakistan, the competing elements turned to the party for expertise—down to the form of the ballot—in conducting an election. The proportional representation method employed at Jama'at's suggestion was the electoral form denied to it in Pakistan's electoral politics where, under a single member district plurality system, the party is placed at a disadvantage.

18. *The New York Times*, November 16, 1988.

19. *Frontier Post*, April 17, 1990; *Pakistan Times* (Islamabad), April 15, 1990. Report from *Nawa-i-Waqt* in *Afghan Jehad*, Vol. 4, no. 3 (April–June, 1991): 256.

20. *Muslim* (Islamabad) February 8, 1990; *Frontier Post*, February 4, 1990. At a Jama'at-i-Islami-sponsored conference on Kashmir in Lahore in January 1993, a Jama'at leader boasted that his party had sent 35,000 mujahidin to fight in Kashmir. He claimed to the embarrassment of government officials in attendance

that these mujahidin had earlier been engaged in the Afghan jihad. *Newsline* (Karachi), February 1993, p. 86. For a discussion of the ISI's role in planning and coordinating Pakistan's support for the Kashmiri cause, including the observation that the Jama'at operated training camps, including ones inside Afghanistan, see Robert G. Wirsing, "Kashmir conflict," in Charles H. Kennedy (ed.), *Pakistan 1992* (Boulder: Westview Press, 1992), pp. 148–149.

21. *The New York Times*, May 23, 1990.

22. Ibid., May 25, 1989.

23. Riaz Khan, *Untying the Afghan Knot*, p. 227. According to Riaz Khan, the Pakistan's Foreign Office was sensitive to the charge of having stalled the process of finding a peaceful solution at the United State's behest but that it never seemed to affect Zia. Ibid., 91.

24. Rasul Bux Rais, *Asian Survey*, Vol. 29, no. 2 (February 1989): 200.

25. *Frontier Post*, January 31, 1990.

26. Following her dismissal, Ms. Bhutto admitted that she had done so against her better judgement. She was reported as saying "They asked to look after Afghanistan. I [was] not very happy with the way they were handling it. I allowed them great liberties." *The New York Times*, August 8, 1990.

27. *Muslim*, May 5, 1989. But so strong is the belief in the ISI's omnipotence that other sources insisted that the military intelligence had instead taken a leading role in organizing the Islamic Democratic Alliance. *The New York Times*, May 31, 1989.

28. D. Shah Khan in *Muslim*, October 3, 1989.

29. Ijaz S. Galani, "The Four "r's" of Afghanistan" (Islamabad: Pakistan Institute of Public Opinion, 1985), pp. 8-9. Also, in a public lecture "Public Opinion and National Security," delivered at the Institute of Strategic Studies, Islamabad, March 31, 1986, Galani indicated that Gallup Pakistan had found three of four Pakistanis supporting continued government assistance to the refugees. Robert G. Wirsing, "Pakistan and the War in Afghanistan," *Asian Affairs*, Vol. 14, no. 2 (summer 1987): 66.

30. Nasim Zehra in *Nation* (Lahore), May 18, 1989. Claims surfaced after the deposing of the People's Party-led government, allegedly based on documents found by the caretaker government that succeeded her, that Ms. Bhutto had in fact suggested to her Intelligence Bureau that they organize "peace processions" throughout the country to undermine support for the jihads in both Afghanistan and Kashmir. Shahid Saleem, in *The Pakistan Times*, September 6, 1990, reported in FBIS, South Asia, September 7, 1990, p. 69. In any event, these processions did not take place.

31. Ahmed Rashid, *The Herald* (Karachi), March 1990, p. 20, had made a similar observation before Bhutto's fall.

32. *Muslim*, May 4, 1989.

33. Ahmed Rashid in *Nation*, September 15, 1989.

34. Mushahid Hussein in *The New York Times*, January 31, 1988.

6

Pakistan and the Negotiations

Pakistan was indispensable to any efforts, political or military, to bring the conflict to a close. The Afghan resistance's capacity to pursue a military victory as well as its interest in a compromise diplomatic settlement was largely determined by how the government in Islamabad defined its own interests and the lengths to which it was prepared to go to pursue its objectives. Much as there could have been no sustained armed resistance without Pakistan, neither could negotiations leading to the Soviet withdrawal have occurred without the Islamabad government's persistence and, in the end, willingness to agree to the terms of a Geneva accord. Pakistan continued to play an influential role in events leading to the fall of the Kabul regime and in efforts to install an interim government of Afghan mujahidin. Throughout the conflict, the decisions in Islamabad leading to a settlement reflected domestic factional and partisan struggles together with the weight of international pressures and sense of threat. Many of the same factors can be expected to carry over into Pakistan's policies in the postwar era.

Pakistan's leaders never reached anything approaching a consensus on how to bring the war to an end most quickly and favorably to the country's interests. Moreover, neither in aiding the Afghan resistance nor in pursuing a settlement did officials in Islamabad ever manage to square Pakistan's covert and overt policies. What the Islamabad government professed publicly was often at considerable variance from its behind-the-scenes role.

At the core of Pakistan difficulties with the Afghan issue was the lack of a coherent set of policies. For most of the war, Pakistan remained divided about what it sought and how to best attain its objectives. Absence of a clear, consistent course aimed at ending the conflict and prescribing a postwar role for Pakistan often resulted in a near paralysis of policy at the national level. Most of its choices, to be sure, appeared to involve critical and painful decisions forcing Pakistan's government to deal with the domestic political ramifications of unavoidably controversial polices. The inconsistencies in policy were, as we have seen, often a result of disagreements among those at the centers of decision making in the country, namely the prime minister, the president, the military (especially its Inter-Service Intelligence [ISI] directorate), the Punjab-based parties in the National Assembly, and the Foreign Ministry. The differences were sometimes highly personal, often part of an effort of officials to avoid criticism and responsibility for their acts. Just as often they reflected long-standing institutional rivalries.

On some issues of Afghan policy there existed a convergence of views among policy makers, shared by a wider public. The belief that Pakistan should not be alone saddled with the burden of the war and care of its Afghan refugees found a near consensus. Similar wide agreement held that however the fighting ended, it should not lead to an Afghanistan government unfriendly to Pakistan. Both of these views were widely felt to be compatible with the belief that no solutions could be forced on the Afghan people, who were ultimately expected to decide their own future. There was far less agreement on who could rightly speak for the Afghan people, on what degree of cooperation between the two countries was necessary, and on how much external pressure on the Afghans was constructive and legitimate.

Pakistan's role in bringing about an Afghan peace had been much of the time affected by a number of miscalculations and misperceptions. For many Pakistanis there existed a tendency to simplify the Afghan conflict—once viewed as merely an artifact of the cold war and then interpreted all too readily as mere tribal rivalries. Officials continued to believe, even against contrary evidence, that the Pashtunistan issue—the tribal and ethnic threat to Pakistan's territorial integrity—was always prone to revival, and that every decision had to be weighed by its meaning for the adversarial relationship with India. Further, policy makers had badly underestimated the staying power of the Kabul government and overrated the possibilities of coordination among the mujahidin. There had been slowness to appreciate in Islamabad the changes that followed the Soviet military withdrawal and how the priorities of the U.S. administration and commitment of the international community might alter with the end of the cold war. By contrast, in discerning how a continuing conflict in Afghanistan could impede opportunities in Central Asia following the Soviet Union's demise, policy makers in Pakistan showed early awareness along with concern. The prospect of the joining of Pakistan to the new Muslim states through an Afghan corridor left a government in Islamabad amenable to the kind of compromises and settlement that had for so long been rejected outright.

The Geneva Process

Pakistan had taken the lead, as already described, in rallying the international community's condemnation of Soviet aggression and succeeded in attracting military assistance for itself and the mujahidin. But with little prospect that the Soviet Union could be defeated in an armed struggle, Pakistan also soon opened up the diplomatic track to a negotiated settlement. At the United Nations, Pakistan argued for the appointment of a special representative in order to promote a negotiated peace. A meeting of the 45-member Organization of the Islamic Conference (OIC) held in May 1980, although not fully committing Islamic countries to talks, authorized Pakistan and Iran to explore possibilities of a political solution leading to a Soviet withdrawal.

Officials in Islamabad rejected face-to-face talks with the Kabul government in Geneva or anywhere else, lest this confer legitimacy and recognition on the communist regime. Concern was also that Moscow might use the talks as a tactic to confuse and weaken the mujahidin and soften international opinion.[1] Although Pakistan had a poorly developed concept of a possible settlement, so-called proximity talks commenced in June 1982 under the supervision of the U.N. Secretary General's special representative Diego Cordovez, with the United Nations acting as intermediary between Islamabad and Kabul, and the United States and Soviet Union as observers. The U.N. mediator was obliged to go back and forth between the parties, often in the same building, throughout the periodically held negotiations. The talks excluded the Afghan mujahidin, who publicly rejected the process. But it was also clear from the outset that Pakistan had little interest in sharing the diplomacy of negotiations with the Peshawar parties.

Very early in the negotiating process, the Islamabad government dropped Soviet withdrawal from Afghanistan as a precondition for the talks. Thus the talks that dragged on for more than five years focused, above all, on a timetable for a Soviet pullout of troops, Pakistan demanding at most a few months, the Soviets asking for years and later holding out for at least 18 months. Even after Mikhail Gorbachev's declaration in 1987 of a willingness to negotiate a withdrawal of forces from Afghanistan, the view in Islamabad remained cautious. The Soviets seemed willing to pull out, but only after they could be assured that a pro-Soviet regime would be left behind in Kabul.

Suspicious of Soviet intentions, President Zia ul-Haq was given to remark, "Perhaps it can be the miracle of the 20th century if the Soviets withdraw."[2] Zia believe that the Soviets, while holding out the possibility of an implicit offer to recognize the Durand Line, were intent on causing difficulties for Pakistan in hopes that Islamabad would become more conciliatory in the Geneva negotiations. He was convinced that Gorbachev had been trying to browbeat Pakistan, destabilizing it by creating rifts in Pakistani society. He saw the hand of Soviet and Afghan intelligence in the repeated terrorist bombing in several Pakistani cities. But Zia's determination remained strong that Moscow's sowing the seeds of discord in Pakistan would not lead his government to succumb to pressures.

The official view in Pakistan of Soviet intentions had changed by the end of 1987. Evidence had mounted that the Soviets desired to play the role of international peacemaker and that a demoralized military and increased losses might have induced Moscow to quit Afghanistan.[3] Zia continued to question whether the Soviets would in the end desert their friends and face the full consequences of a withdrawal.[4] Many doubts were removed, however, with Gorbachev's announcement in February 1988, that the Soviet Union was prepared to negotiate a withdrawal over a period of less than a year, with 50 percent of its 115,000 troops out of Afghanistan in the first three months.

The war in Afghanistan became increasingly an obstacle in the Soviet leadership's efforts in the Gorbachev era to recast the international image of the Soviet Union as a more open, economically efficient society at home and a sincere advocate of negotiated solutions abroad. While Moscow had felt that it had already paid the price internationally of its intervention, its political goals took on increased significance. The Soviet standing in the Islamic world was unlikely to improve until its armed forces stopped killing Muslims and behaving as neo-colonialists. In South Asia, a Soviet diplomatic offensive remained contingent on a settlement of the Afghanistan issue. Withdrawal by the Soviet military promised to give Moscow a more serious opportunity to again float the idea of an Asian security pact with India and others. Soviet concessions on Afghanistan could be part of a concerted policy by Moscow to woo China, meeting one of its preconditions for better relations. Progress on Afghanistan was certain to color on-going disarmament talks with the United States in Geneva. Most of all, the Soviets were anxious to deny the Americans the moral edge that Washington had held while Soviet combat forces remained in Afghanistan. One sure way to reduce U.S. influence in southwest Asia was to wind down the Afghan war.

Only with the prospect that the Kabul regime might soon fall was there any sense of urgency about the composition of a future mujahidin-led government and how that government could be installed. Previously, in mid-1987, Diego Cordovez sponsored a plan to convene a *loya jirga* or grand assembly of all the interested parties to the conflict, including representatives of the former king and the communists, to choose an interim government. The plan received only lukewarm support from

Pakistan and United States, however, and no commitment from Moscow. Cordovez was reportedly blocked by Pakistan from circulating his proposal among the resistance. Although he succeeded in using intermediaries to bring it to their attention, the response among the Peshawar parties was hardly positive.[5]

Until this time, the Soviets had insisted that there be an interim government, including important elements of the People's Democratic Party of Afghanistan (PDPA), in any political settlement. They had tried to link their departure with the consolidation and legitimization of the communist rule in Kabul. But at the insistence of Pakistan and the United States, the Soviets agreed during the fall of 1987 to drop their demand as a precondition for agreeing to a shorter timetable containing a specific date of final withdrawal. In effect, by giving up on plans for a "government of national reconciliation," Moscow had abandoned the idea of the irreversibility of the Afghan revolution.[6]

In January 1988 the idea that an interim government be in place at the time of the Soviet withdrawal was instead taken up by General Zia. Significantly, Zia and other senior Pakistani officials even conceded the need to include at least some members of the communist regime, probably excluding President Najibullah, in a transitional government. The Pakistani president was said to have suggested a formula for a coalition government following a cease-fire that included a one-third participation for the PDPA. He also suggested that Islamabad was ready for a simultaneous cut-off in military aid to both the Kabul government and the resistance.[7]

The logic of Pakistan's demand that a transitional government be created was clear. Only a compromise that brought together all of the warring factions provided any guarantee that the fighting would end with the Soviet departure. Without a political settlement the war could go on indefinitely and with it the probability that the Afghan refugees would remain in Pakistan for the duration. Zia's demands for an interim solution and revision of the terms of the settlement promised to seriously complicate the negotiations, however. Pakistan's formulation required extensive negotiations with the Soviets about the composition of the interim government and, most of all, agreement by the mujahidin that would allow active members of the PDPA to participate. General Zia had never dropped his insistence that any new Afghan regime would have to be acceptable to the mujahidin. But the resistance leaders were far from an agreement among themselves on a future power sharing and what role, if any, the communists could have; in any case, they objected to negotiations in which they were not participants.

Repeated attempts were made to make the Afghan resistance leaders appreciative of Pakistan's problems and to convince them of the gains possible with some flexibility. By nurturing the impression that the Peshawar alliance would go along with a settlement when the time came, the ISI led Pakistan's Foreign Office to badly overestimate its ability to induce pragmatism among the mujahidin leadership, much less to prompt initiatives from the Peshawar parties.[8] In fact, the ISI under General Akhtar Rahman was at the same time encouraging the mujahidin leadership to hold out for granting the Soviets no more than two to three months to withdraw, rather than the ten months finally agreed to by President Zia.

The government's critics refused to believe that Zia himself did not in fact prefer the conflict to continue as a means of sustaining U.S. aid and of keeping Washington from pressing Islamabad too hard on the issue of nuclear nonproliferation. Others felt that Zia was not so much interested in a compromise agreement as he was in seeing the Najibullah regime defeated completely.[9] There was, after all, reason to conclude after 1987 that the Soviets would be forced to leave anyway, and that it was unnecessary to concede very much. Pakistan's military assured the politicians that once Soviet forces had withdrawn, the mujahidin would be capable of dealing a crushing blow to the Afghan communists. Even assuming Zia's sincerity in wishing to reach a diplomatic solution, negotiations were bound to influence domestic political alliances between the government and Pakistan's religious parties that together with hard-line Afghan Islamists insisted that fighting continue until Afghanistan became an Islamic state, free of communists.

Others elements in the Islamabad government were anxious to have any agreement that promised to lessen Pakistan's role in the war and reduce the conflict's effect on the society. In particular within the Foreign Office, key officials worried about the negotiating process collapsing. Zia's prime minister, Mohammad Khan Junejo, became convinced that the resistance would not be persuaded to compromise. He lobbied in favor of the view that Pakistan should sign an agreement, even one without the provision for an interim Afghan government. After a calling a special session of the National Assembly to debate the issue, Junejo convened a meeting of all Pakistani parties in an effort to create a national consensus for signing an accord in Geneva. While these consultations pleased the regime's opposition, they sat less well with President Zia. Later, Prime Minister Junejo would be subjected to the accusation from Zia's loyalists that he had failed to bargain enough in the way of gaining concessions from the Soviets.

Officials in Washington were dismayed by Zia's demand for an interim arrangement, made without the usual coordination of policy. They remained convinced that it would be impossible to get the resistance to participate in such a plan. While the United States and others giving aid to Pakistan agreed in principle with the desirability of a broad-based government, they feared the breakdown in the Geneva talks—that the Soviets would be given an opportunity to back out of their commitment to withdraw. A personal phone call from Ronald Reagan to Zia is reported to have convinced him to back down.[10] U.S. officials denied extraordinary pressure, although they concede that Zia knew very well the priority that Washington gave to an agreement that would bring a Soviet military pullout. Even without threats, Zia apparently feared becoming an odd man out, watching a superpower deal being cut over his head leading to the United States' loss of interest in Pakistan.[11]

In Zia's decision to sign the accord, he no doubt concluded that this was probably the best Pakistan was going to get and, indeed, most of its core requirements had been met. In many respects, the Soviet departure—to be accomplished within a period of nine months beginning on May 15, 1988—could be scored as an enormous victory for Pakistan, which had so steadfastly stood with the mujahidin, maintained international pressures, and kept the negotiating process alive. Pakistan could manage to save face by citing that the quest for an internal settlement would go on through brokering activities by the United Nations. Cordovez had pledged to continue his efforts toward the formation of a transitional government after the signing of the agreement. Even without this, if the military experts were to be believed, the Afghan communist leadership would be close on the heels of the Soviets in leaving the country. Following the communists' defeat in final series of battles, a weak coalition of commanders and parties would probably emerge to form a new government.

With nothing in the Geneva accords to assure the cessation of hostilities, the thorny issue of continued aid to the belligerents remained. The approach most likely to hasten an end to the conflict would have been an understanding between Washington and Moscow that neither side would supply weapons to their former clients. "Negative symmetry" had actually been floated as an idea in 1986 when it was rejected by Moscow. But by 1988 the Soviet leadership was ready to accept the concept. Expecting the imminent fall of the communist government, the United States saw nothing to lose with negative symmetry. However, there was little prospect for this agreement between the two powers so long as Pakistan, Saudi Arabia, and others were not also pledged to withhold arms; their participation would be essential to implement the policy in the border areas. Neither Pakistan nor Saudi Arabia was ready to disappoint its supporters among the resistance, denying them weapons for the military victory that the mujahidin leadership felt was close at hand.

In the end, the arms issue was finessed by adopting the concept of "positive symmetry," an unwritten agreement between the United States and the Soviet Union, formal guarantors of the Geneva agreements, that neither would be precluded from furnishing weapons during the troop pullout at something like equal and balanced levels. Whether resolving the differences between Washington and Moscow on the basis of positive symmetry also assumed that this supply of weapons could continue indefinitely is debatable but this, in effect, is what happened. Almost certainly, it was the way that President Zia and the ISI envisioned it, and "positive symmetry" enabled them to become reconciled to signing the agreement in Geneva.[12]

The understanding on arms, in fact, contradicted that provision in the accords committing the parties to "noninterference" in Afghanistan's internal affairs.[13] Specifically, the first instrument of the accords asserted that neither Afghanistan nor Pakistan could intervene or interfere in the internal affairs of the other country, and that organizing, training, and financing of individuals and groups was prohibited. Pakistan would be in direct violation of the agreement with its more or less open facilitation of the flow of arms to the resistance through its territory. Yet to many observers, all of this seemed academic given the predicted early fall of Kabul's communists. Only when that victory failed to occur as predicted did Pakistani policy makers have to face the question not only of their international obligations but also the choice between a military and political solution.

The Two-Track Policy

Pakistan's two-track approach aimed at ending the war in Afghanistan, so apparent during the years of Zia ul-Haq's presidency, remained the controlling policy after his death in August 1988. Governments in Islamabad proclaimed their desire to end the conflict peacefully but continued their support for the mujahidin's armed efforts. The latter objective for Pakistan's policy-making circles focused on the necessity of a military defeat of the Kabul's communist regime, both to bring the right kind of government into power in Afghanistan and to assure its survival against rivals. The military route would also best assure that India could be stymied in its anticipated future attempts to exercise influence in Afghanistan. Through better coordination among the mujahidin and more effective use of the arms available, Pakistan's military intelligence personnel, together with their CIA partners, remained committed to seeing things through to a decisive victory.

Perceived Soviet determination to stay and the differences among the resistance factions over a settlement of course reinforced arguments for a hard line.

An opposing view held that a military victory was probably impossible and that, in any case, in view of the diversity of political forces, a negotiated settlement in advance of a change in power in Kabul was required if there were to be long-term stability in Afghanistan. The danger always existed that the pursuit of a military solution would increase the chances that a more radical Islamist group or groups would assume power in Kabul. This strategy also furthered the possibility of a rise in Islamic sectarianism, pitting Iran and its minions against the Saudis and their favorites. Further, a delayed solution could help fuel ethnic rivalries among the Afghans. Chances were better for a national consensus allowing for a stable regime if a peace resulted from a political agreement that preceded a transfer of power from the communists. A minority of resistance leaders, the so-called moderates or traditionalists, acceded to this point of view, including its corollary that power would have to be shared with at least some officials of the previous communist regime.

The two approaches toward a conclusion to the war were not necessarily mutually exclusive, and advocates of a military solution included many who expected that the right kind of political solution could only follow the route of military victories. Tangible gains on the battlefield were needed to obtain the best terms or accelerate a settlement, specifically, to gain major concessions from the communists. In general, it was not unusual for the authorities in Islamabad and their U.S. intelligence contacts to be urging the mujahidin to mount more attacks while working toward improving conditions for negotiations with the Soviets and Kabul government.

The projected quick fall of the Afghan communist government after the February 1989 Soviet pullout had renewed attention to the possible role of an interim government. Without central authority in Kabul, drawn from many elements, a civil war loomed as a distinct possibility. Moscow anticipated, along with many in the region and the West, that the Najibullah regime would have at best only a decent interval before succumbing to the mujahidin. The Soviets were believed to be prepared to settle for an orderly transfer of power, leaving elements of the regime, if not its top leaders, to join a broad, mujahidin-dominated government.

With the Soviet departure imminent, the Islamabad government had, however, lost interest for the time being in diplomacy. There appeared no reason to compromise on any points when officials believed that the communists would soon be ousted. Following their troop withdrawal, the Soviets, uncertain about the staying power of the Najibullah regime, had sent high ranking officials to Islamabad, including Yuli Voronstsov, First Deputy Foreign Minister and Ambassador to Afghanistan, and Foreign Minister Eduard Shevardnadze. Pakistani officials, now sure of a military victory, were not especially interested in a Soviet formula that would have the PDPA settle for a 30 percent share in a future government.[14] When only a few months later the Pakistan government was ready for serious discussion, the Soviet position had hardened.

The mujahidin's failed military campaign at Jalalabad might have pushed Pakistan back toward the political track. However, Pakistan's military leadership, which had orchestrated much of the attack on the far eastern city, felt the need to redeem itself. Reasoning that the Afghan resistance was politically and militarily weak, Pakistan's generals opposed early negotiations. Moreover, before there could be successful direct talks with the Kabul's communists and their Soviet backers, the military argued that the Peshawar party alliance, the AIG, needed to bring into the fold the more independent commanders and the Shi'ite parties based in Iran.

Pakistan's leadership, military as well as civilian, also remained concerned about creating strong resentments and security problems for Pakistan if it pushed the resistance parties in Peshawar too hard. Ministry statements to the effect that Pakistan's interests might demand policies independent of mujahidin were undermined by the military's insistence that the Afghan resistance be satisfied that its aims had been attained. Pakistan's call for a just and equitable settlement, acceptable to all parties, meant continuing a policy that gave hard-line Afghan groups a virtual veto on policies affecting a settlement. The Afghan resistance was convinced, then, that it had little reason to fear a break with the Pakistan government, or need to concede anything politically.

The coup attempt in Kabul by Afghan General Tanai in March 1990, demonstrated how anxious were Pakistan's civilian and military leadership for a short cut in bringing the war to a conclusion through a quick military solution. However, with the failure of the leftist-cum-Islamist coup to topple Najibullah, and the resistance's inability—principally the forces of Hekmatyar—to capitalize on opportunities in the countryside, Pakistan once more reasserted its commitment to a two-track strategy. Public statements stressing diplomacy were revived and the military returned to the blueprint that called for the kind of patience that would produce a string of smaller military victories leading to the desired results. This strategy was best demonstrated in the fall of Khost, a strategic garrison city close to the Pakistan border, at the end of March 1991.

Interestingly, instead of the success at Khost strengthening the hand of those seeking a military solution, it helped to make a case for those in the leadership anxious to prevent further bloodshed.[15] Khost's fall, after a difficult campaign, brought home the extent to which Pakistan would be obliged to get directly involved in the conflict if there were to be further mujahidin victories. Based on the experience of taking and occupying the city, it was obvious that the resistance parties were not sufficiently unified to win a series of similar victories. Pakistan, which had provided weapons to several mujahidin groups (probably more to Hezb-i-Islami than its presence warranted at Khost), was clearly embarrassed by the behavior of the mujahidin in Khost. The resistance had been unable to control its militias in their looting the city and battling among themselves for arms and ammunition, and other spoils of war. The Khost victory confirmed the worst fears of some over what a mujahidin military success could bring: that given the political diversity and ethnic heterogeneity, the military route could not produce a governable society.

The defeat of the Kabul regime at Khost, although not in itself significant in altering the political or military balance of power, was nevertheless thought to be valuable for improving Pakistan's position in negotiations.[16] Yet, as had occurred before, when the Kabul government appeared ready for a political settlement, the mujahidin and their friends in the ISI, sensing a military breakthrough, pulled back from political discussions. For a number of reasons, however, a larger planned offensive by the mujahidin on the Khost model never materialized.[17]

Pakistan's civilian and military elites both agreed that a broader-based, legitimized, more representative Afghan resistance leadership would be required for either a military victory or a negotiated settlement. To bring the Afghan leaders together and in the process take from them some of their perks and power could be accomplished, however, only with popular backing created by the national appeal for a consensus. Greater public support would also help the Islamabad government if it hoped to discourage Saudi Arabia and others from encouraging their hard-line protégés in the resistance.[18] Popular agreement over the proposition that the refugees leave sooner rather than later had always been present. Otherwise, Afghan policy did not enjoy a national political consensus within Pakistan. Indeed, none had ever been built by Pakistan's political leaders, in large part because so much of the Afghan operation had remained secret, confined to a small number of policy makers.

It was plain, as described in the previous chapter, that while Benazir Bhutto was in power, a clear direction toward a political solution was unlikely; instead policy drift was evident. She was deeply concerned about how a continuing and possibly intensified war could raise the danger to Pakistan's integrity and security. Moreover, Ms. Bhutto was less supportive than Zia of particular mujahidin groups, rejecting what she believed was Zia's attempt to impose a government on the Afghan people.[19] But beyond her preference for a negotiated outcome to the war, Bhutto had at best vague goals and was unable to articulate policies to implement them.

Modalities for a Settlement

Throughout 1990 and until May 1991, rounds of intense international diplomatic activity took place, although very little of it became public. Above all, the negotiators preferred quiet diplomacy both because they felt that more could be accomplished with no one being blamed for failure, and because they wanted to keep from appearing to impose a solution on the Afghans. At times the talks took on some urgency as a result of the belief, wrong as it turned out, that the Soviets were ready to drop their $300 million-a-month support of arms, food, and fuel to the Kabul regime.

Negotiations had to take into consideration that, with the Soviet army out of Afghanistan, intrinsic differences in goals among the mujahidin were more visible than ever, while the Najibullah government had shifted to more conciliatory policies toward its opposition. Also, a settlement had realistically to reflect the transformations inside Afghanistan after years of war, namely the uneven survival of the traditional power structure, the emergence of strong local militia and commanders, the experiences and aspirations of the long-exiled Afghans, and the strengthened hand of the Islamists and their foreign backers. There was also the reality that years of communist rule had so altered the country's urban population as to put constraints on the type of postwar regime that would be acceptable and viable. This included evidence that, however unpopular Najibullah might be in his country, sizable numbers of Afghans in the capital and elsewhere preferred the social freedoms of an essentially secular regime to an anticipated Islamic dictatorship.

The superpowers reached agreement by mid-1990 on the broad outline of U.N.-supervised voting for a shura inside Afghanistan and within the camps. Both Washington and Moscow could agree that stability required that the Afghans be allowed to choose their own leaders, and that the choice be an open one. The key was in Najibullah's resignation, which could set the stage for negotiations and would presumably bring the resistance leadership to the table. The Afghan president was unwilling, however, to relinquish power, at least in advance of the U.N.-supervised election. He demanded to be allowed to remain in office during the transition, sharing power during the election period.

The several Peshawar resistance party leaders differed on the degree of participation they could foresee for Najibullah's followers in a future vote and after. The more hard-line ruled out those individuals associated with repressive acts by the communists, a definition open to wide differences in interpretation and application. At most, if any "good Muslims" could be found, they might play a role in a future regime. Some in the resistance spoke openly of the need to subject Najibullah and others to trials for their crimes. But on the proposition that communist leader Najibullah should step down in advance of any election, the views of the mujahidin leaders largely coincided.

Moscow continued to hold out for a transitional government to be installed with a role for former government officials and party members. Pro-Soviet elements in the country, it was felt, could not be protected if Najibullah were deposed prior to the holding of an election. Yet Najibullah was not, in fact, the major stumbling block. For the Soviets had signaled their readiness to dump the Afghan leader were a reasonable alternative figure found. Even so, nothing the Soviets saw could convince them that any arrangement likely to be negotiated could guarantee an Afghan regime of moderate Muslims willing to co-exist with those former communists who would stay on.

The preferred political solution for Pakistan remained what it had been for some time: a broad-based government in Kabul acceptable to the mujahidin. However, many Pakistanis, most vocally the intelligentsia, were increasingly of the view that the Afghans had to be pushed to a settlement. In their opinion, Pakistan was "morally bound" to interfere to override Afghan group interests and, in effect, save them from "ideological interests alien to Afghan society."[20] Above all, it would be necessary to neutralize the Peshawar-based resistance parties. One way would be to nominate people to stand for elections in districts within Afghanistan as well as in the party-dominated camps inside Pakistan. The repeated declaration that the Afghan people should decide their future raised the question of whether this merely meant a majority or whether there had to be some consensus among all major elements. The Afghan ethnic minorities were concerned that their interests would be overridden by the Pashtun majority. Anyway, it was difficult to determine where the majority stood without elections.

Pakistani authorities revived efforts in early 1990 to form a new coalition among the squabbling resistance factions in Peshawar. To salvage the reputation of the Afghan parties and legitimize mujahidin authority, officials pressed for elections to a representative assembly that could ratify a negotiated agreement and serve as the basis for an interim government. It was reasoned that even if the Kabul government were overthrown through military means, hopes to avoid a civil war turned on an effective interim arrangement. The civilian leadership hoped that a *shura*, by opening the path to a full political solution, would help to isolate the more radical Afghan elements. The key part performed by Army Chief of Staff General Aslam Beg in these efforts to galvanize the resistance parties was both a token of the military's continued key role in Pakistan's decision making structure and recognition of its close ties with the mujahidin.[21]

The plan, widely discussed, envisaged that each of the 216 districts of Afghanistan would nominate ten representatives, by whatever means they chose, who would then elect one member to a new shura. The shura would then choose a head of state and government. Although some resistance commanders argued that free and fair elections were not widely possible for the time being, the indispensability of a shura was acknowledged. Where the various elements failed to agree was on the modalities. There was no consensus over who would be permitted to vote, how the vote would be supervised, and who could be elected. Nor was there agreement on where the proposed shura would convene, whether within or outside of Afghanistan. Particularly vexing was the inability of the Sunni majority to agree to the kind of representation in the shura and an eventual government acceptable to the Iran-based Shi'ite resistance parties. In general, none of the mujahidin groups were prepared to back a proposal for elections that did not maximize their representation in a future government.

Former king Zahir Shah provided an answer to those seeking a leader who could attract support and enhance the legitimacy of an interim government. To many U.S. and Soviet officials, but also at least two of the more moderate, traditionalist resistance parties, Zahir Shah offered the key to a peaceful transition. His role was envisioned to be a temporary one, with no return to the monarchy contemplated. Ideally, the former monarch, acting as the symbol of unity for the nation, would lead the country into a new system, particularly one that tolerated political differences. Najibullah dropped hints that he might be willing to step aside in favor of Zahir Shah. Many suspected Najibullah of using the prospect of the former king's return as a means to split the Afghan mujahidin leadership and to separate it from the rank and file refugees, where Zahir Shah had a strong popular following.

Prior to the Soviet withdrawal, high-level discussions took place between the Pakistani foreign minister and those close to the former king. (Representatives of Zahir Shah had earlier had serious talks with Foreign Office officials in Pakistan—in 1981 and 1983.) Meetings continued into September 1989 between senior Pakistani officials in the

Benazir Bhutto's government and aides to Zahir Shah. While the diplomats were willing to talk to those speaking on behalf of the former king, and by late 1987 were willing to envision a role for him in the future, the military intelligence branch and the Islamic Democratic Alliance (the major opposition party front), were adamantly opposed. Even among officials in the Bhutto government there remained suspicion of the former king, who was felt to have been partial to India while he was in power. Reports of contacts between Zahir Shah and Indian envoys made it more difficult for Pakistan's governments to consider the king seriously in a political solution. For their part, the more hard-line leaders among the Afghan Islamists contended that Zahir Shah had long ago forfeited his right to play any role in Afghanistan's future. To many, including the Afghan Shi'ite parties in Tehran, he had been, if unwittingly, a puppet of the Soviets.

It was a widely held belief that Pakistani and U.S. intelligence held the key to the resistance's intransigence. A threat to withdraw arms and other forms of aid, especially when combined with material incentives, was thought sufficient to force the mujahidin into serious negotiations and major concessions. Whatever their stockpiles of weapons, it was doubtful whether the mujahidin could sustain their military effort from within Pakistan at anywhere near the same level without the approval of the Islamabad government. Yet, notwithstanding that Islamabad had so well managed and manipulated Afghan politics within its borders, it was another matter whether Pakistan had very much influence over the resistance in forcing terms for peace. Anything resembling an imposed settlement would probably not work with the mujahidin, and threats to withhold resources would only stiffen opposition to new policies. Hard-line resistance elements already interpreted doubts about a military victory as proof that the superpowers and others, maybe even some Pakistanis, were conspiring against self-determination for the Afghan nation.

It was a frequent mistake to underestimate the determination of the Afghan resistance leadership. Most party leaders and commanders held a clear vision of their country's future—be it an Islamic state or the restoration of traditional authority—on which they were loathe to compromise. They dismissed the idea of neutrality as alien to their nation's ethos.[22] The resistance leaders were fond of pointing out that at the war's beginning they managed to carry the fight without the West and with minimal help from Islamic countries, and that they could, if forced, carry on alone in the future. Additionally, the leverage of Pakistan's ISI over the Peshawar parties did not extend appreciably to commanders inside Afghanistan, should they independently decide to continue with plans to fight. Not unimportantly, the composition of a post-communist regime would also have to be acceptable to the Saudis and Iranians who, like Pakistan's military, remained determined that their favorite resistance factions prevail.

International Pressures

Through their material and political aid, overt and covert, various countries, and the international community in general, had always been in a position to exert some influence over the course of negotiations. The leverage that existed on Pakistan was most apparent, but the Afghan resistance was hardly immune. While the donors denied trying to dictate to the Afghans, military and humanitarian aid to the mujahidin, as well as the promise of programs for the reconstruction of the country, provided incentives capable of influencing the timing and shape of a settlement. Particular parties and mujahidin groups had their foreign benefactors, governmental or private, whose preferences could not be ignored. There was also a very real threat that intransigence and infighting among the resistance elements could prompt their international supporters to walk away from involvement in the ongoing conflict as well as from the subsequent rehabilitation of Afghanistan. Officials in Islamabad constantly worried about the possibility that Pakistan might be deserted by allies tired of backing the Afghan resistance.

At the same time, an international convergence of views on the need for an early political settlement served the interests of those in the Pakistani leadership wishing to revise policies. The Islamabad government found it easier to accept compromises—criticized by domestic groups and resistance parties—by blaming irresistible international pressures. Accusations by mujahidin leaders of foreign collusion with the Kabul government and Moscow reflected their concern that an international consensus could accelerate if not force a political settlement opposed by them.

Throughout most of the war, the national interests of Pakistan, the goals of most of Pakistan's allies, and the aims of the resistance were essentially compatible, at times identical. Only with the changes in the wider international environment did the strategic equation alter and the underlying strains among former partners in the anti-communist, anti-Soviet struggle become manifest. The decision in Moscow to withdraw from the Afghan battlefield was no doubt the most important of these changes, widely altering priorities and leading to a reassessment of threats by resistance supporters. On a wider scale, the end of superpower military confrontation and, specifically, the intent of both the United

States and Soviet Union to disengage from regional conflicts had a major, if somewhat delayed, impact on the Afghan conflict and efforts to bring it to a conclusion. In a post-cold-war era, neither the Afghan resistance nor the Pakistan government could take for granted continued military and economic assistance or assume that others would accept their visions of a future Afghanistan.

The Persian Gulf war and responses to it within Pakistan and among the mujahidin leadership cast further doubt on the continuity of policies, including those of Saudi Arabia and Iran. The failed August 1991 putsch in Moscow left Soviet policies even more uncertain. What remaining interest the Soviet Union (later the individual republics) had in the war was their mutual concern that Afghanistan not become the bastion of a fundamentalist regime, conceivably linking up with similarly ideological regimes in Iran and possibly Pakistan.

The divergence of Washington and Islamabad over Afghan policy is most clearly marked as beginning with the Soviet military withdrawal in February 1989. The subsequent Jalalabad debacle underscored the need for a new approach. To be sure, in the immediate aftermath of Jalalabad, Washington continued to support the view that the mujahidin had to be strengthened through continued arms supplies before any serious renewal of negotiations. U.S. officials, observing the Soviet buildup of weapons for the Kabul regime, saw no reason to cut off arms supplies any time soon. But even many long-time supporters of the Afghan cause in Washington had become convinced that a military solution any time soon was out of the resistance's grasp and that a political compromise with Kabul was unavoidable. With the abortive March 1990 coup in Kabul, Washington became increasingly committed to an approach to negotiations that bypassed the Peshawar-based parties altogether. The United States sought an early conclusion to the conflict, preferring that moderate elements prevail if possible but prepared to accept almost any kind of leadership in Kabul. The official position in Pakistan remained insistent, however, on an Afghan solution that gave strong promise of close and amicable ties with future governments in Kabul.

Domestic critics of Islamabad policies had long claimed that Pakistan had no Afghan policy independent of U.S. interests and objectives. These elements had always believed that their country was fighting an American war and argued that a settlement was blocked or at least slowed by Pakistan's dependence on the United States as well as Zia ul-Haq's reliance on the conflict in order to remain in power. In fact, as described in Chapter 3, Washington had largely deferred to Pakistan on the pivotal decisions involving who should receive military assistance and how it should be used. Pakistan also shaped the diplomatic agenda, such as it was. Even with the more active, post-Geneva role of United

States in efforts to find a solution, Washington was ready to follow gladly any flexibility on Pakistan's part on negotiations. Much of the U.S. diplomatic initiative was as a result of still largely reactive—at least until mid-1991—Pakistan government policies.

While the Soviets held sway in Afghanistan, leftist elements in Pakistan had renewed the contention that a peace settlement could be accelerated with a full Pakistani-Soviet rapprochement. The idea was to plan for a new bilateralism in the establishment of relations with the Soviet Union that better reflected Pakistan's unfavorable geopolitical circumstances and its economic interests. It was not clear how much incentive the Soviets would have felt in risking their relations with India if that were the price of a more cooperative Pakistan. For, in economic terms, Pakistan could never compete with India in its value to Moscow as a trading partner.

The idea of playing a Soviet card was revived after the cutoff in U.S. economic assistance in late 1990. Not only was this thinking short-lived as the Soviet empire crumbled, in the post-cold war circumstances the threat of warming relations with Moscow could not be a very useful lever to pry loose American aid. At best, through 1991, Islamabad could do little more than remain hopeful that with better relations with the Soviets, Moscow would halt arms shipments to the Kabul regime and, in its new demands for hard currency payments for food and other supplies, further weaken the Najibullah rule.

Diminishing concerns in Beijing about Soviet military intentions meant that China, long Pakistan's most reliable ally, had less reason to lend material and political backing to the mujahidin. Yet close political ties with China, even though only marginally useful in times of real crisis, were certain to continue give both countries lasting suspicions of India. And with a cooling of relations between Islamabad and Washington, relations with the Chinese took on added meaning. It was of some importance, then, that by mid-1991, the Chinese had gone over to a policy of encouraging Pakistan to seek a political solution of the Afghan problem.

The Islamic government in Tehran consistently proclaimed that it supported the legitimate demands of the Muslim people of Afghanistan, including the establishment of a nonaligned Islamic government. With its large Afghan refugee population, Iran could hardly ignore the war on its eastern border, despite its preoccupation with its difficult fight with Iraq on the west. Iran rejected repeated Soviet suggestions that an accommodating attitude toward Moscow on the Afghan issue could earn Iran greater assistance against its Arab enemy. Iran had also declined to become directly involved in the negotiations in Geneva. Although leaders of the Islamic Republic refrained from criticizing Pakistan's role, they were none too pleased with Islamabad's sponsored Afghan Interim Government, especially after the failure to accommodate Shi'ite resistance parties within this Sunni-dominated Peshawar-based alliance. Tehran also had its doubts about Pakistan's dependence on both the United States and Saudi Arabia. In turn, the Islamabad government was dismayed by Iran's support for a proposal calling for a regional conference on Afghanistan that notably omitted the Saudis and Americans, and by Iran's improving political relations and trade with the Soviet Union. Pakistani officials had been particularly suspicious about an August 1989 meeting in Tehran between the Indian foreign secretary and Shi'ite Afghan mujahidin leaders.[23]

The Islamic Republic kept close tabs on their client Afghan Shi'ite groups based in Tehran and, in 1990, encouraged eight of the factions to form a single Islamic Unity (Wahdat-i-Islami) party. In an effort to expand its influence beyond the Shi'ite minority among the Afghans, Iran's leaders also kept up a dialogue with several moderate Afghan parties as well as Burhanuddin Rabbani's (non-Pashtun-dominated) Jamiat-i-Islami. In Tehran's desire, at the same time, first to normalize relations with the Soviet Union, and then to follow the international community, Iranian leaders gave reason to believe that they favored political means over a military solution. Although Tehran had only reluctantly gone along with the Geneva accords, in mid-1989, Iran let it be known that it preferred an intra-Afghan dialogue to decide the modalities of an international peace conference.

The increased flexibility of the Tehran government was notable in the position it took late in 1990, dropping an earlier insistence that the Kabul government step aside and a transitional government be in place for the holding of elections. The Islamic Republic's leaders at one point seemed to be arguing that communists could remain in power during elections with control of security forces still in the hands of Najibullah, a position they urged on the mujahidin.[24] Tangible signs of improving relations between Iran and the Kabul regime were evident in food aid for floods in Afghanistan and landing facilities for the Afghan national airline in Iran. Cultural relations with Afghanistan were also further developed. Inside Iran, the Rafsanjani government stepped up threats during 1991 to expel Afghan refugees and had attempted to levy income taxes on Afghan labor. Sectarian differences aside, Tehran's policies alienated several of the more radical Afghan resistance parties, most notably Hezb-i-Islami, which accused the Iranian authorities of terrorism and interfering in Afghan affairs.[25]

Tehran had reservations about a Pakistan-supported mechanism for an intra-Afghan dialogue and, for some time, opposed a convening of a Loya Jirga, the traditional means of installing a new government—since this promised to favor the Sunni Pashtuns. But differences never overcame the need for Pakistan and Iran to maintain close cooperation based on common goals regarding the importance of an Afghan settlement for regional security.[26] The two countries continued to work together (with Turkey) in the region's Economic Cooperation Organization, and neither, as a matter of national policy, sought to take advantage of the other's internal weaknesses to destabilize it. Like Pakistan, Iran came to desire a regime in Kabul sufficiently stable to cooperate economically and able to withstand extra-regional political and economic dependencies. Eventually the patience of both would wear thin, and government leaders in Tehran, along with those in Islamabad, would focus on the Afghan fighting as an obstacle to economic and cultural openings with Central Asia's former Soviet Muslim republics. Above all, Tehran had demonstrated that it expected to be a player in negotiations to resolve the Afghan conflict and settle on an Islamic government.[27]

Close relations with Saudi Arabia had for many years acted as a constraint on those Pakistani policy makers willing to press the mujahidin toward a diplomatic settlement. The Saudis firmly supported a decisive military victory, and particularly the ascendance of Wahabi-Sunni groups. The financial assistance, direct and indirect, that was provided by the Saudis during the Zia years and that continued under Benazir Bhutto gained them a sympathetic hearing in Islamabad. During Ms. Bhutto's tenure in office, there was, moreover, always the fear that, if offended, the Saudi leadership would side with the domestic religious opposition who were forever on the verge of seeking a ruling that a woman could not head an Islamic government. The Gulf crisis and war offered the clearest sign that a government in Islamabad was obliged to remain sensitive to the Saudi royal family. Notwithstanding highly vocal domestic critics, the Islamabad government sent 11,000 volunteers to Saudi Arabia for the declared purpose of defending Islamic holy places— not to liberate Kuwait.

Yet the war also prompted considerable revision by the Saudi regime in its attitudes toward the Afghan resistance and the diplomatic process. Three mujahidin factions, including two that had received generous assistance from Saudi Arabia, had sided with Iraq in the crisis. In the war's aftermath, not surprisingly, then, Saudi Arabia withdrew some of its financial backing for these Peshawar-based parties. Even so, Saudi shipments of Soviet-built Iraqi arms, including tanks and other heavy equipment captured in the Persian Gulf war, reached mujahidin forces in the late spring and summer 1991. With the ISI handling the distribution and private Arab funding available, the supposedly punished Hekmatyar and Sayyaf groups continued as recipients.[28] Privately donated, large sums of money also continued to flow to mujahidin for the financing of thousands of Muslim volunteers, mostly Arabs, training and fighting alongside the resistance parties.

While continuing to insist that the Afghan people be allowed to make their own decisions, most concerned states were ready to conclude that the resistance elements, left to their own devices, were incapable of agreeing on a peaceful solution. To have a political settlement, however, the international community would, first, have to reach a consensus among themselves. This was largely accomplished within the broad framework of a U.N. plan offered in May 1991 by Secretary General Javier Perez de Cuellar. Second, the involved states had to be prepared to use both the carrot and stick: promises of postwar assistance and also threats to withdraw all material, especially military support. As in the political settlements in Angola and Nicaragua, progress, above all, required the coordinated efforts of peacemakers in Moscow and Washington, specifically their willingness to halt all military supplies to the combatants.

The participation of the Saudis and Iranians was especially critical. They could each now be counted on to throw their considerable weight beyond a political settlement. With the strained relations between Iranians and Saudis somewhat eased, Saudi Arabia, after prodding from Washington, joined the call in late 1991 for a peaceful solution through the United Nations. In cooperation with Islamabad, the Saudis pressed the mujahidin to halt their bickering. Renewed diplomatic relations with the Soviet Union (later Russia) also created an improved international climate, which prompted Saudi support for direct talks between the mujahidin and Moscow.[29] Importantly, the willingness of Saudi Arabia and Iran to seek an accommodation made it politically safer for Pakistan to pursue the same policy.

New Priorities

Even among political figures who had criticized Zia's Afghan policies, most were forced to concede that Pakistan's steadfast policy of aiding the resistance elements had succeeded. No doubt, had Zia's death preceded Moscow's decision to withdraw, his successors might have succumbed to the Soviet campaign of destabilization and intimidation against Pakistan, and reached an agreement in Geneva partial to the communists in Kabul. Those counseling no weakening in support for the mujahidin argued that to desert the Afghan resistance now was not only morally wrong but might delay, perhaps preclude, the refugees' early return.

Mohammed Nawaz Sharif, who assumed the post of prime minister in October 1990, had in opposition voiced these convictions. Yet it soon became apparent that his government was determined to give the Afghan issue new direction. The Islamabad government's energized diplomatic activities in pursuit of a political settlement occurred, ironically, as already noted, in the wake of the mujahidin's success at Khost. Pakistani policy did not turn its back entirely on the military approach; the supply channels to the resistance forces were kept open. The Islamabad government had, however, breathed new life into the venerable two-track strategy by trying to fashion a solution and finding cover from expected critics in an international consensus. Contacts aimed toward a peaceful resolution of the conflict were stepped up with Iran, Saudi Arabia, the Soviet Union, and the United States, as well as in the United Nations.

Those officials in Islamabad who had argued for the need to bypass the Peshawar-based Afghan parties were now given a better hearing. Under the circumstances, Pakistan's leaders came increasingly to recognize that they could not be supportive of the ISI's creature, the AIG, and also be in favor of a solution deriving from a broadly based government that included the field commanders inside Afghanistan and Iran-based Afghan parties, much less former Afghan communists. Some in Islamabad were privately ready for direct, face-to-face talks between high ranking Pakistani and Kabul government officials—against the wishes of the AIG leadership. Informal, secret contacts were in fact undertaken in mid-April 1991 in Geneva between the then ISI head, General Asad Durrani, and a close advisor to Najibullah, Afghan General Tukhi.[30] By some accounts, Durrani also met with General Ghulam Yaqubi, head of the renamed Afghan intelligence service, WAD.[31]

Clearly, there remained some in positions of authority in Islamabad holding out for installing an Islamist-dominated government and resisting any effort to throw Pakistan's weight behind a negotiated agreement. In this camp was most notably Ejaz ul-Haq, son of the late president and a member of the Sharif cabinet, and Qasi Hussain Ahmed, whose Jama'at-i-Islami was a constituent of the government coalition. Most of these elements remained committed to the Hezb-i-Islami as future partners, even if not necessarily the preeminent force in Kabul. The inclusion of a high-level representative and son-in-law of Hekmatyar in the April 1991 Geneva meeting seemed to confirm this fact.[32] About the same time, Hekmatyar's ally of convenience, former Afghan general Tanai, was believed to have traveled to Moscow, also for the purpose of exploring the chances of a deal involving Hezb-i-Islami that would bring a new regime to Kabul; Moscow's probable motive was to assure itself of some influence with more radical elements in the event of Najibullah's fall.

Meanwhile, renewed contacts between the officials of Pakistan's foreign ministry and representatives of the former king Zahir Shah took place in June 1991, probably without the full endorsement of the ISI.[33] Importantly, these representatives were welcomed publicly in the country and allowed to make their case in meetings with Nawaz Sharif and Afghan resistance leaders.[34] This was followed up with a meeting in Rome between new Army chief Lieutenant General Asif Nawaz and the former king's son-in-law, Abdul Wali, in early January 1992. For the first time, a Pakistan government was prepared to seriously consider the former monarch's active participation in a political settlement, though only in a transitional government. It seemed also to presage a willingness in Islamabad to include a fuller spectrum of Afghans acceptable for the task of shaping the country's future, including personalities and parties with some considerable following among those in exile.

There was good reason for the shift in thinking in Islamabad. In terms of Prime Minister Sharif's domestic aims, Afghanistan had clearly become an obstacle. On balance, whatever its earlier value, continuation of the war did not seem in Pakistan's interests. A decision had been reached in a January 25 meeting of the government's Afghan policy cell composed of the country's top military and civilian leaders that a political settlement now be pursued seriously and that lines of communications with the Soviets be opened.[35] Opinion in Pakistan appeared to be coming closer to the view of one of the war's long-time critics that the country's "national interests were rendered hostage to the needs and interests of particular mujahidin leaders or groups."[36] Resentment in Pakistan also grew in the belief that the government was prolonging the war and that time was ripe for a political solution. Although every effort needed to be made to avoid forcing distasteful terms on the resistance, the popular sense in Pakistan seemed to be that the country would have to stake out a policy freer of the mujahidin.

More than ever, with international assistance dwindling, conditions for the early, safe return of the refugees were imperative. Sharif's desire for sweeping economic and social changes in Pakistan was believed held back while the country continued its involvement in the Afghan war. Pakistan would continue to see a drain on its resources as a result of the conflict, with the probability that the demands on its treasury would increase with the decline in international support. The domestic violence, notably in the Sindh, showed signs of foreign involvement, allegedly Indian but possibly with an Afghan connection. Sought-after investment from abroad was considered unlikely until a more peaceful Pakistan was realized. Without Afghanistan, popular and elite pressures for an accelerated nuclear program could diminish. As a result, new U.S. and Western aid might be facilitated.

Defections from Sharif's ruling coalition and the rapidly deteriorating law-and-order situation across the country beginning in mid-summer 1991 weakened the prime minister's government. Even so, the prime minister was in a far stronger position to stand up to Pakistan's military than his predecessor, Benazir Bhutto, had been. The possibility increased that Afghan policy might be taken from the generals and specifically out from under the direction of the military intelligence. The reduced role of the military as the conduit for arms to the resistance from the United States and other foreign suppliers no doubt promoted a greater willingness to allow the civilians to take political command on the Afghan issue.

In any case, the civilian leadership had assumed the forefront in a streamlined Afghan policy.[37] The willingness of President Ghulam Ishaq Khan, by the end of 1991, to press the mujahidin leaders on the need to seize the opportunity for a political settlement was especially significant in view of his influence with a military that had so recently opted for jihad against Kabul and had helped to undermine domestic, secular forces in Pakistan. Yet not until the retirement of the outspoken General Aslam Beg could Prime Minister Sharif feel reasonably secure in his authority. During the Gulf war, Beg had led political attacks that castigated the Nawaz Sharif government for its "anti-Muslim" stance.[38] To some extent, Beg's line of policy had been discredited by Iraq's defeat. Still, rumors of a Beg-led coup were widespread throughout June and July 1991. When Beg stepped down on schedule as armed forces' Chief of Staff, replaced by Asif Nawaz, a man with none of his predecessor's ties to Islamic groups and no obvious political ambitions, it was thought to augur well for civilian rule.[39] The military stood far closer to a consensus with the elected government than it had for some time.

The appointment of General Nawaz appeared to mark the assertion of influence by a more liberal, modernist generation of officers, in effect, a transition within the military away from the conservative generals who Zia had brought along. This coincided with Nawaz Sharif's ascendance to power and the urban, more progressive middle class that he represented. Both contributed to the policy shift that preferred a peaceful solution to the Afghan conflict, and entailed some break with the Islamist mujahidin.[40]

Under Asif Nawaz, a series of power plays leading to personnel changes in the command structure gave indication of a military more reconciled toward ending the conflict in Afghanistan quickly. The modification in thinking appeared to go beyond mere strategic calculation. Key figures in the army were now ready to see a reduction in the influence of Pakistan's Islamist parties and their militant, radical agenda. A telltale sign of change was the demotion and premature retirement from the Pakistan army of Lt. General Hamid Gul, former head of the ISI and a continuing voice in opposing a shift of policy on Afghanistan. ISI chief and Beg loyalist, General Durrani, was also replaced, although the change in Afghan policy was affected before his departure in March 1992.

The Afghan issue continued to carry domestic partisan ramifications in Pakistan. Were the conflict put behind Pakistan's government, Nawaz Sharif could envision feeling less beholden to the religious parties in his governing alliance. At the same time, alliance building may have increased the voice of a partner in the ruling alliance, the National Awami Party, in its pleading for more flexibility in dealing with the Kabul regime. With Ms. Bhutto and her party out of office, the ousted former prime minister had resumed her criticism of Pakistan's policy. As mentioned, while Benazir Bhutto held office, the politics of maneuvering to stay in power had taken precedence over the Afghanistan issue despite her believed interest in a negotiated solution. The People's Alliance, as the Bhutto-led opposition was now called, revived its contention that a military solution was unlikely and that Pakistan should establish cordial relations with whatever regime came to power in Afghanistan through fair and free elections. Ms. Bhutto restated her view that conditions must be created to allow for the early return of the refugees and that Islamabad should extend support to Afghanistan for reconstruction.

If the Afghan war was proving politically troublesome and economically detrimental for Pakistan, a conflict without some closure also seemed to militate against the country's larger security requirements. The realities of the post-cold war were appreciated anew as Pakistan was once again left largely alone to confront its regional problems following the fall 1990 suspension of U.S. economic and military aid as a result of the country's nuclear program. Plainly, if it were necessary to choose, the country's limited resources would be used to defend against India. Meanwhile, unless the war could be concluded soon, the chances of Indian economic and political involvement filling the vacuum left by Soviet disengagement from Afghanistan had increased.

The possibility of Pakistan's taking on fuller responsibility for the Afghan war was becoming clear with the crumbling support for the Afghan cause in Washington. The U.S. Congress had trimmed $50 million out of $300 million in annual military aid to the resistance in the 1990. A complete arms cut-off of U.S. weapons to the mujahidin was a growing possibility. In fact, some resistance groups inside Afghanistan had not seen U.S.-supplied arms for many months.

A new, more vigorous effort to find a diplomatic solution became imperative if Pakistan hoped to avoid having to simultaneously sustain both continuing conflict on the Afghan frontier and heightened danger of armed confrontation with India with the revival of the Kashmir issue. By the end of 1991, Pakistan was nurturing talks under way between mujahidin leaders and representatives of the soon-to-collapse Soviet state that were aimed at forming an interim Afghan government. The mujahidin had been convinced to drop their formal demands for war reparations as a precondition after assurances from Pakistani officials that they could expect money for reconstruction from Moscow. Military operations against Kabul, though still supported in Islamabad, were intended primarily to win better terms for the resistance at the negotiating table.

Political Compromise and Military Collapse

A critical juncture in the Afghan war was reached in March 1992. Either the conflict might rapidly become de-internationalized but likely to settle into a protracted civil war, or the framework for realizing a political compromise had been found. The strategic options for Pakistan had greatly altered. With the patronage of superpowers formally ended, the attention of Pakistani officials focused even more sharply on concluding the war. International and regional events appeared to be conspiring to force as well as entice the Afghans toward a compromise solution. If the endgame was finally in sight, the untiring mediation by U.N. representatives was given most of the credit. Fresh from its brokering and monitoring of peace in several former regional conflicts and carrying some momentum from its association with the successful Gulf war, the world organization seemed well positioned to break the impasse. The necessary decisions from the more recalcitrant mujahidin seemed unlikely without Pakistan's participation in the U.N. initiative and its determination to close off other options for the resistance. As it happened, the United Nation's timetable and design for a compromise settlement were overtaken by events in mid-April.

Until then, the Sharif cabinet had looked particularly to the U.N. Secretary General to play an active role in facilitating a peaceful solution. The May 1991 U.N. initiative, no doubt encouraged by the shifting attitudes in Islamabad, was designed to bring a settlement through an Afghan dialogue. The five-point plan—more a collection of principles than a detailed plan or specific mechanisms for a settlement—envisaged a halt to the supply of weapons to both sides and elections to establish a broad-based government in Kabul. Through Perez de Cuellar's personal envoy, Benon Savon, the United Nations pressed the search for a group of more independent Afghan personalities to assume interim government roles. Savon's consultations involved Saudi Arabia, Iran, the United States, and the Soviet Union, as well as Pakistan.

A notable effort to win backing for the U.N. initiative was a late-July 1991 quadrilateral meeting of officials from Iran and Pakistan together with leaders of the mujahidin from Peshawar and Tehran. The purpose of the conclave, as conceived by Pakistani officials, was to find positive elements in the May plan. In the end, the conference held in Islamabad offered little more than an opportunity for the dissidents to air their feelings. Only the more pro-Western Sunni mujahidin organizations, those led by Ahmed Galani, Sibghatullah Mojadeddi, and Mawlawi Muhammadi, were in large measure in agreement with the U.N. plan. A follow-up meeting took place in late August in Tehran with, importantly, the ISI formally part of the Pakistan team.[41] A surprising degree of accommodation and understanding marked relations between the Tehran-supported and Peshawar-based groups. On this occasion, however, three of the mujahidin's Sunni parties refused to send representatives.

The major sticking point in any early progress in negotiations was the continued insistence among the more radical Islamists that all members of the communist hierarchy be excluded from participation in a coalition government or have a political future in Afghanistan. They were particularly insistent that Najibullah himself not participate. In calling for an intra-Afghan dialogue, the U.N. plan appeared to leave a role for Najibullah's Watan (Nationhood) party, renamed from the People's Democratic Party of Afghanistan (PDPA), and perhaps Najibullah himself. Rather than debate the merits of the U.N. plan or its possible modification, the more radical Islamists indicated a fresh resolve to force a military solution and interpreted the talk of a political solution as deliberately intended to divert their attention from the jihad.[42]

As the AIG's Prime Minister, Islamist leader Rasul Sayyaf publicly rejected any political solution that would include negotiations with the communists and vowed to fight on in the jihad until final victory of the mujahidin and a true Islamic government in Afghanistan. Any dialogue was considered traitorous, and the U.N. representative was labeled a "devoted servant of Zionists and international colonialism."[43] Hekmatyar threatened any mujahidin leaders who might agree to cooperate in trying to forge an interim regime. Retired ISI chief Hamid Gul expressed the belief that a conspiracy was underway in the U.N.

effort designed to pit Pakistan against Afghan mujahidin, leading to Islamabad's being compelled to disarm the resistance.[44]

In April 1991, Nawaz Sharif had reopened dialogue with the Soviet government. A high-level Soviet delegation that was supposed to visit Islamabad in May 1991 canceled its trip. Even so, Pakistan's Secretary General for Foreign Affairs, Riaz Muhammad Khan, traveled to Moscow at the end of May in order to keep the exchanges going. On August 11, a Soviet foreign ministry delegation arrived in Islamabad to renew talks, with particular focus on the U.N. Secretary General's plan. Yet negotiations had become more complicated with the apparent increased influence of the military in Moscow in the spring and summer. The Soviet Union appeared less flexible in finding a solution for Afghanistan. Hard-liners were determined not to entirely desert their former allies in arms. The lobby in the Soviet parliament calling for a continuation of "internationalist aid" to Afghanistan appeared strongly entrenched, intent on blocking an agreement on negative symmetry.[45] According to one source, 500 to 600 Soviet military advisers were still assigned to Afghanistan, with an additional 1,500 Soviet civilians.[46] Progress on talks between Soviet and U.S. representatives was clearly stalled, mainly over differences in the powers to be enjoyed by Najibullah during the transition. The Soviets were disturbed by the offense operations during the Khost campaign and by reliable evidence of direct Pakistani involvement in the military operations, despite claims of innocence made to Moscow and others.

The failed Soviet coup of mid-August 1991 removed the remaining obstacles to direct superpower cooperation. With the ascent of the reformers and the rapid decline of military and KGB influence in political circles in the coup's wake, the very elements that saw continued support as a moral obligation to the Soviet soldiers who fought in Afghanistan as well as to a brotherly communist party had been pushed aside. In view of the deteriorating budgetary conditions and transport difficulties inside the Soviet Union, continued economic aid to the Najibullah government was certain to be curtailed. Russian President Boris Yeltsin was on record asking for a reexamination of Soviet military and economic aid to the Kabul regime. It came as little surprise, then, when in September 1991, the Soviet Union and United States announced a mutual, complete halt in arms to the warring sides beginning in January 1992. The joint communiqué also pronounced its support for the United Nations' attempts to mediate a settlement, although without specifying the need for a formal caretaker government in the transitional period. Inadvertently, however, the developments of August and September 1991 worked against a peaceful resolution.

Until this time, a consensus had formed among most policy makers in Pakistan that a mujahidin military victory over Kabul was out of reach. The Islamabad government had worked to put together a caretaker government, composed of figures who would not be candidates for leadership in a future, elected government. However, the failed coup in Moscow and joint U.S.-Soviet declaration on arms, which Pakistani officials welcomed publicly, brought new concerns and opportunities, and reactivated the military track for ending the war. Once again, with the Najibullah regime seemingly having its back to the wall, there was renewed interest in Islamabad as well as among key resistance leaders in pushing a military solution. Although the Kabul government was thought to have up to a two-year supply in weapons and ammunition, continued supply of food and fuel was in doubt, especially with Moscow's newly imposed hard-currency purchase requirements. The ability of the Kabul government to sustain morale in the cities and loyalty among its army officers was also problematic.

On the diplomatic front, the Islamabad government argued for some time for a package settlement along with the negative symmetry, one that would include a cease-fire, an interim government, and arrangements for the return of refugees. For without these provisions, once Washington and Moscow had entirely washed their hands of the conflict, the fighting was believed likely to go on for some time, especially given the ability of the warring sides to finance their operations with drug money. As leverage, the Islamabad government refused for months following the U.S.-Russian declaration to commit Pakistan to following the lead of these countries to halt arms shipments to the combatants. Islamabad's diplomatic efforts to mobilize regional backing for comprehensive settlement was meant to give added content to the U.N.'s five-point plan and go beyond the concept of negative symmetry.

By the end of 1991, renewed military offensives on Jalalabad city and Gardez in Afghanistan had fissiled out, owing largely to differences among the mujahidin field commanders and the superior firepower of the Kabul regime forces. Even more, the mujahidin, despite the continued presence of Pakistani army officers providing logistical and tactical advice, appeared unable to gear up for a sustained fight. The reasserting of the military approach against the Kabul regime, approved in Islamabad, had only delayed, not derailed the political process. Pakistan appeared to run out of options. Although the ISI was from most indications resigned to finding a political way out, the extent of the military intelligence's willingness to fully implement decisions in Islamabad was still to be tested. AIG president and mujahidin moderate Mujaddedi raised claims of continued interference by the Pakistan military, insisting that his efforts in discussing a peaceful solution were marred by Pakistan's military intelligence. Indeed, Mujaddedi claimed that the fighting in Gardez and Jalalabad was started without the knowledge of the AIG.[47] There were other mixed signals. The appointment of a known religious ideologue (affiliated, however, with a party opposed to Jama'at-i-Islami) as new ISI chief, General Javed Nasir, was seen by some as a setback but by others as signifying a "balancing act," intended to coopt the intelligence community, thereby assuring greater stability to the civilian government.[48]

Events moved quickly. The Sunni-monopolized alliance, the AIG, in effect dissolved at the end of 1991. The most auspicious of the changes was the beginning of a dialogue with the Soviets, later the Russians, in Moscow and subsequently in Pakistan. Prodded by Pakistan to open talks, only the most radical Islamist groups boycotted the mid-November Moscow meeting. The endorsement by both Iran and Saudi Arabia of the mujahidin-Soviet meetings was apparent with the participation of the Tehran-based Shi'ite resistance parties and the stopover of the Peshawar delegation in Saudi Arabia before proceeding to Moscow. From these direct negotiations the leaders of the-then-disintegrating Soviet state had indicated their acceptance of the proposition that the interim government should be an essentially Islamic one.

While trying to remain true to the promise that the Afghan people would be permitted to determine their own future, Pakistan's civilian leadership was finally committed to a process that seemed to leave the mujahidin few good alternatives to a negotiated settlement. During January 1992, Islamabad finally went along with "negative symmetry," declaring its intention to end military support for the mujahidin. The Sharif government pressed openly for acceptance of the U.N. program, warning that peace would not be "held hostage" to the opposition of a few resistance groups and that they would be "left behind" if they posed obstacles.[49] Defying objections from radical Islamist parties and Pakistan's own religious right, the government endorsed the idea of a pre-transition council, which would rule for 45 days and lead to a U.N.-sponsored assembly of 150 representatives from the various Afghan groups to be convened in Europe. A council elected by the assembly was slated to assume authority in advance of national elections.

Just when it appeared that the necessary groundwork for the U.N. plan was in place, the Kabul government's hold on power rapidly dissolved. Najibullah agreed to resign once the interim government was formed. His announcement, however, had the immediate effect of hastening his fall, as it appeared that the president was deserting his followers. Many of his army officers began to negotiate their defection with the resistance.[50] The ISI again became optimistic about a military outcome.

132   *Pakistan and the Negotiations*

Recognizing the dangerous course of events, Najibullah moved to assert his authority over the northern command—located around the largely ethnically Uzbek city of Mazar-i-Sharif—by putting Pashtuns in key posts and particularly in replacing General Mohammad Momin, the leading Tajik officer in the region. This in turn led dissident non-Pashtun army officers headed by General Abdul Rashid Dostam to conclude an alliance with mujahidin groups, notably those under the command of Masoud. The military defections occurred against a background of dwindling supplies of food and fuel in the cities, a crisis sufficiently acute that Pakistan, the United States, and others had begun shipping wheat to Kabul, intended both to stave off hunger and maintain the regime long enough for it to administer an orderly transition of power. When the mujahidin closed in on Kabul and Najibullah was observed trying to flee, government forces across the country gave up the fight.

It was left to the contentious mujahidin to determine how and when peace would finally come to Afghanistan. Once a compromise solution had been superseded, it was clear that moderate elements had lost their chance to find a role for Zahir Shah. If Afghan factions insisted on settling old personal and ethnic scores among themselves and felt the need to take retribution against their ideological enemies, the former communists, there seemed.to be little that outsiders could or would try to do. With former patron-client relationships bound to be weakened if not broken, no one other than the Afghans themselves would decide who would eventually emerge to lead the country.

While in the short term Pakistan still had an indispensable role to play, as the time came for the Islamic forces to take power in Kabul, Islamabad's loosening grip on the Peshawar leaders was evident. The negotiations to put together an interim ruling council and agreement on the transfer of power among mujahidin leaders (reached on April 25, 1992) was once again an ISI production. But Pakistani officials had not been able to foresee and plan for the rapid developments leading to Najibullah's defeat. Nor were they able to fully control their protégés during a series of meetings in Peshawar and Islamabad. For days it appeared that the infighting among parties would preclude any agreement, despite the strong intercession of Prime Minister Sharif and foreign ministry officials. The prime minister was joined in Peshawar by Saudi Prince Turki-al-Faisal, King Fahd's special envoy. At the same time, Mir Hamid Musavi, a former ambassador to Pakistan, was deputed from Tehran to assure that the deal to form a new government incorporated Iranian interests. Unable to move the factions, frustrated Pakistani officials brought the Afghans together with leaders of several of Pakistan's religio-political parties, including Jama'at-i-Islami's Qazi

Hussain Ahmed, who were asked to use their influence with various Afghan groups to reach a consensus—to no avail.[51]

In the end, the Peshawar-based leaders agreed to a formula mainly out of fear that if they delayed any further the field commanders, notably Masoud, would take matters into their own hands and bypass the parties. A majority of party heads settled on a 50-member council—with unspecified responsibilities—made up of 30 field commanders, party and religious leaders, a complicated arrangement transferring executive power, and the promise of national elections. The future of the plainly jerry-built plan designed to get a government settled in Kabul as soon as possible was predictably dim after the decision by Hekmatyar—expected to take the second position in the government as prime minister—to designate in his place a party lieutenant.

When the convoy of autos carried the interim government leaders into Afghanistan, their security was assured by an armed Pakistani escort.[52] Pakistani authorities were also anxious to show their confidence in the new government . On April 29, Sharif flew to Kabul together with his army chief of staff General Nawaz, ISI head General Nasir, and Saudi Prince Turki to demonstrate Pakistan's backing for the interim government headed in the planned first stage by Sibghatullah Mojadeddi. They endeavored, without success, to get hold-out Hekmatyar to accept a cease-fire and in fact join the political arrangement. Implied was the threat that Pakistan would stand with the new moderate government against Hekmatyar should he carry out his threat to attack Kabul. It marked the first official break with Hekmatyar, Islamabad's long-time client, and put the government clearly on the opposite side from its ally Jama'at-i-Islami, still Hekmatyar's prime backer in Pakistan. It also opened up a potential rift with Saudi Arabia. Despite their public support for a compromise among the mujahidin, the Saudis had moved for the time being toward Hekmatyar's camp, at least as far as to assure his participation in a regime intended to balance off what was seen as Iranian influence among ethnic minorities or at least Persian speakers within the new government.[53]

Prime Minster Sharif's government and the dominant group among the country's policy makers—who had always assumed they could count on Hekmatyar for Pakistan's long-time patronage, found they had good reason to be angry with Hekmatyar. In his confrontation with troops loyal to Masoud (a Tajik), and General Dostam (an Uzbek), the Hezb-i-Islami leader had for the first time resorted to an ethnic appeal among the Pashtun-dominated mujahidin parties.[54] Curiously, Pakistan had now come to covet a connection with the Afghan minorities. Islamabad concluded, unrealistically it would eventually prove out, that Masoud and his forces were the key to putting the country together and, importantly, opening up the road routes through the north. In overestimating Masoud's military reach, Pakistan's planners also underestimated the grip of former communist, General Dostam, over the area.

With the installation of an Islamic regime in Kabul, Pakistan's relations with the Afghans entered a very different stage. By its actions, Islamabad had kept faith with the resistance and won the renewed appreciation of most resistance forces. In spite of some erosion, Pakistan had managed to retain the international good will that the country's leaders acquired in their forthright stand over the decade of the 1980s. Attempts to negotiate a conclusion to the conflict had in the end shown that left to their own devices, the Afghans were incapable of reaching a compromise either among themselves or with the Kabul government. While no governing institutions or particular power configuration was likely to be imposed on the Afghans by outsiders, the mujahidin leaders found it necessary to weigh the incentives and disincentives presented them by others. Only when the resistance forces together with the Kabul regime came to believe that Pakistan and the international community, most notably the United States and Russia, were serious in their determination to see an end to the conflict, did the necessary pieces fall into place.

Notes

1. Riaz M. Khan's *Untying the Afghan Knot; Negotiating Soviet Withdrawal* (Durham, N.C. and London, Duke University Press, 1991), p. 99. Riaz Khan offers the most comprehensive and definitive study of the negotiating process leading up to the Geneva accords.

2. *Pakistan Affairs* (Embassy of Pakistan, Washington D.C.), Vol. 40, no. 14 (July 16, 1987): 1.

3. Foreign Broadcast Information Service (FBIS), December 29, 1987, p. 63 from an interview with President Zia on German television.

4. Arnaud de Borchgrave's report of an interview with President Zia, *The Middle East Times*, January 3–9, 1988, p. 23.

5. See Barnett R. Rubin, "An Avenue Out of the Afghan War," *The New York Times*, August 14, 1988, and Edward Girardet, "Kabul-Soviet Offers at UN Talks Could Stymie Afghan Resistance," *Christian Science Monitor*, September 9, 1987.

6. Oliver Roy, "The Lessons of the Soviet-Afghan War," *Adelphi Papers* #259 (Summer 1991), p. 65.

7. *The New York Times*, January 13, 1988, and February 19, 1988.

8. Riaz Khan, *Untying the Afghan Knot*, p. 191.

9. Rasul Bux Rais, *Asian Survey*, Vol. 24, no. 2 (February 1989): 200.

10. Mushahid Hussein, *Nation*, (Lahore) February 18, 1991. See also discussion in A.T. Sheikh, "Afghanistan: An Appraisal of Soviet Withdrawal Strategies," *Pakistan Horizon*, Vol. 42, nos. 3 and 4 (October 1989): 26–27.

11. *Pakistan Affairs*, Vol. 40, no. 14, July 16, 1987, p. 2.

12. Riza Khan, *Untying the Afghan Knot*, p. 269. The author reports that Zia and Junejo telephoned President Reagan and Secretary of State George Shultz to suggest an agreement based on continuing the supply of arms for both sides (p. 274). Robert G. Wirsing offers an extensive discussion of the explanations given for Zia's motivations in *Pakistan's Security Under Zia, 1977-1988* (New York: St. Martin's Press, 1991), pp. 67–71.

13. See discussion by Richard P. Cronin, *Asian Survey*, Vol. 24, no. 2 (February 1989): 208–211. Another of the bilateral agreements between Pakistan and Afghanistan guaranteed the voluntary and orderly return of the Afghan refugees.

14. Mushahid Hussain, "Prospects for a Peaceful Settlement," in Suroosh Irfani and Fazul-ul-Rahman (eds.), *Afghanistan; Looking to the Future* (Islamabad: The Institute of Strategic Studies, 1992), p. 5.

15. BBC Foreign Service in *Afghan Jehad* (Islamabad), Vol. 4, (July–September, 1991): 224.

16. Roy, "The Lessons," p. 25.

17. Barnett R. Rubin, "Political Elites in Afghanistan: Rentier State Building, Rentier State Wrecking," *International Journal of Middle East Studies*, Vol. 24, no. 1 (1992): 95.

18. See Ahmed Rashid, "View From the Bunker," *The Herald* (Lahore), March 1990, p. 18.

19. Interview with Benazir Bhutto, *Pakistan Times* (Islamabad), July 20, 1989.

20. Nasim Zehra, *Nation*, January 28, 1990.

21. Mushahid Hussein, ibid., February 18, 1990.

22. Riaz Khan, *Untying the Afghan Knot*, p. 241.

23. Mushahid Hussain, "Prospects for a Peaceful Settlement," p. 6.

24. Foreign Broadcast Information Service (FBIS), Near East and South Asia, December 7, 1990, p. 43.

25. Ibid., September 11, 1991, p. 39.

26. Nasim Zehra, "A Common Cause for Pakistan and Iran," in the *News* (Islamabad) August 3, 1991.

27. See the discussion in Graham E. Fuller's *The Center of the Universe; The Geopolitics of Iran* (Boulder: Westview Press, 1991), pp. 230–231.

28. *Frontier Post* (Peshawar), September 19, 1991, and *The Economist*, June 15, 1991, p. 33. *Afghan Jehad*, Vol. 4, no. 4 (July–September): 293. With Bush Administration approval, 7,000 tons of captured Iraqi weapons were destined to go to the mujahidin, this despite the mounting disillusionment in Washington with the Afghan resistance. *Los Angeles Times*, May 19, 1991.

29. FBIS, October 29, 1991, p. 58, from Islamabad Radio, October 24, 1991.

30. *Nation*, May 5, 1991, pp. 1 and 12. Reported in FIBIS , May 9, 1991 p. 44.

31. Ahmed Rashid in the *Far Eastern Economic Review*, October, 17, 1991,p. 21.

32. Roy, "The Lessons," p. 42.

33. Afghan Information Centre, *Monthly Bulletin*, nos. 123–124 (June–July 1991): 13.

34. *Kausar-I*, June 12, 1991, in *Afghan Jehad*, Vol. 4, no. 2 (April–June 1991): 173.

35. Khawar Malik, *Frontier Post*, February 7, 1992. The author makes note, however, that the Pakistan President, Ishaq Khan, who ordinarily presided over the cell's meetings, was not present when this basic policy change was debated and agreed on. Whether or not his absence indicated displeasure is debatable; more certain, it represented a retreat on his part. Benazir Bhutto told Malik that the decision was a victory for the PPP and its desire for a political solution.

36. Eqbal Ahmad, "The Spoils of War," *The Herald*, December 1989, p. 93.

37. Salamat Ali, in *Far East Economic Review*, June 27, 1991, p. 18.

38. *The Herald*, February 1991, pp. 22–33.

39. Beg in retirement accepted the view that Pakistan did not have sufficient military resources to help the Afghans reach a military victory over the Kabul government. BBC Foreign Service, September 28, 1991, in *Afghan Jehad*, Vol. 4, no. 4 (July–September): 319.

40. *Christian Science Monitor*, February 4, 1992.

41. FBIS, August 27 1991, p. 34, from *Muslim*, August 27, 1991.

42. FBIS, July 25, 1991, p. 41.

43. *Pakistan Times*, April 4, 1991; FBIS, July 5, 1991, p. 36.

44. *Afghan Jehad*, Vol. 5, no. 2 (January–March, 1992): 240, from an interview with General Gul by the editor of *Jang*, a Pakistani daily, March 31, 1992.

45. Rusian Budrin, "The Endless War," in *Far Eastern Economic Review*, August 1, 1991, p. 21.

46. *Jane's Intelligence Review*, June 1991, p. 245, from comments by U.S. Senator Gordon Humphrey, March 12, 1990.

47. *Afghan Jehad*, Vol. 5, no. 1 (October–December 1991): 133, 158.

48. Najam Sethi, *The Friday Times* (Lahore), March 12–18, 1992, p. 3.

49. *Frontier Post*, February 7, 1992; *The New York Times*, February 18, 1992.

50. Anwar ul-Haq Ahady, *Christian Science Monitor*, April 30, 1992.

51. Zaffar Abbas, *The Herald*, May 1992, pp. 34–37; FBIS-NES, May 27, 1992, p. 70, from Radio Islamabad, May 25, 1992.

52. *The New York Times*, April 30, 1992.

53. Abbas, *The Herald*, pp. 36c and 36d. The strong competition between the Saudis and Iranians was plainly evident when, at the end of May, a high-ranking Iranian delegation was in Kabul to talk with the interim government president and others, having brought with them planeloads of relief supplies. Meanwhile, two Saudi officials based in Pakistan, one the head of an institute for orphans, the other an Islamic leader, were also in the capital for talks. FBIS-NES, May 20, 1992, from AFP in Hong Kong, May 19, 1992.

54. To show displeasure with official Pakistani government policy, Hekmatyar's forces stalled the movement outside of Kabul in May 1992 of 170 trucks carrying food from Pakistan. Rogue elements within the ISI were at the same time still working to instill Hekmatyar as head of the transitional arrangement. *The New York Times*, April 29, 1992. Evidence could be found in the

fact that Hekmatyar had massed forces, including tanks, on the Pakistani side of the border prior to moving them into Afghanistan following Najibullah's fall. Pakistani authorities on the scene had made no visible effort to impede this massing of forces, which was expected to be used against the very interim government that officially the Islamabad was busily erecting.

7

Resettlement and Rehabilitation

It is almost a truism to say that the destinies of Pakistan and Afghanistan are bound together. The war that brought many Afghans and Pakistanis closer, more aware of one another, pointed up the reality of interdependence. Political instability and economic stagnation in either Pakistan or Afghanistan are bound to have a profound effect on the other country. A Pakistan that is politically troubled and economically prostrate will retard the recovery of Afghanistan, and a delayed economic revival resulting from civil strife in Afghanistan can undermine Pakistan's economic growth and political security. Pakistan's policy makers have particular reason to be concerned about whether the future rulers of Afghanistan are cooperative or antagonistic and how the power struggle in Afghanistan and delayed rehabilitation and reconstruction will affect the return of refugees. Pakistan's leaders are faced, most of all, with putting their relationship with Afghanistan on a secure and cooperative basis, realizing that the relationship turns on events in Afghanistan mostly beyond their control.

With the collapse of the Kabul government, Pakistan had appeared to be uniquely positioned to facilitate some degree of unity and concerted action by the mujahidin leadership during a period of transition. It was quickly to discover the limits of its influence once the party leaders had returned to Afghanistan. Policies seen in Pakistan's interests that may have had some rationality over the years of fighting came back to haunt the country at the end when its goals required compromises among the resistance elements. Zia's legacy of dividing the Afghans, with the picking of clear favorites, and specifically the building up of Hezb-i-Islami, would be an obstacle when it came to trying to forge unity for a negotiated peace that would lead the Afghans toward a workable, broad-based government in Kabul.

Pakistani authorities had long felt uncertain over the kind of state they preferred to see emerge in Afghanistan. Many of the country's leaders harbor a deep-seated suspicion of Afghan intentions in the postwar period. Above all has been the hope that any successor regimes in Kabul not be unfriendly ones. Officials in Islamabad have repeatedly commented that they did not take the risks associated with the war only to have an Afghanistan emerge much like the one that preceded the long conflict. Pakistani officials are anxious to avoid a revival of the controversies and disputes that marked so much of the pre-1978 period. But in a postwar Afghanistan the degree of centralized authority and independent policies compatible with Pakistan's interests has been subject to debate.

Some in Pakistan have argued that instability and a feudal, decentralized Afghan state could serve Islamabad's purposes by preventing a strong, autonomous, and potentially antagonistic regime from emerging. Until the collapse of the Soviet state, it was not of too great consequence, then, if the Afghan war dragged on, except that it would probably delay the return of the refugees. Ideally, Pakistan would have preferred a government of its own choosing in Kabul. But if this proved impossible, the weakness of an Afghan state at least guaranteed that such an entity would be unlikely to pose the threat of renewed Afghan irredentism. In its preoccupation with internal problems and dependence on Pakistan, a weak state was also thought to be in no position as well to reinvite Soviet influence or rehabilitate its relations with India.

As previously described, over the years the policies of Pakistan's military intelligence, whose operatives rather cynically manipulated the resistance groups based inside Pakistan, seemed designed to keep mujahidin leaders and parties at times divided, at least dependent. Moreover, a disunified mujahidin assured that Pakistan would lead the diplomatic effort to reach and define a settlement. Military and political assistance went disproportionately to hard-line Islamic parties with the aim of eventually installing authority in Kabul that felt sympathetic or beholden to Pakistan for its war-time support, even at the almost certain cost of continued factional fighting among the Afghans.

The largely successful submersion of older tribal and local loyalties in the shared life of the camps seemed for some time to present a challenge to host Pakistan. The idea of a largely cohesive and well-armed Afghan refugee community had worried Pakistan's policy makers. In theory at least, the same weakened primordial loyalties could be expected to make Afghans more amenable to national integration and stronger government in Kabul once most refugees had returned to a country at peace. The customary concessions to tribalism and regional authority would presumably be less necessary. Yet it was to become quickly evident that the basis of a new national consensus had not been created. The glue that had held the Afghan community together in exile was not easily transferable, as might have been predicted by the decentralized military leadership in Afghanistan during the conflict. Also, traditional local leadership would in many places be revived. What had more certainly been destroyed was the traditional central authority that had involved for many "a magical charm" associated with the royal family.[1]

As the struggle against the Najibullah regime approached an end, the possibility that Afghanistan might carry on a protracted civil war became an increasingly unattractive prospect to Pakistan. Should the victorious resistance leaders fail to put together a broad-based Islamic government, the resulting ethnic fractionalization of Afghanistan could potentially threaten Pakistan's territorial integrity. As discussed below, a de facto Pashtunistan in Afghanistan might well emerge in the event of the country's political disintegration. If so, it could be expected to intensify and spread ethnic nationalism, and sooner or later covet the inclusion of the Pashtuns of Pakistan's northwest. The security risks for Pakistan could also come with a political vacuum in an embattled Afghanistan, increasing the possibility of wider outside intervention. In particular, along with continued manipulation by Iran, Saudi Arabia, and Pakistan, after some time Afghanistan might become vulnerable to renewed Indian influences.

A postwar Afghanistan ruled by regional commanders acting as local warlords could have other serious drawbacks. In the absence of a strong state, there would be no authority to disarm local militias and keep them from carrying out revenge killings. Few questioned the possibility of a Lebanon-like outcome to the war, an ensuing civil war among the militias of Afghanistan. Policy makers in Islamabad reasoned that in a badly fragmented, embattled Afghan countryside, Pakistan could be tempted to take sides and would likely experience a new influx of refugees. Without a full peace, the task of resettlement and rehabilitation could be expected to be delayed if not derailed, and chances for a quick return of the refugees and a reduced drain on Pakistan's resources sharply diminished.

Very plainly, a fractious Afghanistan would block Pakistan's ambitions in Central Asia. Afghanistan is critical to plans for Pakistan to furnish an economic corridor and cultural bridge to the newly independent Muslim republics of the defunct Soviet state. A stable, peaceful, and largely moderate Afghanistan seems imperative if Pakistan hopes to compete with Iran, Turkey, China, and India for the markets and loyalties of the peoples of Muslim Central Asia. A radical regime in

Kabul, liable to export revolutionary Islam, would be an impediment to close ties to the area by both Afghanistan and Pakistan, at least while most of these republics continue to be headed by secular leaders. Although some kind of Islamic state in Afghanistan is probably inevitable, there has long been doubt that a centralized, oppressive authority—alien to many traditional Afghan social and political norms and a segmentary society—would be acceptable. Much as Najibullah, however repentant, had no place in building a peaceful future for a geographically whole Afghanistan, neither does Hekmatyar nor any other radical Islamist adequately suit the part.

Refugee Repatriation

In a worse case scenario for Pakistan, the war against Kabul's communists would have continued indefinitely, few refugees choosing repatriation, and international aid groups soon tiring of their relief role. The onus of financing the refugees and their rehabilitation would then be expected to fall heavily on Pakistan. Authorities had reason to be concerned that over time the local economy would find it difficult to support the disproportionately young, poorly educated refugee population, who would be unable to find jobs and liable to grow into a restless mass, prone to crime and violence. The situation would certainly have become desperate if many of the Pakistanis working abroad were forced to return to the domestic work force, a taste of which was provided by the loss of jobs in Iraq in 1990.

Had Pakistan's leaders agreed to a negotiated solution that was opposed as a sell-out by the mujahidin and their allies, an uprising among the refugees against national authority might have followed. A government in Islamabad, feeling that it had popular domestic support, would have stepped up pressure for the resistance leadership to approve an agreement and for the refugees to leave. Afghans housed in refugee camps might have resisted the strong efforts by authorities to repatriate them. Pakistan's military had long been uneasy about the large stock of weapons in the hands of resident Afghans. Certainly, economic pressures would have been applied long before any military-supported measures, very likely the denial of relief subsidies in the camps. In any case, as many had long feared, direct confrontation with the Afghans could have had dire consequences for the survival of any Pakistani government and acted to undermine the state itself.

Although displeased with the international community's weakening sense of obligation, Pakistan was spared from watching the international community wash its hands entirely of the refugees—as might have happened if Islamic forces had not prevailed when they did. Yet even with the ascendance of the mujahidin in Kabul, the Pakistanis remained concerned that large numbers of Afghan refugees would be reluctant to return. Many city-dwelling Afghans, well established in the local economy, were expected to maintain a presence in Peshawar and other cities, even while some members of their families returned to Afghanistan, often to start planting. The more affluent, those without the need for relief services, look on retention of their financial interests in Pakistan as a form of insurance, to be abandoned only under the greatest pressure.

The first to depart were those refugees who had faced a hard time finding steady work in Pakistan. They were taking their chances in returning to Afghanistan, leaving the security of the camps for the uncertainty of obtaining food, fuel, and shelter. Those returning to the more heavily populated valleys faced the acute problem of having no wood for the rebuilding of houses and, even more serious in the immediate future of resettlement, little water for irrigation and consumption. And then there was the concern about the uncharted land mines, certain to pose an obstacle to farming and grazing. More than 10 million are believed to be scattered around the country. By 1992, after three years of de-mining operations by various agencies working under U.N. auspices, no more than 35,000 mines—by other estimates no more than 22,000—had been cleared.[2]

Despite this, more than 600,000 people had crossed the border since the beginning of 1992, and in June alone, 225,000 were repatriated from the rapidly emptying and partly dismantled camps. (By comparison, only 40,000 had returned in all of 1991.) The heavy exodus that began following the communists' fall, most of it to the politically more stable and accessible areas in the southeast of the country, was spurred by many factors, including desire to reclaim property rights and scout the conditions at home. Fears were also raised that rations in Pakistani camps might soon run out. Wheat rations in the camps had already been reduced with the falloff in international assistance. A year after the collapse of the Najibullah government, as many as 1.5 million Afghans had returned, most of them from Pakistan. Over the following months, roughly 12,000 refugees were leaving monthly. Additionally, by August 1993, some 750,000 refugees from Iran, mainly from its Khurasan and Seistan-Balochistan provinces, had been repatriated to Afghanistan.[3]

U.N. officials refrained from pressing the Afghan refugees hard to go back. But to provide some incentive and facilitate their departure, each family was promised by the UNHCR the equivalent of about $130 in cash and approximately 140 pounds of flour on turning in their ration passbooks.[4] Yet the cash-short U.N. representatives were always on the verge of running out of money to provide the returnees—and sometimes did for short periods. Only $15 million of the $53 million that the UNHCR had requested for its repatriation program in 1992 had been received by July, in large part owing to the demands elsewhere on U.N. refugee funds. Financing was no better in subsequent months. The understaffed ten encashment centers established in the NWFP experienced unruly crowds, with at least some refugees not planning to leave immediately taking the money in expectation of its being unavailable later. Wheat distribution was also subject to irregular deliveries. Distribution centers, some managed by Pakistan's Commissionerate for Refugees, often failed to receive wheat that was first claimed by Pakistani traders or stuck in government warehouses.[5] Those refugees impatient to leave had often sold their wheat coupons to local traders at half their value rather than wait for new shipments to arrive. Although there had been no riots over food or money, UNHCR officials nonetheless feared massive unrest inside Pakistan if they were forced to turn away would-be returnees as a result of the agency's under-funded payment program.[6] Because most available funds were earmarked for repatriation grants alone, transportation home, using hired trucks and buses, came at the refugees' expense. This left very little assistance for farmers in need of aid for buying seeds to replant their fields.

It was not the availability of cash payments to refugees that slowed their flow back to Afghanistan beginning most notably in August 1992, however. With the outbreak of fighting among forces loyal to the government and those aligned with Hezb-i-Islami (as well as armed conflict between a loose coalition of eight pro-Iranian Shi'ite parties, and Sayyaf's Saudi-supported Ittehad-i-Islam), there began a streaming out of Kabul. In all, half a million residents fled the city where they faced severe shortages of food, water, and fuel, and where in time more than half the city's houses had been damaged or destroyed. Tens of thousands of them crowded the highway back to Pakistan, over 30,000 in August alone. By March 1993, as many as 70,000 had taken refuge in Peshawar.[7] Those who had previously returned from Pakistan had already given up their refugee status, and forfeited their right to financial assistance. Consequently, they were dependent on relatives, small amounts of aid from private relief groups, or finding sources of employment. These refugees also put strains on public services in Pakistan once again. This led at the end of August 1992 to an action that marked a departure from Islamabad's long-held position on refugees: an announced policy, if short-lived, to close the borders to Afghans seeking sanctuary in Pakistan.

Afghans escaping from the devastating rocket attacks on Kabul—at least 10,000 killed—had been preceded in their escape to Pakistan earlier by Kabulis of another stripe. As former military officers and party officials of the defunct regime, these new refugees were not anxious to test the tolerance of an Islamic government. By one account, more than half of the ministers and deputy ministers in the Najibullah government, Khalqis and Parchamis, had found refuge in Pakistan, settling largely with family and friends in Peshawar.[8] The larger influx beginning in August 1992 included others who, while not in positions of authority under the communists, had lived throughout the war in the capital. Among them were better educated Afghans, most of them professionals, lower level bureaucrats, and intellectuals. They had been accused of being collaborators by the mujahidin and saw their homes attacked and women intimidated. But even in taking refuge in Pakistan these refugees continued to be terrorized, usually by Hezb-i-Islami gangs. The party, whose offices and printing presses in Peshawar work in close coordination with Pakistan's Jama'at-i-Islami, launched a campaign of vilification against the refugees on their arrival in Peshawar.[9]

While most Afghan resistance groups have moved their headquarters to Kabul, their representatives and the larger part of their staffs remain in Peshawar. Mujahidin leaders and party activists not only continue to travel regularly to Peshawar but have left their families in the city. Early in 1993, the Pakistan government had threatened to shut the offices of the Afghan parties, not only closing their printing presses but forbidding Pakistani presses to print Afghan publications. In fact, business continued much as usual, as it had with a threat to deport illegal Arab immigrants and shut down unregistered PVOs. The government also failed to carry through on its threat to renew permits for resistance leaders and their bodyguards to carry arms in the NWFP. Peshawar remains as well the base of activities for liberal and moderate Afghan intellectuals, who would find it impossible for the time being to return in safety or operate effectively in Kabul. Aside from security for themselves in the anarchy of the Afghan capital, they could expect to find a radical Islamist-dominated Kabul little more hospitable than have the city's former communists.

Owing to the tendency of many Pakistanis to stress the distortions to local economies created by the refugees during their long stay, the positive economic stimulus of the Afghans to the border provinces was often depreciated, if at all acknowledged. At least some of the infrastructure created by their presence is permanent, including water systems, and will remain for local populations. The effect of repatriation can be expected in fact to vary greatly with locality. Most clearly, Pakistanis in their government's refugee bureaucracy will be left unemployed, and the impact of the lost income will no doubt have massive effects, especially on the NWFP. The closing of the AIG ministries by the end of 1991 had put upwards of 20,000 Afghans in Peshawar out of work, also with obvious impact on the local economy.

With the $107 million total aid budget of the private agencies, their eventual exodus could be expected to bring new hardship to those refugees not as yet able or willing to go home.[10] Afghans employed by the relief groups may retain their jobs by following PVOs into Afghanistan once conditions in the country permit—assuming that these groups have not given up the effort by then. Not long after the setting up of the interim government, most organizations involved with running cross-border assistance programs had petitioned the mujahidin-led government in Kabul to permit them to direct their operations from within the country. Until the heavy fighting in Kabul among mujahidin factions had erupted, the departure of aid workers from Pakistan seemed likely to accelerate as the Pakistan government put pressure on the PVOs by refusing, in many cases, to extend workers' visas and removing the certification of some groups. Still, through 1993, the great majority of government and nongovernment Afghan aid groups remained based in Peshawar, along with their training programs and most of their Afghan staffers.

Pakistani authorities did not expect to see all problems eliminated with the refugees gone. Although, on one hand, with fewer refugees much of the smuggling of guns and consumer goods would probably drop off, many repatriated Afghan farmers will depend on drug money in an effort to survive when they return to devastated farms and villages.[11] An effective program of drug control on both sides of the frontier cannot occur until alternative, marketable crops have been introduced. A farmer on a small plot can expect to earn six times more from opium than he would from wheat grown on the same parcel of land, even after the local drug mafias take their cut from the area's raw opium trade.[12] During the course of the war, the drug trade between the tribal areas of Pakistan and Afghanistan helped to finance resistance groups and their friends. Following the withdrawal of most external military assistance, armed Afghan groups have become even more involved in poppy cultivation. A U.S. government survey found that between 1991 and 1992, opium cultivation and production had increased 12 percent in Afghanistan. Informal sector financing stands as an attractive substitute source of money as the squabbling factions—many with connections to the international drug trade—become desperate for resources. This has occurred at the same time that the demand in South Asia and abroad has increased and new land routes through Central Asia are opening up.

Although Pakistani officials boast of having reduced the number of laboratories and acres under poppy cultivation, they admit that the resources to fight drugs have declined and corruption has soared. Despite this, government-furnished resources to cope with narcotics production and trade have been reduced.[13] The Pakistan government may turn to its traditional aid donors for additional financial assistance, describing its own problems of rehabilitation as a result of having welcomed the refugees, including the need for the country to repair the damage they left, especially to the environment. But in view of the halt in U.S. economic assistance to Pakistan and the donor fatigue evident among traditional Western sources, the prospects are not good. More important, in light of the strong contribution of drugs in Pakistan's gray economy, there are many who have begun to question whether a successful program against the drug trade is in fact in Pakistan's best interest, and whether there can be a sincere commitment, given the almost certain involvement of so many high ranking politicians.[14]

Pakistan and Reconstruction

Prior to the conflict, Afghanistan was a strong but complex society and a weak state. There had developed a modus operandi that permitted regimes in Kabul a restricted though not inconsequential area over which to exercise authority. Over time the society had become increasingly less autonomous of the state, and a desire to share in the material, developmental benefits handed out by Kabul became the key instrument of state power. Chances for establishing a viable postwar Afghan state could improve through the resources provided by Pakistan and especially extra-regional powers and international agencies. A strategy that centralizes much of the distribution of the outside aid can be expected to play a meaningful part in creating a strengthened state.[15] Presumably it could produce incentives to cooperate for those divided by language, sect, and ethnic, tribal, and regional loyalties.

At the same time, a reasonably stable government in Kabul laying plans for postwar reconstruction is indispensable for Afghanistan to be a credible claimant for foreign assistance. International aid agencies usually find it awkward to work outside the authority of central governments. The funneling of assistance through such a government and its ministries can be part of the overall, if necessarily slow, process of rebuilding the state. Resources for rehabilitation and reconstruction enable the central government to extend its authority outside the capital and improve its claims to legitimacy. Without it there may be small chance of putting the more productive and self-sufficient areas of the north under Kabul's effective control. A central authority in a peaceful Afghanistan also offers a better chance of contributing to regional security arrangements and serving as an economic partner to neighbors rather than as a burden.

Much of the planning for Afghanistan is premised on the view that fundamental changes have occurred in Afghan society. The experiences of the refugees in Pakistan, under different systems of authority in military and elected governments, will undoubtedly affect Afghans' expectations about their own future. For better or for worse, Pakistan has set an example for those Afghans seeking to revive their state through institutions that are both competent and accountable.

The next generation of Afghans will no doubt be a more difficult people to govern. While competing primordial allegiances have eroded somewhat, the individual Afghan is also less passive, more politicized. Exile has established higher standards for government that will make resettled Afghans less easily satisfied, more critical, and more distrustful of those exercising authority. Returned rural and city dwellers alike will no doubt demand of their government services in the future that previous Afghan governments were not accustomed to providing. Refugees are unlikely to quickly forget the educational and medical assistance they found for the first time in Pakistan. They may also be less tolerant of the traditionally ineffective Afghan government. Feelings could be intensified if a weak new regime in Kabul is unable to address the reconstruction problems in the devastated country and things appeared better under the communists, particularly in the cities. While at their best the changes in expectations could create the basis for a more responsible political system, they could also produce a public cynicism and dissatisfaction that could be a source of political instability. This is especially so since many of those who are claimants for power in Kabul may not feel especially accountable to the masses' opinions, especially where they believe that their principal task in ruling is to carry out God's will.

Afghans did not have to learn about political pluralism in Pakistan. Theirs is a different kind of pluralism and, if anything, is already too healthy. The task is to contain it or at least to create a modus operandi, an institutional framework, in which the competition among interests can be rendered constructive. The defeat of the Kabul regime had, however, only increased mutual resentments based on ethnic differences. Feelings toward Pashtuns are strong among Afghanistan's minorities who believe that the Pashtun central authorities have always sought to dominate them politically and culturally. Mutual respect may have increased in the camps and in the course of fighting a common enemy, but minority leaders are determined that their groups' subordinate position not be restored once the war is over. Conversely, many in the Pashtun majority believe that their way of life is threatened and that minority Tajiks and others among the urban elites had too much power during the monarchy of Zahir Shah.

In the immediate future, the Pakistani contribution to efforts at reconstruction in Afghanistan could be sizable, even critical. Pakistan is expected to put its relatively more developed infrastructure at the international community's disposal. A number of studies by U.N. agencies and PVOs have identified areas in which Pakistan can assume a particularly active role.[16] Aside from lending logistical support for the voluntary repatriation of refugees, the studies single out Pakistan's short-term food aid, its assistance in such areas as agricultural inputs, road repair and construction, raw materials for building shelters, and creation of health facilities, including the supply of medicines. Pakistan has also been expected to contribute to water supply schemes and in the lending of professional manpower.

All of these sectors of support would be expected to draw on Pakistan's indigenous technological base and development experience. Pakistan can be the source of commodities and manufactured goods needed in the Afghan rehabilitation. Providing construction materials along with technical and professional expertise can create confidence that the Islamabad government sincerely desires to help in the timely reconstruction of the shattered Afghan economy. Restoration of Afghanistan's telecommunications system, its telephone, radio, and telex links with the outside world, is critical to a restored economy, and Pakistan has much expertise.

Pakistan's private sector has an equally significant part to play. Private investment in Afghanistan, mainly small scale joint ventures, will be of considerable value. A consumer goods production base in Afghanistan could be restarted, for example. Private investment in Afghanistan might also be integrated with business projects planned for Central Asia. The attraction of these investments will no doubt be enhanced if they are secured through some institutional framework, although the best guarantees for the private investor are a stable political-economic environment.[17]

Pakistan has been slow, in fact, in gearing up for the possible role in reconstruction. Along with the international community, chances of generous investment by Pakistan in Afghanistan's reconstruction diminished steadily with the delayed settlement and later with the intercine warfare among factions. The Pakistan government had dissolved its high level Afghan cell, responsible for strategic decisions, and in April 1992 created a new cell, headed by the finance minister, and charged with considering how Pakistan could best help in the reconstruction of Afghanistan.[18] Pakistan responded quickly to the need for aid, delivering large quantities of wheat and other foodstuffs by truck to Kabul in the weeks following its liberation, and promising construction materials and other items essential for reconstruction. Pakistan's emergency assistance continued into 1993 in response to both the factional fighting that devastated Kabul and a serious cholera outbreak. Yet overall, surprisingly little thinking about Pakistan's role in reconstruction occurred within the ministries in Islamabad.

In anticipation of what will be needed to develop economic ties with Afghanistan, particularly in the reconstruction period, Pakistan has shown scant foresight in going to international funding agencies for help for improving its own infrastructure. Nor has it sought assistance for producing the kinds of commodities, such as cement, that will be in high demand during rebuilding. Pakistan's transport system needs upgrading if it is going to be the major conduit for goods. A rail line from Karachi to Kabul is a possibility and, indeed, an understanding with the interim Afghan government was reached in November 1992 to begin construction between Kabul and the border town of Landikotal—as soon as circumstances in Afghanistan permitted. The road system is already badly clogged, and a controversial new motor way from Karachi to Peshawar, and possibly to the Afghan border, is only in the earliest stages. Although Pakistan does not provide Afghanistan's only link to the sea, the port of Karachi is surely the most convenient outlet. Additionally, though also costly, construction of a highway connecting Afghanistan more directly with an Indian Ocean port on the Baluchistan coast could be an economic stimulus for both countries. Less worrisome is the flexibility of Pakistan's private transport sector. With a sense of where profits can be made, this sector is likely to be more responsive than government authorities in meeting the opportunities created by reconstruction.[19] In general, Pakistan may be able to offer more if reconstruction is not undertaken on a grand scale but is attacked realistically in a large number of mini-projects, spread out over time.

The economic bonds between Pakistan's NWFP and Afghanistan's eastern provinces are bound to remain strong. During the immediate postwar period, Pakistan should have enormous trade advantages, most of all because of recently exiled Afghans operating on both sides of the border. Pakistan's markets are critical to a balanced postwar trade. To an Afghanistan that will desperately need to stabilize its currency, a flourishing bilateral trade with Pakistan can help to build reserves that will strengthen the Afghan currency over the long term. Much of Afghanistan's agricultural surpluses are sold in Pakistan, which in the future could become a customer for Afghan iron, copper, and hydroelectric power. Natural gas from Afghanistan could flow to Pakistan should a pipeline prove feasible. Even when the war was most intense, a flourishing trade took place across the usually porous border. Rice and vegetables from Pakistan, for example, continued to go to Kabul in the winter months. Year-round, a great proportion of all imported goods reaching Afghanistan from Europe and the Far East was smuggled across the border to provide black-market items in the Pakistani economy. The two-way trade occurred with the approval of the mujahidin, who took payoffs to let the goods pass through occupied areas.

Where once Afghanistan worried about dependency, in a postwar period the devastated country must be far more concerned about the availability of international aid, without which any significant reconstruction becomes impossible. Major reconstruction no doubt requires generous help from Western countries, including the United States. The prospect is, then, for long-term dependency on foreign powers. Early in the tenure of the interim Islamic government its leaders issued a call to all states and international organizations for urgent financial and technical assistance to rebuild their country.[20]

At the same time, the Afghans are likely to resist an outside power that tries to dictate the path of rehabilitation and reconstruction. Any suggestion that Pakistan might be trying to play big brother to Afghanistan by taking a dominant part in reconstruction is certain to be resisted. Pakistanis will have to be careful not to repeat past mistakes by appearing to impose a set of development policies. A government in Pakistan that insists on firm guarantees and major rewards for its decade of generosity is almost certain to revive old antagonisms. There is, instead, much that Pakistan can do to avoid the often patronizing and exploitative pre-war relationship. If Pakistan is to feel secure that a future Afghanistan does not again see its national interests better served through ties to India, officials in Islamabad will have to be more sensitive than in the past to charges that they are behaving as a hegemonic neighbor. This may require concessions, especially economic ones, to allay Afghan suspicions.

Resentment against Pakistan's influence was plainly evident during the war, most so in its closing years. In general, attitudes among Afghans toward Pakistan have been ambivalent. On the one hand, there is gratitude for hospitality and brotherly assistance in a sacred war. On the other hand, there exists a strong residue of resentment over Pakistan's manipulation of Afghan refugees and resistance politics. Many Afghans believe that Pakistan is likely to be interested mainly in shaping the postwar balance of tribal power and in heading off any revival of a strong Pashtun nationalism.

A desire to keep Pakistan out explains to some extent the degree of coordination reached late in the war among Afghan commanders and their success for a time in brokering agreements between antagonistic resistance parties in Peshawar. No small part of the drive to reach agreement among the Afghan leaders was the broadly held feeling that they wanted to free their policy, as best they could, from the direction of Pakistan's military. A prime example of a conflict over priorities occurred in late 1991 between the more moderate mujahidin parties, concerned about postwar reconstruction, and Pakistan's military intelligence. The ISI was accused of being all to ready, in the quest of military successes, to participate in the wrecking of Afghanistan's power grid and the dynamiting of several of its major dams.[21]

To treat Afghanistan as a regional equal would be disappointing at the least for many Pakistanis, especially elements of the military. President Zia had not discouraged thinking about a federation with Afghanistan as part of a strategic Islamic consensus for the region. Like many other Pakistanis, he misjudged the temperament of the Afghans in believing that Pakistan, through its support and hospitality, had earned the right to play Afghanistan's mentor. Zia would have soon learned that any mujahidin-led government, even the befriended Hezb-i-Islami, would resist Pakistan's efforts to shape Afghanistan's foreign or domestic policies, whatever its sense of appreciation. It was highly unrealistic to expect to exercise as much influence on the Afghans in their own country as Pakistan agents had wielded with Afghans in exile.

While Pakistani officials can hope to facilitate cooperation among the Islamic factions, Islamabad is unlikely to be able to impose a leadership in Kabul. Indeed, among the independent-minded Afghans, having Pakistan as patron can be a disadvantage. Even among those who benefited from Pakistan's favors, few would want to be seen in a postwar period as willing tools of the Pakistanis. The nationalism that strengthened during the course of the war has assured that Afghanistan will become no one's client state. Whichever factions emerge ascendant in Afghanistan are certain to insist on national self-determination. The pride and sense of identity shown by the Afghans in their long struggle is ample demonstration. As a result, Pakistan can be expected to settle for a government in Kabul that, while not anti-Pakistani, will not be entirely pliant toward Islamabad. A more neutral Afghanistan becomes acceptable in exchange for a reassuring new set of bilateral relations.

Prospects for cooperation between Pakistan and postwar Afghanistan are nevertheless reasonably good. Indication that Pakistan would continue to be a presence in Afghan life was strengthened by an agreement with the first interim government to admit Pakistani TV programs and its news agency, and to allow the circulation of a Pakistani newspaper in Pashtu, in exchange for Pakistan's aid in rehabilitating the state printing house and film and TV facilities in Kabul.[22] Both countries might find their economic and political futures in South Asia, a reality which can be formalized by bringing Afghanistan into the framework of SAARC, the fledgling organization of South Asian countries seeking to further economic cooperation.

However, Afghanistan may be instead drawn into Pakistan's approach to the future which often seems to have conceded South Asia to India. The two governments were perhaps likely to be drawn together by their mutual affinity toward countries to the West and Central Asia rather than to South Asia. They could seek out the needed economic and strategic security, and find in Central Asia an area in which to profit and play a meaningful role, reducing their having to live in the shadow of a hegemonic India. This was most readily realized through a Muslim organization, such as that represented by the Economic Cooperation Organization (ECO), successor to an older alliance including Pakistan, Iran and Turkey, and in 1992 joined by five Muslim republics of the former Soviet state.

Anxious to help Afghanistan realize political normalcy and acquire greater legitimacy, the ECO-affiliated countries granted the Kabul government membership in November 1992.[23] A regional grouping that includes Afghanistan offers one way of avoiding the almost certain sense of inferiority that a postwar Afghanistan is bound to feel in its relations with Pakistan. In any case, regional economic bonds may offer the best chance for the two countries to develop complementary, cooperative relations rather than revive their traditional differences, most of all over a Pashtun state.

Pashtunistan

Logically, the Pashtunistan issue should not be expected to reemerge any time soon. Pakistan's leading advocates of a separate nation largely disqualified themselves as spokesmen as a result of their war-time pro-Moscow proclivities. Afghan radical Islamists, long preferred for leadership by Pakistan, have stressed a universal religious identity rather than a secular national allegiance. While given sanctuary in Pakistan, none of the Afghan parties were inclined to antagonize their Pakistani hosts, and any new Afghan regime will hesitate before destroying what good feelings remain as a result of Pakistan's wartime assistance. In October 1992, a representative of the interim Afghan government in Islamabad explicitly rejected the idea that the issue could ever be raised again in light of Pakistan's role in the Afghan jihad.[24] Even among some nationalistic Pashtun tribes in eastern Afghanistan, the cause of Pashtunistan had lost much of its appeal during the war since most felt no desire to come under the control again of the Durranis, the former ruling family of Afghanistan. Afghanistan's ethnic minorities, unlikely to accede to a postwar restoration of Pashtun ascendance in Kabul, can also be expected to counter proclamations of Pashtun nationalism—assuming that the country remains intact.

All the same, a future Afghan government may be tempted to revive the Pashtunistan issue against a Pakistan perceived as asserting an overbearing influence. A more immediate concern about Pashtunistan comes with the possible disintegration of Afghanistan as a sovereign entity in a stalemated civil war. Should interim governments prove incapable and elections fail to occur or gain sufficient legitimacy, the prospect of Afghanistan fragmenting into separate ethnic, sectarian, and ideological pieces becomes very plausible. In this, Pakistan might try to carve out a sphere of influence, but it is likely that other dependencies will come into being—Shi'ite Hazaras with Iran, Uzbeks and Tajiks with ethnic cousins in the Central Asian republics, the radical Islamists and Wahabis in the east and southeast with the Arabs.[25] Divisions could evolve quite naturally as local commanders continue to administer areas under their control, with or without outside help. Some of these ethnic enclaves might be led by individuals and parties that are anti-Pakistani.

Not only would many refugees still remain in Pakistan but, as has occurred with heavy fighting among the mujahidin, new waves could be expected to arrive from Afghanistan, including those from areas which had been pacified for some time. Pakistan's leadership, always concerned about Pashtunistan, might additionally be loathe to watch the division of Afghanistan along ethnic lines because of its own problems in keeping its regional-ethnic differences from erupting with greater force and crossing the border. Endemic conflict and anarchy in Afghanistan could envelop Pakistan's tribal regions, as well as increase the siphoning off of food and other essential items through smuggling.[26]

Above all, an alliance of northern ethnic forces and the possibility of a rump Pashtun state in a fragmented Afghanistan might be the very issue that revives the Pashtunistan cause in Pakistan.[27] In a fractured country, Afghan Pashtuns may look toward their Pakistani cousins to form a new political unit to replace their lost multi-ethnic country. A harbinger of this was seen in the way many Pashtuns, not identified earlier with Hezb-i-Islami, had rallied to the side of Hekmatyar when he faced other ethnic forces in the fight for Kabul; the Islamic leader had become the new, if unlikely, standard bearer of Pashtun nationalism. Pakistani authorities appreciated that if Hezb-i-Islami were able to keep a stable coalition government from forming in Kabul, the de facto emergence of a Pashtun state would be a strong possibility.

In the short term, Hekmatyar was more interested in preserving the integrity of Afghanistan, presumably as a Pashtun-dominated country. The leader of the old-line secular Pashtun nationalist party, Afghan Millat, paid tribute to Hekmatyar while denouncing others for conspiracies to disintegrate the country.[28] Even Hezb-i-Islami's arch enemy, the Awami National Party of Wali Khan, became an ally in decrying the movement toward a division of Afghanistan on ethnic lines. Should the Pashtuns fail to regain ascendance, they seem posed to create their own enclave. This could give the signal for the Baluchis in Pakistan, Iran, and Afghanistan to try to come together. In the end, the Punjabis might be left alone as Sindhis went their separate way. Under conditions of a disintegrating and warring Pakistan, all plans for a Pakistani role in Central Asia are bound to be canceled along with hopes for Afghanistan's effective participation in regional organizations.

Notes

1. Sayid B. Majrooh, Afghan Information Center (AIC), *Monthly Bulletin*, no. 75 (June 1987), p. 4.

2. By fall 1992, the higher figure was reported by Radio Moscow, October 11, 1992, in *Afghanistan Forum*, Vol. 20, no. 6 (November 1992): 5. Also see Justin Burke in the *Christian Science Monitor*, May 14, 1992. The 10 million estimate is according to a November 1991 U.N. survey that also concludes that 200,000 people were killed during the war by mines, and 400,000 maimed over the course of the 14-year war.

3. *The News* (Islamabad), August 2, 1993, and *Frontier Post* (Peshawar), August 5, 1993, both from a United Nations High Commissioner for Refugees report. The UNHCR estimated that in mid-1993 there remained 2.2 million Afghan refugees in Iran. *The New York Times*, October 18, 1993.

4. Ibid., August 31, 1992. By comparison, refugees returning from Iran were not initially given material inducements to return home. This was despite an agreement that had been reached with UNHCR in summer 1992 for the voluntary repatriation of 500,000 Afghans that would provide the Tehran government with $15 million—far less than what Iran felt it spent on the refugees and a small fraction of what Pakistan had received, thanks largely to Western aid. Understandably, in the months following the fall of Kabul to the mujahidin, only 176,000 refugees from Iran had left for home. The pace of repatriation picked up considerably by fall 1993. Although denying that Afghan refugees were being forced across the border, Iran was reportedly confiscating identity cards, making it impossible for Afghans to remain legally. The 1,500 crossing daily into Afghanistan in October also reflected a new agreement with the United

Nations that encouraged voluntary repatriation; departing refugees were offered a 110 bag of wheat and $25. Iran, experiencing severe economic difficulties, including high domestic unemployment, welcomed the arrangement that obliged the United Nations to buy the wheat from the Tehran government and transfer to Iran the refugee payments in dollars which were then converted to Iranian riyals for distribution to those leaving. *The Economist*, October 16, 1993, p. 40.

5. A full discussion of the problems with repatriation is found in Sylvie Girard, *Refugees* (September 1992), reprinted in *Afghanistan Forum*, Vol. 20, no. 6 (November 1992): 22.

6. Hamish McDonald, *Far East Economic Review*, July 30, 1992, p. 11.

7. *The Herald* (Karachi), March 1993, p. 49-50. *Pakistan Times*, March 31, 1993, put the figure at 86,000 of new refugees arriving in Pakistan after six months of heavy shelling of Kabul.

8. FBIS-NES, *Daily Report*, June 3, 1992, p. 44, from *Muslim* (Islamabad), June 2, 1992. Also, *The Nation* (Islamabad), August 21, 1992.

9. *The Herald*, March 1993, p. 50.

10. Colin Barraclough, *Christian Science Monitor*, May 21, 1992.

11. Sheila Tefft, ibid., September 28, 1989, p. 3.

12. *Frontier Post*, November 4, 1992.

13. *The Washington Post*, April 29, 1993.

14. A study commissioned by the U.S. Central Intelligence Agency concluded that the involvement had "penetrated to the highest political circles" as well as top military personnel. Heroin traffickers are alleged to have financed Pakistan's ruling party, bought seats in the National Assembly, and gained access to both the prime minister and president. Knut Royce, "Pakistan: Heroin Country,"*Newsday*, February 23 1993.

15. Marvin G. Weinbaum, "The Politics of Afghan Resettlement and Rehabilitation," *Asian Survey*, Vol. 29, no. 3 (March 1989): 293–298.

16. The several sectors for possible contribution are noted in Fazal-ur-Rahman, "Pakistan's Role in the Immediate Reconstruction of Afghanistan," *Afghan Jehad*, Vol. 5, no. 3 (April–June, 1992): 129–130.

17. Ibid., p. 130.

18. FBIS-NES, April 30, 1992, p. 40, from an address by the prime minister, PTV Television, on April, 29, 1992.

19. I am indebted to Ashraf Ghani, currently with the World Bank in Washington, D. C. , in an interview in Peshawar in late April 1990, for a number of the suggestions for areas of future cooperation.

20. FBIS-NES, June 17, 1992, from a statement issued by the Foreign Ministry on Kabul Radio.

21. Irina Lagunina, *New Times*, Vol. 47 (1991), reprinted in *Afghanistan Forum*, Vol. 19, no. 4, December 1991: 13. AIG President Mujaddedi accused Pakistani military officers of trying to destroy the Kajaki Dam in Helmand Province in 1990, and during late 1991 of planning to destroy the Naghloo and Daroonta dams. *Afghan Jehad* (Islamabad), Vol. 5, no. 1 (October–December 1991): 133, from *Afghanistan Qulb-e-Asia*, November 9, 1991.

22. *AFGHANews*, Vol. 8, no. 16, August 15, 1992, reprinted in *Afghanistan Forum*, Vol. 20, no. 6 (November 1992): 27.

23. Membership had been promised from the outset of the Islamic regime. FBIS-NES, May 28, 1992, p. 52, from Islamabad Radio, May 26, 1992.

24. *Pakistan Times*, October 15, 1992.

25. A possible model was the mini-Wahabi kingdom of Pashtuns already in place and funded by Saudi princes in the Kunar Province and the area around Jalalabad. See Ahmed Rashid, *The Herald* (Karachi), May 1992, p. 26.

26. *Frontier Post*, September 1, 1992.

27. For this argument, see among others, Graham E. Fuller, *The New York Times*, March 23, 1992.

28. FBIS-NES , May 18, 1992 from *The News*, May 16, 1992.

8

Regional and International Context

Afghanistan has quickly receded in importance for much of the international community. States that once played a significant humanitarian role and which may have aided the resistance militarily, have largely turned away, leaving the Afghans to fight, if they must, among themselves. Sectarian, ethnic, tribal, as well as ideological conflict in a weak Afghan state contributed most toward internalizing Afghanistan's problems. With global attention having shifted in the early 1990s to the Persian Gulf, developments in Eastern Europe, and most of all the breakup of the Soviet state, the conflict in Afghanistan had become to many an annoying side show. For those anxious to come to the rescue of beleaguered peoples, Cambodia and Somalia offered more than sufficient opportunity. It is doubtful, then, that Afghanistan can again be, as it was for the 1980s, a focal point of international attention, viewed widely as a direct threat to world peace.

Nevertheless, states within the region can be expected to place their bids for influence and advantage in a postwar Afghanistan, using if necessary domestic surrogates to realize their sometimes clashing aims. Initially, to be sure, there seemed much that was convergent in the interests of the key regional players. The idea of an independent, nonaligned Afghanistan won wide support across the region. Pakistan found support in Tehran and the Arab states in appealing to the Afghans to end their political wrangles over forming an Islamic government.

The first two postwar accords reached among the Afghan factions, intended to install an interim government in the capital, were brokered by Pakistan, Iran, and Saudi Arabia. High-ranking envoys from the three monitored the understandings reached among the Afghan leaders in negotiations that took place in Islamabad in March 1993. Participants at the meeting, held at the initiative and in the home of Pakistan's prime minister, were expected to form a broad-based government to replace the poorly conceived arrangements in the Peshawar accord of April 1992. Iran, anxious to demonstrate its commitment, offered to send a peacekeeping force to Afghanistan to implement the proposed plan. And in what was supposed to be a religiously symbolic legitimization of the document, the ten Afghan factional leaders who participated at Islamabad traveled to the holy city of Mecca at the invitation of Saudi Arabia.

Two months later the same Afghans approved an elaborated version of the agreement in Jalalabad, one more fully tailored to meet the demands of ever-constant spoiler Gulbiddin Hekmatyar. On this occasion, to counter criticism that the accord was, as in the past, a foreign creation, the talks were deliberately held on Afghan territory. The point was underlined when the city's military commander kept the ambassadors from Pakistan and Saudi Arabia from even approaching the meetings of party leaders.[1] Pakistan may have lost some of its ability to manipulate the mujahidin leaders, but, like Iran and Saudi Arabia, it was hardly ready to turn its back on Afghanistan. In face of the expected international disengagement from Afghanistan and the continuing de-facto political disintegration of the country, a scramble among regional powers for influence among the parties to the civil conflict seemed increasingly likely. Pakistan surely had the most at stake.

The underlying competition between Iran and Saudi Arabia complicated Pakistani policy toward Afghanistan and undercut a broad Muslim position for the region. Without the cooperation of Iran and Saudi Arabia, religious and ethnic factional differences were expected to stymie any effort to rebuild an Afghan state.[2] The Tehran government seems intent on assuming a larger role in Afghan affairs than it did previously. Pakistan has reason to be concerned that a surrogate-fought war between Iranian and Saudi foreign policies has escalated, with Afghanistan as the battleground. And whereas in the distant past Afghanistan had turned to Turkey to counter the influence of Iran, like it or not, it now finds Saudi Arabia playing the part.

Regional Tensions

Pakistan, marginalized like many other states in the Third World in the absence of cold war competition, finds itself forced to reassess many of its regional policies. With Pakistan's international role diminished, it becomes imperative for it to forge regional alliances that promise to compensate for the country's economic loses and military and political deficiencies. Most of Pakistan's opportunities regionally are contingent, however, on stabilizing developments in what is for the present an ungovernable Afghanistan. Virtually unchanged in Pakistan's strategic thinking is the belief that national security turns primarily on the country's endemic confrontation with India.

In a post-Afghan war era, India and Pakistan need not feel as clients of superpowers, in effect going beyond their national interests out of obligation to their patrons. Paradoxically, however, bilateral relations between New Delhi and Islamabad may become more adversarial. For along with the freedom from the instigation of external powers comes the loss of the constraints against military confrontation once felt while the Soviet Union and United States were counted on as allies. Much may depend on the ability of countries of South Asia to forge new, workable regional security arrangements.

Pakistan's strategic aims involving Afghanistan include trying to assure that India will not be in a position to rebuild good relations with a Kabul government, ties that are seen as sure to involve mutual opposition to Pakistan. Policy makers in Pakistan firmly believe that the Indians will work hard to nurture close links with any Afghan government as a means of keeping Pakistan off balance. President Zia and others had earlier conceived of a fundamentalist Muslim regime in Kabul as the best way to safeguard against such an eventuality. The dependence of an Afghan government on conservative Arab states for financial backing was to provide additional insurance.

Conversely, India's prime fear has long been the ascendancy of radical Islamic forces in the region, particularly should Pakistan try to assume a leadership role. The Kashmir uprising gave India a frightening demonstration of militant Islam at work. As a result, officials in New Delhi stubbornly maintained their support for the communist regime in Kabul. So long as the Soviets satisfied themselves with the pacification of Afghanistan and contained any obvious geo-strategic ambitions in South Asia, India never pressed Moscow very hard to end the drawn-out Afghan war. The price of this policy for Delhi, in the rearming of Pakistan by the United States, was willingly paid as long as the Soviet Union maintained its own arms arrangements with India. Not only did it largely countenance the Soviet role in Afghanistan, the Indian government went out of its way in early 1989 to befriend Afghan President Najibullah—at a time when Moscow's leadership seemed ready to write him off. Meanwhile, for India, Pakistan's distraction over the Afghanistan struggle was welcome.

In face of quantitative and qualitative military inferiority with India in conventional defense, Pakistan sought to provide itself with the nuclear option to overcome this imbalance. Once the development program was in a position to produce weapons, however few in comparison to the Indian stockpile, Pakistan had probably succeeded in deterring a future Indian initiated massive ground attack and in lessening the likelihood of a conventional war. However, the program also assured that should war occur, it would be highly lethal, conceivably threatening Pakistan's very survival. The possibility of nuclear war through miscalculation is real enough, given the degree of mutual suspicion. It is logically increased by the incentive for preemptive use of nuclear weapons in light of questionable second-strike capabilities, especially on the part of Pakistan.

The fall of the communists from power in Kabul did little to remove Pakistan's sense of insecurity and thus influence its plans for nuclear weapons. Indeed, it is more likely to have accelerated the decision to go ahead, once the country would be arguably more vulnerable without some of its war-time benefactors. Islamabad's nuclear program has been driven, moreover, by many domestic imperatives, including national pride in having a bomb, which Pakistani governments have themselves consistently fostered. In any case, only in the event of the imminent use of nuclear weapons in the Indian subcontinent, where an international stake is self-evident, are major nonregional powers likely to be tempted to impose solutions.

Pakistan has no immediate reason to be concerned about Indian influence in Afghanistan. Whatever government may emerge in Afghanistan, Afghans who fought the communist regime are not likely to overcome ill-feelings toward India any time soon. The hostility toward India among the more radical Islamist groups is particularly bitter. India has greater reason to worry about Afghan support of Muslim militants in Kashmir. The danger was expected once the factions in Kabul had sorted out their differences. But there was evidence of Hezb-i-Islami fighters along with Arab volunteers having already joined the Kashmiri insurgency—even while the Afghan factions were still contesting for power.[3] The possibility of a de facto ethnic division of Afghanistan generates further apprehension in New Delhi as it tries to control its Kashmiri and Sikh separatists.

If in the short term India's role in the Afghan recovery will necessarily be limited, older, more friendly ties could indeed reassert themselves over the longer run.[4] Trade between the two countries has long been a staple of the Afghan economy, and the Indians first helped Afghanistan to internationalize its commerce. Likely to return eventually to Kabul are many Hindu and Sikh traders with strong links to the Indian and international markets. Should Pakistan appear in the future to be exerting too great an influence on Afghanistan's economic choices, a Kabul government may look to New Delhi as an alternative, as it did in the past. Complaints in Pakistan alleging the misuse of transit facilities by Afghan importers, and demands by Afghan authorities that Pakistan live up to a 1965 agreeement on the free flow of goods had already surfaced in mid-1993. Economic motives, then, make it possible that India will eventually again figure strongly in Afghan economic and even political plans. Many strategically minded Pakistanis believe that the best way to head this off is to include Afghanistan in a meaningful regional economic bloc and press the idea that India poses a threat to Islam itself.

The Afghan war and Pakistan's involvement has already impacted the wider region. An international brigade of Arabs and other Muslims in Pakistan and Afghanistan, described earlier, carried their own aims and national goals to the conflict. They were never a decisive factor in the fighting in Afghanistan; nor did they amount to a major disruptive influence in Pakistan. However, these foreign Muslims, backed by governmental and private Arab financing, strengthened selected mujahidin commanders and party leaders. As such they came to be an issue in themselves among many Afghans—resented along with Pakistanis for trying to turn the war to their advantage. To the moderate Afghan elements, the Arab volunteers were viewed as fanatics. They were believed to have participated in retaliatory border raids across the Amu Darya River in the later stages of the Soviet occupation.[5] The Arab volunteers were considered ruthless, accused of assassinating rivals and executing Soviet and Afghan government soldiers who surrendered. The success for a time of Saudi-connected elements in gaining political and military control over most of Afghanistan's Kunar Province, adjoining Pakistan, was a conspicuous example of Arab intrigue and involvement.

Thousands of these expatriate Arab fighters with the mujahidin returned home during the Gulf crisis where large numbers became a force in their country's politics. Many had been domestic political dissidents and security risks earlier, and were further radicalized in their association with the Afghan resistance. Returning Arab volunteers may have played a role in the popular surge of the Islamic Salvation Front in Algeria and similar radical movements in Jordan and Tunisia. Intensifying pressures from Islamic militants on the Hosni Mubarak government in Cairo came in no small part from the several thousand who had gone to Pakistan as warrior-pilgrims with the support of Egypt's Islamic Brotherhood. After their return, many of these veterans of the Afghan war were arrested by Egyptian authorities for taking part in attacks against the police and Christians.

It had been long feared that the volunteer fighters could pose a powerful obstacle to a negotiated peace for Afghanistan. Had that been the case, Pakistan might have had to face earlier the question of how far it was prepared to go to force them to leave the area. Once the mujahidin had returned to Kabul, believing that the volunteers constituted a potentially disruptive element in Pakistan, the Islamabad government felt freer to act against the jihad-seekers from abroad. In spring 1992, Nawaz Sharif, responding to the entreaties of several Arab governments as well as domestic criticism that he was not doing enough to supervise them, signed an order to block new visas for Muslim fighters that was also supposed to discourage the 1,500 to 3,000 still in Pakistan from remaining.[6]

In January 1993, citing objectionable activities, the Islamabad government at first ordered all Arab private aid organizations to close their offices, and then merely insisted that the unregistered ones legalize their stay. Not only was it a little late to be accusing these groups of overstepping their charters—some had been operating for more than 10 years—but given the sympathy within elements of Pakistan's military for the Muslim volunteer warriors and their ties to Pakistan's Jama'at-i-Islami, reputable Arab Islamic organizations, and influential Arab patrons, there was no immediate or wholesale attempt to coerce the Arabs to leave. Even the more marginal Arab private groups found their expulsion deadlines repeatedly extended. And of more than 200 Arabs arrested in Peshawar in April 1993, having been described as suspected terrorists by the United States, Egypt, and other friendly Arab countries, most were soon released. At least 1,000 volunteers were believed to have relocated in Afghanistan, where they were not only participating in factional combat but were believed taking part in armed cross-border operations against the governing authorities of Tajikistan.

Arab governments had become increasingly worried about the volunteers receiving assistance in Pakistan that could be used against their regimes at home. Countries such as Egypt became particularly sensitive about the continued activities of Arabs in Pakistan and Afghanistan following the bombing of the New York World Trade Center, which was blamed not only on Islamic activists but on individuals who had first met and trained in Peshawar. The city received special attention when it was revealed that Sheik Omar Abdul Rahman, alleged spiritual leader if not mastermind of radical activities in Egypt and the United States, had visited Peshawar at least three times. The sheik who had been active in recruiting Arabs to join the jihad, was believed to have met with Hekmatyar, the last time in mid-1990.

Policies toward the Arab expatriates had most to take Saudi Arabia into account. It was private Saudi funds which had earlier provided many of the volunteers with air transport and financing, and facilitated their training with the mujahidin. The Saudi government was now, however, desirous that Pakistan maintain closer supervision of potentially troublesome battle-trained Arabs. Saudi Arabia had continued to provide Islamabad with development loans, even if not at the level of budgetary support that Islamabad sought for its Persian Gulf-related economic losses. At least 80,000 of the 85,000 Pakistanis working in Kuwait and most of the 35,000 employed in Iraq were repatriated during fall 1990. Pakistan estimated that it suffered a decline of $300 million annually in foreign exchange remittances. Oil price increases and the ban on U.N. exports to Iraq were projected by the Pakistan government to leave an annual domestic impact of between $1.5 and $2 billion.[7]

The Pakistan government's sense of obligation to Saudi Arabia contrasted with that toward Iraq which, in fact, had never sided with Pakistan in its international disputes, whether over Afghanistan or Kashmir. The official Pakistani position equated Iraq's attack and incorporation of Kuwait with Israel's control over captured Arab lands and the Soviets' former occupation of Islamic Afghanistan. Islamabad offered to contribute an 11,000-member military force to defend Saudi Arabia. The deployment was never represented as an alignment with the U.S.-led coalition—no Pakistani troops were in fact assigned to the fighting front—but was rather portrayed as in keeping with long-term understandings between Islamabad and Riyadh.

The Islamabad government's use of its "Islamic brotherhood" with the Saudi government as a means of pacifying domestic public opinion always carried the risk of backfiring. The same theme, after all, had been the rallying cry of those who also sympathized with Iraq. However, once the war had concluded with a decisive allied victory, government officials treated it as a vindication of their stand and considered that its support had earned Pakistan an economic role in the rebuilding of Kuwait. The extent of domestic opposition in Pakistan had, just the same, disappointed the Gulf states' leaders and, it was feared, could conceivably jeopardize future economic support for Pakistan.

During the Persian Gulf crisis, prominent mujahidin leaders had also pledged to defend Saudi Arabia's holy places.[8] Although only about 300 of a promised 2,000-man Saudi-financed Afghan contingent joined the multinational force in February 1991, the decision created one more source of friction within the resistance alliance. Those mujahidin sent to Saudi Arabia were drawn almost exclusively from the more moderate Afghan resistance parties. The decision to heed the call from Saudi Arabia and the United States for an Afghan armed presence once again divided the Afghan moderates and hard-line Islamists on a highly visible issue, jeopardizing some improvement at the time in the Pakistani-directed coordination of resistance groups.

The division was surprising only in that several key Islamist leaders previously identified with Saudi Arabia deserted their traditional financial backer in disavowing the action. These leaders led the chorus of

Afghans who joined Pakistani opposition parties as well as some factions of the ruling party alliance to criticize the Gulf conflict as an unjust war imposed on Iraq, motivated by an American desire to control the region and usurp its resources.[9] Pakistani police in Peshawar stopped Afghan student demonstrators after they came out to protest the decision to send mujahidin fighters, injuring several of them.

Another illustration of the export of the Afghan conflict is the acquired military skills by several thousand Kashmiris in the course of training and fighting with the mujahidin.[10] Despite Pakistan's continued assertion that its support for the Kashmiris' right of self-determination is only diplomatic and moral, elements in Pakistan's security forces were anxious to apply to the Kashmiri rebels contesting Indian authority lessons learned in keeping the Afghan mujahidin as a viable fighting force. Most Kashmiris associated with resistance parties based in Peshawar where they were welcomed into the mujahidin camps located just across the Pakistan border in Afghanistan. Members of Jama'at-i-Islami facilitated links to the Afghans, thereby allowing the Islamabad government to issue its repeated disclaimers about direct involvement in training Kashmiris. From 1987 onward, Kashmiri contingents fought in the major mujahidin battles in eastern Afghanistan. On their return home, the Kashmiris took the helm of those forces confronting Indian troops and, like the Arab volunteers, conceived of themselves as Islamic warriors in a jihad. The Muslim rebels could count on weapons from the Afghan conflict being smuggled to them.

Officials in Tehran have long worried that with the establishment of a fundamentalist Sunni regime in Kabul, a pro-Arab set of interests will prove detrimental to the minority Shi'ites in Afghanistan as well as Pakistan. Iran was uneasy that the Islamabad government, faced with the Kashmir crisis, seemed to look upon Saudi backing as ever more imperative. Strong support from the Tehran government for Pakistan's position in Kashmir was undoubtedly meant to draw Pakistan closer to Iran. At the same time, Iran's increased political activity in Afghanistan by late 1991, in particular its relief missions to Shi'ite communities of ethnic Hazaras in central Afghanistan and aid to Hesb-i-Wahdat-i-Islami (Islamic Unity Party) militias after Najibullah's fall, signaled that Tehran expected to be active both in the peace process and reconstruction, as well as in defending the interests of the Shi'ite minority in the postwar period, even if it meant challenging Pakistani-supported groups.

Although Pakistan may serve as a more appropriate model for development for Afghanistan, Iran offers the Afghan economy expanding possibilities for trade and trans-shipment of Afghan and other goods to the West, especially should Tehran agree to finance the building of a rail link. Western Afghanistan has traditionally maintained economic ties to Iran, and a pragmatic, development-oriented regime in Tehran could return to its once economically supportive role toward Afghanistan, if also its patronizing attitude. Not inconsequentially, Afghanistan's fuel requirements could be met in part by Iran. The only likely customers for Afghanistan's natural gas are some of the new Muslim states to the north. However, Kabul's leaders will no doubt drive a harder bargain than the under-valued equivalent of $300 million that Afghanistan earned yearly from sales to former Soviet Union.

Following the resistance's victory, Iranian-backed Shi'ite militia were very prominent around Kabul, deeply involved in the inter-factional fighting that persisted after the mujahidin takeover. In opposing the Saudi-backed forces of Rasul Sayyaf, the Shi'ites reportedly faced through the summer of 1992 Arab volunteers who, under pressure from Pakistan, had transferred their operations across the border. While Iran officially joined Pakistan in its opposition to the division of Afghanistan on ethnic and factional lines, its leaders were at some odds with Pakistan, or at least elements in the military, in opposing Hekmatyar's Hezb-i-Islami's becoming a full partner in a future Kabul government. Significantly, it was in the border city of Jalalabad, serving in effect as the Afghan Pashtun capital, that Hekmatyar met with intelligence officers from Saudi Arabia and the Gulf States to discuss the creation of a "temporary" pro-Arab, Sunni Pashtun state to oppose spreading Shi'ite and Iranian influences.[11]

In a worst case scenario, Pakistan could find itself in confrontation with Iran as both come to the defense of their respective Sunni and Shi'ite co-religionists. In a sense the problem had already potentially surfaced—within Pakistan. Increased Sunni-Shi'ite tensions were plainly apparent through the country and, in 1993, during the month of Muharam, religiously significant for Shi'ites, violent confrontations occurred throughout Pakistan. The Islamabad government was cognizant of the financial support and direction received by local Shi'ite communities from Iranian sources and the activities of visiting mullahs. Yet, in these incidents as in other activities involving Iranian diplomatic personnel in Pakistan, the official position in Islamabad was to minimize Iran's involvement. While the Tehran government apparently did not hesitate to use its influence with Pakistan's Shi'ites to try to nudge Islamabad's foreign as well as domestic policies, Pakistan has obviously gone far out of its way to avoid offending Tehran and bringing a deterioration of relations. Iran figures too centrally in Pakistan's ambitions for cooperation among Islamic countries of West and Central Asia to jeopardize the emerging political and economic entente.

In an important sense, Iran, like Pakistan has realized far less from its Afghan policy than it had once hoped for. At one time or another, Tehran has funneled money to nearly every Afghan party, and each has sooner or later disappointed Iran. Even the Shi'ites of Wahdat let it be known that they should not be taken for granted. Although obviously needing Tehran's support, there was more than a little resentment by the Mongol-looking Hazaras of being looked down upon racially by the Iranians. Many also had bitter experiences in Iran as refugees. If authorities in Tehran had at one time a grand design for Afghanistan, one that began with the Persian-speaking populations of the West of Afghanistan, and ran through the Hazarajat toward the culturally linked people of Tajikistan, there was little to encourage such dreams of an area of Iranian influence in the early postwar period.

With respect to Afghanistan, the policies of all the key regional states were mainly defensive: keeping the Afghans from moving too close to regional adversaries and forming unfriendly alliances. The outcome of Afghanistan's leadership struggle was believed to have a possible effect in time on the political stability, including the territorial integrity, of neighboring states. The competition over Afghanistan was bound to be fused with the contest over implanting differing versions of Islamic orthodoxy on the country. It would almost certainly involve competition to exploit resources and dominate trade. But policies toward Afghanistan also promised to be forward-looking, envisioning opportunities for Afghanistan to serve as the linchpin for a more prosperous, ultimately more secure region.

Central Asia

In many respects, Afghanistan has become primarily a means to a further end—to realize the opportunities believed by Pakistan and others to exist in Muslim Central Asia. Mujahidin groups, always ready to take the credit for having humbled the Soviet military and begun the unraveling of a superpower, had never denied their efforts to influence Muslims in the former Soviet Union and China. At least some of these plans were laid in Pakistan, often with the approval and support of the ISI. Guided by generals Akhtar Rahman and Hamid Gul, the ISI had envisioned using the mujahidin as a catalyst for Islamic movements in the Soviet Union. The significance of the Afghan resistance for the revival of Islamic consciousness in those republics, while they were still part of the Soviet state, is nevertheless uncertain. In all probability, through most of the 1980s at least, the Iranian Revolution carried a more powerful message than anything spread by the Afghan mujahidin or as fallout from the war. While the Soviet Union remained intact, Moscow was highly sensitive about direct cross-border links between their Muslim republics and groups in Afghanistan and Pakistan. However, the advent of the Sharif government in 1990 eased Soviet worries: it no longer became official, if unstated policy, to support Islamic groups operating against established regimes in Central Asia.

The formation of newly independent states has effectively redefined the entire region in the eyes of both policy makers in Islamabad and among the broad public in Pakistan. The reality of the six Islamic republics is seen as virgin territory, not only for its commercial possibilities, but psychologically as well, opening up the possibility of Pakistan's overcoming or leaving behind many of its familiar problems in South Asia. Viewed geo-strategically, in place of the proverbial two-front threat involving India stands the possibility of a bloc of Islamic countries and the enhanced sense of security it presumably brings. Not only would it appear as a counterweight to the perceived aggressive intent of India, but the cordial and cooperation relations of Islamic states in the region suggested the long-sought-after external pressures for Kashmir's self-determination.[12] The political stalemate over Kashmir, together with the nuclear stand-off and the stagnation of hopes for economic cooperation through SAARC, also contributed to psychological desire to "break out" of South Asia.

Not surprisingly, Pakistan became the first country to establish diplomatic ties with all five Muslim republics of Central Asia and Azerbaijan, and joined in sponsoring them for membership in the ECO. It is this potential market of 300 million people—second only to the European community—across ten Islamic countries that is conceived by many officials in Pakistan and the other states as capable of turning the region into a major economic power. Cooperation is envisioned in various fields such as communications, energy, banking, and human resources, as well as trade.

Pakistan holds considerable potential as a key to economic activity in the region. The port of Karachi, as the closest in terms of mileage for the four eastern new republics, is probably the most desirable sea outlet for expanded trade routes. The leadership in Uzbekistan has expressed its desire for linking Tashkent to Karachi as a means of avoiding a dependence on commerce through Russia. Pakistan signed bilateral cooperation agreements with Uzbekistan and established an air link during 1992. The idea of a new trade link between Pakistan and Tajikistan through the Han corridor of Afghanistan has come under discussion between the two countries. An alternative or supplementary land route for Pakistan to Central Asia's Kyrgyzstan and Kazakhstan is possible through China's Sinkiang province. Some see prospects of Pakistan's exports expanding up to $2 billion in value.[13] Still, for the foreseeable future, any goods moving between the new republics and Pakistan will come through Kabul and north through the Soviet-built Salang tunnel crossing the Hindu Kush mountains.

For Pakistan to become a significant link in international trade with Central Asia and beyond, major infrastructural improvements are required. Communications and transport facilities are already congested. A railway can be envisioned connecting the new Muslim republics though Afghanistan with a southwest Pakistani port on the Indian ocean to supplement Karachi. Peshawar could be revived as a hub of trade, especially if the road links from Afghanistan to the city's rail head were improved or the rail line extended west and north. With the necessary investment, there are opportunities for the import of electricity from Tajikistan. In return, Pakistan has many people with entrepreneurial skills, especially in banking and management, and the capital needed for stimulating private economies in the republics. Pakistan can assist in joint ventures involving mineral development, gas pipelines, telecommunications, and agriculture, among other areas. Under-utilized textile mills in Pakistan are offered up as ready to receive the cotton production of Uzbekistan and other republics. And should entrepreneurs from the republics want to invest in Pakistan, newer liberal economic polices are more attractive to foreign investors.

The possibilities for Pakistan commercially in the republics of the former Soviet Union are, nonetheless, uncertain and likely overstated. Pakistan has limited ability to supply credits or hard currency to the republics which, in the short run at least, are more likely to be in need of food and other forms of assistance that hold out promise of a balanced trade. Pakistan has little acquaintance with these Islamic republics, and very few Pakistanis speak the local languages or Russian. This was particularly evident as the bureaucracy tried to gear up for a coordinated policy toward the new states. Moreover, aside from Sunni Islam, there is little that binds Pakistan culturally to its potential northern partners.[14]

Pakistan's influence in a postwar Central Asia would appear to be challenged by neighboring states with stronger ethnic and linguistic commonalities to the new republics. Certainly Turkey's economic attractions for the other states cannot be matched. Turkey is in a position to invest in local industries in the republics and it offers them a port on the Black Sea, albeit an expensive and distant alternative. Despite historical and cultural links that are more remote in time than is usually acknowledged, Turkey has obvious language advantages. It also has appeal for advocating a more secular or at least nonradical brand of Islam. Turkey's impressive record of economic growth, together with its resilient democracy and Western military ties, has attracted the leaders of the new Islamic states. Still, some believe that Turkey's influence in

Central Asia had peaked by mid-1992, as its various contacts and exchanges fell below expectations. The region's economic problems were beyond the ability of Turkey to do much with its aid and trade credits. Moreover, there were no Central Asian Ataturks to implement the Turkish model.[15] Turkey was itself bogged down with Azerbaijan and that republic's territorial dispute with Armenia. In Ankara's attempts to assert its influence in Azerbaijan, it courted difficulties with an Iranian policy that recognized competitive ethnic ties to the new Muslim state.

Iran is a formidable player in economic terms. It offers a gateway to a port on the Persian Gulf and has promised to build the necessary rail extensions. A rail link between Ashkhabad in Turkmenistan and the northern Iranian city of Meshad, offering a route to the Gulf, is scheduled for completion in 1995. Natural gas production from Turkmenistan could also find an outlet to European markets if construction of a pipeline to Iran's port of Abadan—replacing one through Russia—is realized. The Iranians can trade much-needed oil to the new republics and pay, if they choose, in dollars for their imports.

The government of Hashami Rafsanjani has pushed hard to raise religious and cultural consciousness across the region, and has succeeded in making its strongest penetration in Tajikistan among that republic's largely Persian-speaking population. It is noteworthy that Iran's leaders, while recognizing Tajikistan in particular as a target of opportunity, have thus far refrained from direct political interference in any of the new republics, preferring to work with established governments. Still, for all of the Tehran government's cautious policy in the region, it operates under some handicap. Fears of Islamic fundamentalism, specifically Iran's brand of theocracy and repression, are strong among the ruling elites of the new republics. The republics' leaders have actively sought economic cooperation with Islamic countries to the south. But led most mainly by former communist, now nationalists, these leaders have tried to slow the import of cultural and religious influences and have directly opposed outside—aside from Russian—political and military activities.

Other would-be players in Central Asia include Saudi Arabia and India. Saudi delegations have visited the republics regularly since 1990 and have spent a reported $1 billion, mainly for the revival of Islamic institutions and the rebuilding of mosques.[16] In seeking to export Wahabism, Saudi Arabia is poised to counter Iranian influence much as in Afghanistan. India's commercial interests have considerably more experience in the markets of Uzbekistan, Turkmenistan, and Tajikistan, most of it, to be sure, when these were captive markets in economic arrangements with the Soviet Union. In any case, India offers more developed consumer industries and moderately priced, if not always high quality, consumer goods. Moreover, a large number of Indians, having been educated in Tashkent, speak Uzbek. What India lacks most of all is the ground or sea access to the new states which could, conceivably, become a powerful motive for improving relations with Pakistan. Yet chances for either Pakistan or India to develop trade and technical cooperation with the new republics—in their search for partners to assist them in attaining effective economic independence and modernization—cannot proceed very far without a lasting political settlement in Afghanistan.

In general, Central Asian leaders show little enthusiasm for closer links with Afghanistan's ethnically-alike northern areas, much less political amalgamation. Uzbek and Tajik factional commanders in Afghanistan may in the event of the further fragmentation of their country or a chronically weak central authority in Kabul turn to these new states in hope of trade and security.[17] Regimes in Central Asia could in time look at the fertile lands and untapped mineral resources of northern Afghanistan with more covetous eyes. But, for the time being, their southern neighbor, backward and poor as it is, promises more burden than boon for the new republics.

The potential spill over of Afghanistan politics is worrisome. Islamic forces in Afghanistan have been explicitly warned by anxious leaders not to try to trigger unrest.[18] Beginning in September 1992, the heavy fighting that erupted in Tajikistan between several regionally based clans, more often described as between former communist officials and their Islamic and democratic adversaries, followed the infiltration of Afghan arms and mujahidin fighters from the radical Muslim parties. By early in 1993, as many as 60,000 Tajik refugees had fled across the Amu Darya River to Afghanistan, requiring $2.76 million in U.N.-provided food aid.[19]

If Pakistan cannot expect to compete successfully for influence in Central Asia on economic and cultural grounds, it holds some political advantages. While Pakistan's domestic political instability and poverty no doubt distract from its appeal as a model, the country is not easily open to the accusation that it is trying to convert anyone or market an ideology. Unlike Iran and Turkey, Pakistan has no obvious stake and no ethnic ties that could complicate or compromise its role as a possible mediator, should the states of Central Asia be looking for one. As a relatively moderate Muslim country, Pakistan can be seen as offering a safe option to the rivalries that seem to pit Turkey, Iran, and Saudi Arabia against one another. Indeed, as Afghan-Russian tensions increased over Tajikistan in August 1993, Islamabad offered itself as a honest broker.

Their interests in Central Asia should draw Pakistan, Iran, and Saudi Arabia alike toward good relations with Russia. It had become increasingly clear that with the chaotic conditions in Afghanistan showing little sign of slowing, Pakistan would remain largely cut off. Turkey's involvement in the turmoil in the Caucasus similarly stood as a barrier. Even if Iran had no similar problem of proximity, the three states have come to realize that, whatever the attraction of other Muslim states, the Central Asian republics will necessarily remain dependent on Moscow for some time. Aside from military support for the regimes, Uzbekistan and Tajikistan are dependent on Russia for oil through a pipeline that has long supplied them. The same republics have few better markets for their cotton than Russia's textile industry.

Fear of radical political Islam and its spread into the Russian Federation aside, Moscow's regional interests in the Muslim republics have thus remained strong. In the event that the Central Asian states might be tempted to opt instead for stronger ties to the Muslim ECO, Moscow did not hesitate to threaten that closer ties with Pakistan, Iran, Afghanistan and Turkey might forfeit favorable treatment from Russia in the sale of their products.[20] Although the Central Asian states were unlikely to be so easily intimidated in being asked to choose, Pakistan, Iran, and Saudi Arabia had to conclude that their plans for Central Asia have little chance of being realized if Moscow imposes strong objections.

The International Community

The conclusion to the 14-year Afghan war is likely to have a strong bearing on Pakistan's future relations with those countries outside the region that served as its allies and enemies during the conflict. A Pakistan no longer party to what was, at least in part, a proxy war, has already witnessed the opening of old scars and creation of new strains with the United States. Military and economic assistance to Pakistan acquired less urgency or rationale with the Soviet withdrawal. Even the sense of obligation to give generously toward Afghan reconstruction had weakened in subsequent years in the belief in many quarters in Washington that the Afghan resistance and perhaps Pakistani authorities had become obstacles to a negotiated settlement.

During this time the United States sought ways to extricate itself from the responsibilities of aiding the Afghan resistance and Pakistan without appearing to desert these recipients. The United States preferred a moderate, independent state to emerge and civil war to be averted, but felt little more than a lingering sense of obligation to assist, to the extent that it could, in a postwar rehabilitation, and then most probably through multilateral agencies. By 1993, U.S. aid funding for the Afghans had dropped to $20 million, a 60 percent decline from the preceding year, and a small fraction of the $3.3 billion believed spent by the United States during the course of the war.

It was difficult for many Pakistanis and Afghans to believe that either Washington or Moscow, having invested so heavily, could simply walk away from the war in its final stages. Convinced that much in the protracted conflict was at the behest of the superpowers, skeptical observers could not imagine that the same countries were not in the weeks before Kabul's fall still pulling strings, albeit more quietly, and that they would stay involved. Ironically, some who in the past criticized outside intervention now welcomed a more active role for Washington and even Moscow. Their hope became that the former patrons would exercise something like their previous influence in helping—possibly through the United Nations—the Afghans to resolve their differences and specifically to assure that most radical Islamists were prevented from coming to power.

In the sense that it existed in the 1980s, the United States no longer required Pakistan as an ally. It has become sufficient in Washington that Pakistan be reasonably independent and economically viable. What remains of a deeper U.S. interest in Pakistan is Washington's preference that there be regional stability, expected to be contingent on the survival of democratic governments in the subcontinent and on Pakistan's (and India's) refraining from embarking on a full-scale nuclear weapons development program. Yet the United States is unprepared to invest very much to bring this about.

Even were stability in the region threatened, it is highly doubtful that the United States would follow a course resembling what it did in the Persian Gulf in 1990–1991. Intervention in a conflict in the subcontinent has never been seriously envisioned, notwithstanding Washington's concern about the potential danger of a new Indo-Pakistan war. In any case, the economic costs and political debts incurred in taking up the leadership of an international coalition in the Gulf, where Washington recognized greater stakes and felt it could decisively make a difference, has only increased the United States' reluctance to become involved elsewhere anytime soon.

It matters little in Washington which faction or factions come to power in Kabul so long as their infighting does not carry over into Central Asia and draw large Russian involvement. The concern is less what happens among Russia's Muslim neighbors, than what are the implications of large-scale fighting on the integrity of the Russian Federation and on possible political fallout in Moscow. Even the desire to quash the drug trade from Afghanistan, the number two global source of heroin, has not assured Washington's continued attention, much less a commitment to stay politically engaged in the region. Although a hostile regime in Afghanistan might be uncooperative with the United States in trying to stop the spread of opium and heroin, few expect dramatic successes in halting drug production in any case. Washington might find that while an Islamic state has in fact less tolerance for narcotics use, a weak Afghan government will be unable to affect the cultivation of crops. In any case, even with some reduction in poppy growing, other producers in the area, in Central Asia as well as Pakistan, could quickly take up the slack.

The estrangement between Washington and Islamabad occurred over a matter of years and involved disillusionment on both sides. The ousting of the Benazir Bhutto government in 1990 once again exposed the shallow roots of democracy in Pakistan. Many in the U.S. Congress who admired Ms. Bhutto were initially inclined to punish Pakistan for its unceremonial dumping of the first woman prime minister of an Islamic state by a president whose office carried no popular mandate. The subsequent resounding defeat of her party in an arguably fair election only partly alleviated the disappointment and desire to press Pakistan harder. While applauding her successor's market-oriented economic policies and the military's constraint in face of the usual partisan fratricide, the United States showed little interest in the possible connection between its halt in assistance to Pakistan and the difficulty in stabilizing democratic rule under Prime Minister Sharif.

When Sharif was himself subject to removal by the same president, Ghulam Ishaq Khan, the subsequent reversal of the decision by Pakistan's Supreme Court, and the August 1993 resignation of both officials under pressure from army chief General Abdul Waheed, the United States saw its misgivings about Pakistan's ability to sustain democracy confirmed once more. But instead of the military declaring marshal law, a civilian interim government was installed leading up to new elections in October. The well-supervised elections brought the return to office of Benazir Bhutto, heading a coalition government, followed in November 1993 by the selection in the national and provincial assembies of her party's nominee for president. Indeed, in light of the visible struggle and stalemate in Pakistan between the feudals and bureaucrats on one side, and the industrialists and middle class on the other, the army had become, ironically, the guarantor of democracy— if one were in fact sustainable.[21]

U.S. policies toward nuclear nonproliferation have for a long time been viewed in Pakistan as discriminatory. The Pakistanis are especially upset by what they perceive to be a double standard: that the Pressler Amendment that mandates a cut-off of aid because the country's nuclear program is deemed to have a military orientation is not a criterion similarly applied to India. It is universally recognized that the nuclear issue would not have been raised—the U.S. President would have continued to provide the necessary statutory assurances for the aid program—were the Soviets still ensconced in Afghanistan. In October 1990, financial assistance for the following fiscal year—already reduced to $237 million including $90 million in direct military aid—was suspended.

By halting its economic and military assistance to Pakistan, the United States had also forfeited most of what leverage it had over policy makers in Islamabad, not only on drug issues but also over nuclearization and human rights. Without the Afghan war to cement the relationship with the United States, new doubts arose among Pakistan's leaders over the country's security, a development likely to promote or at least not slow acceleration of the country's nuclear program. Although Pakistan's political and military leaders put a brave face on the impact of the suspension of U.S. aid on Pakistan's defense capability, citing their own defense industries, they soon felt obliged to shop around for credits to buy a substitute for U.S.-supplied F-16As.

The halt in assistance strengthened suspicions in Islamabad that the United States harbors a deep inclination to support India, and that once Pakistan had lost its importance to Washington in the containment of the Soviet Union, U.S. ties with New Delhi would improve, dropping Islamabad in the process. Prodded by the alleged pro-India lobby in Congress, the United States was believed ready to go beyond a mere tilt toward India to countenance India's assuming hegemonic power in South Asia. At best, Pakistan critics of U.S. policy interpreted Washington's cessation of its aid program as pressure, if not blackmail, aimed at getting Pakistan, first, to toe the line on the Afghanistan issue and then, more importantly, on Islamabad's nuclear program.

Unmistakably, by the beginning of the 1990s, wide public resentment had developed in Pakistan against the United States, not only in the usual intellectual, mostly leftist circles, but now in the bureaucracy and military, and increasingly in popular opinion. The curtailing of economic assistance strengthened the perception that Washington was trying to dictate a foreign and nuclear policy to the Pakistan government. The coalition of parties aligned against Ms. Bhutto's People's Party inflamed feelings further in stressing her close—to some even treasonable—links with the United States (and India) as part of their propaganda to keep the former prime minister from returning to office. Resentment also increased as the United States has been perceived as seeking to discourage Pakistan from playing a direct role in Afghanistan's political future. These sentiments had coincided with increased anti-American sentiments among Afghan resistance factions following the U.S.-Soviet (then Russian) deal to cut off their arms shipments to the warring sides.

Like the Afghans, many Pakistanis, while often grudgingly acknowledging that covert U.S. policies were indispensable to defeating the Soviets, nonetheless stress that policies after the withdrawal of the Red Army is evidence of how little Washington really cared about the Afghan cause or the security of Pakistan. Although the Islamabad government had lost its major patron and much of its development budget, the case was made that Pakistan might be better off without so heavy a dependence on the United States.

Still, the Sharif government during its tenure sought to avoid allowing differences with the United States from growing too wide, lest Washington be pushed closer to New Delhi. By looking for compromises on differences with the United States on the nuclear issue and, in particular pushing the concept of regional denuclearization, which the Indians rejected, the government in Islamabad found opportunities to defuse the more threatening aspects of the relationship with Washington. Signs of Islamabad's reasonableness included its formal acceptance of the five-point U.N. plan for ending the Afghan war and its willingness early in 1992, despite powerful domestic opposition, to join in withholding arms for the mujahidin. These policies won Pakistan a brief reprieve in the U.S. aid cut-off, with permission to buy spare parts for its planes.

The prospect of more normalized ties between Pakistan and the Russian Federation are strong. With the once profitable economic and political entente with India largely in the past, Russia will try to expand bilateral cooperation with Pakistan and explore new areas for agreements.[22] In October 1992, Russia agreed to give Pakistan a $95 million credit for expansion of the Soviet-constructed steel mill in Karachi. Earlier Moscow had hinted that the Soviet Union might help Pakistan with a nuclear power station. However, it is doubtful that Russia or any of the new states that have emerged will be in a position to offer substantial development assistance any time soon. More conceivable are military sales to Pakistan by a Russian government anxious to market its virtually only exportable items to a country in search of new, less expensive military hardware.

Uppermost in the mind of Russian policy makers—when they can divert their attention from domestic economic matters—have been events in Tajikistan and their threat not only to regimes within the tenuous Commonwealth of Independent States (CIS) but to the Russian Federation proper. Moscow is most concerned that Pakistan be in agreement that peace in Afghanistan and Central Asia is essential for security across the region. In particular, Moscow seeks Pakistan's cooperation in containing within Afghanistan's boundaries the post-Najibullah civil war. In September 1992, Russia augmented its troops stationed in Tajikistan to help police the border and offer protection to

the Russian ethnic population. By mid-1973, more than 3,500 were trying
to stem the flow of arms and men, and aircraft had been thrown into the
conflict, striking at targets on both sides of the border with Afghanistan.
Soviet aircraft launched raids on targets inside Afghanistan in a manner
reminiscent of the concluded Afghan war.

More broadly, Moscow hopes to work with other powers, including
Pakistan, Iran, and the United States, to halt the flow of weapons to the
combatants in Afghanistan that might end up in Central Asia. The
Russians accused Kabul of aiding the Muslim dissidents by harboring
armed Tajik rebels. Mainly, Moscow had in mind the provision of
weapons and military training to anti-government elements by the forces
of Masoud and Hekmatyar, one motivated by ethnic bonds, the other by
ideological reasons.[23] Aside from trying to export a militant Islam,
Hekmatyar is suspected of trying to stir up hatred between Tajiks and a
large Uzbek minority in Tajikistan, with the hope that the antagonisms
created may also serve to split the ethnic coalition opposing him inside
Afghanistan.

The Islamabad government has tried to allay suspicions in Moscow
that Pakistan is itself involved. Anxious to keep alive its possible links
with the Central Asia republics, the Islamabad government publicly
disavowed many of the once backed jihad-minded mujahidin who had
taken the fight to Tajikistan. In August 1993, Islamabad forced a leading
Tajik dissident leader who had been seeking and receiving support from
Jama'at-i-Islami to leave the country. Pakistani authorities also worked to
convince the shaky Kabul government that it should distance itself from
the rebellion and join in the call for a political solution. Although
Pakistan flinched at the heavy-handed Russian military actions on the
Tajik-Afghan border, it plainly had no intention of sacrificing its dreams
in Central Asia for the adventures of radical Islamists.

Pakistan's relations with China in the wake of the Afghanistan war
will be modified even while they may remain mutually beneficial. Russo-
Chinese relations can be expected to affect those between Beijing and
Islamabad. But ties between the two countries run deeply, and so long as
both Pakistan and China continue to view India suspiciously, they have
reason to collaborate. Indeed, their motives could increasingly converge
as India showed signs with the Soviet Union's breakup of moving
aggressively to establish its own economic and political ties in Central
Asia.[24] The Chinese-built Karakorum highway in northern Pakistan
offers China its own, alternative land route to the new Muslim republics,
as well as to South and West Asia. The Beijing government promises to
help Pakistan unconditionally in developing a nuclear energy industry
and is believed to have been involved earlier in aiding Pakistan to design
a nuclear weapon. It had also offered to assist Pakistan in building a

modern jet trainer aircraft. If the Chinese leadership provides less in the way of military aid in the future, it will only be as a result of increased international pressures, especially from the United States, against proliferation and sale of ballistic missiles. Most worrisome for the Chinese are the possible effects of ascendant Islamic forces in Afghanistan, and conceivably Pakistan, on China's own minority Muslims. A breakup of Afghanistan could, according to the view in Beijing, strengthen backing by mujahidin leaders, most notably Hekmatyar, for a well-established underground separatist Islamic movement in Sinkiang, China's westernmost province bordering Central Asia.[25]

In the end, it may be impossible to avert periodic civil war in Afghanistan without a persisting international role, even a peacekeeping force. The probability is, of course, that U.N. resources required for such undertakings, currently so severely taxed globally, will be unavailable—even if the international organization is disposed to act. Conceivably a few peacemaking cards are available to Iran, Saudi Arabia, the United States, and Russia, most effectively if they are prepared to act in concert, using the positive and negative incentives available in funding reconstruction and food relief. Of course, Pakistan is best positioned to intervene militarily in Afghanistan in order to force the sides to halt bloody conflict and the slide to disintegration, much like the Syrian intervention in Lebanon. But as in that case, Pakistan's actions would be read by many Afghans as self-serving, even if it succeeded in bringing a greater measure of peace. For that matter, few Pakistanis would relish an interventionary military role in Afghan political affairs that could enmesh their country in what is perceived as the insoluable Afghan quagmire.

Conclusion

For Pakistan, neither its worst worries nor highest hopes came to pass in the Afghan war. The two-front threat with India and a communist Afghanistan never materialized, but neither did the federation with a pro-Pakistani Kabul regime and its promise of protection inside a larger Islamic bloc. With the conclusion of at least the broad international phase of the Afghan war, it is unlikely that the balance of forces in the region or inside Pakistan will be altered any time soon. Even so, the end of at least this phase of the war carries advantages and disadvantages for Pakistan. Its leaders will be obliged to make some strategic adjustments and more clearly define Pakistan's national priorities.

The immediate impact of a conclusion to the Afghan war on Pakistan's domestic problems would seem to bear on the outcome in Kashmir. The cause of Kashmiri self-determination, as already noted, has drawn inspiration and material assistance from the Afghan conflict and the victory achieved after long perseverance. The possibility that many Afghan mujahidin and Muslim volunteers might transfer their arms and zeal to the Kashmir conflict and further militarize it has long been considered possible. The cessation of Pakistan's assistance to the Afghan resistance forces was not expected to have major, independent effect on the Kashmir rebellion, which had progressed far enough to contain its own dynamic. Ascendance of a hard-line Islamist government in Kabul would likely increase support for Kashmiri separatists. This shift in forces appears blunted, however, by the unresolved power struggle inside Afghanistan and by obstacles interposed by the Islamabad government to creation of a new war front. In any case, the initiative in the rekindled controversy lies foremost with the Muslims of Indian Kashmir.

Similarly, the end of a threat from across the northwestern frontier will not in itself alter Pakistan's nuclear development program. The policy was never intended to help Pakistan face a communist onslaught and has always been India-oriented. It is driven most of all by feelings, both elite and popular, for the need for parity in status with India—even more than by a belief in the deterrence value of nuclear weapons. However, indirectly, with the loss of generous U.S. financial patronage, Pakistan has experienced a revived sense of isolation, strengthening arguments for a nuclear program. The case is made that Pakistan's greater difficulty in modernizing its military without U.S. help assures it a conventional weapons disadvantage that can only be offset by a nuclear option.

Expectations that a conclusion of the war might improve the law-and-order situation inside Pakistan will probably be disappointed. The virulent Klashnikov and drug cultures have already made deep inroads in the society and cannot be removed any time soon. In fact, the stoppage of foreign military assistance and declining humanitarian aid to the Afghans may make drug income more attractive. A proliferation of drug laboratories, both in Pakistan and Afghanistan, is bound to add to the lawlessness in the border areas. Although with the denouement of the Afghan conflict there occurred a more determined effort to deal with banditry in Sindh, the military could only temporarily restore domestic order. The political disarray inside Afghanistan also posed a new security threat: the danger of former mujahidin commanders and their fighters plundering inside Pakistan. In one incident, a fugitive Afghan resistance commander, in possession of Stinger missiles and other heavy weaponry engaged under-armed Pakistani militiamen on the border.[26] Economic depravations inside Afghanistan were also the occasion for increased smuggling of foodstuffs and other goods from Pakistan, not only raising the volume of illegal business but also the price of edible commodities inside Pakistan.

The country's strongly religious parties, which had moved closer to the Islamabad government over their common championing of the Afghan war—some would say holding governments hostage—lost influence with the Sharif government with the war's winding down. In its origins, the IJI leadership in Islamabad, heir to Pakistan's founding Muslim Movement, had little in common with philosophy of Jama'at-i-Islami. Under a democratically elected government, the promotion of religion and accompanying codling of religious parties was no longer perceived as a necessary source of regime legitimacy, as it had been under President Zia.

The Jama'at-i-Islami's support for Hekmatyar had become critical inside Afghanistan, where Sunni fighters aligned with Hezb-i-Islami and Sayyaf's Ittehad-i-Islami were kept well supplied with weapons (paid for by the Saudis) and employed Arab advisors in their efforts to defeat the militias backing the Rabbani-headed government.[27] Prime Minister Sharif severely criticized Jama'at and its leader, Qazi Hussain Ahmad, for blocking the truck deliveries of food to Kabul and contributing to the factional differences among the Afghans. In late April 1992, Pakistani civilian militants associated with Jama'at-i-Islami were reportedly killed after crossing the border to fight alongside Hekmatyar's Hezb-i-Islami.[28]

The Jama'at broke with the Sharif government in early May 1992 over an official Afghan policy that offered backing to those opposed to Hekmatyar's forces, as well as over claims that Pakistan's prime minister had failed to give sufficient urgency and attention to implementing Islamic laws inside the country. While the defection from the government of Pakistan's Jama'at-i-Islami, with only a handful of the parliamentary seats, did not threaten the government majority in the 217-member National Assembly, the Islamic party was capable of making trouble in the streets and maintained a considerable following in some rural areas of the Punjab and the NWFP. Had the war against the Afghan communists continued indefinitely or had Pakistan tried to force refugees to return too early, several mujahidin groups, in alliance with Pakistan's Jama'at-i-Islami, might have defensively tried to enter the national political arena. In the short run, however, the turn of events allowed for the marginalization by the Islamabad government of the more radical Islamists in Pakistan. But if in the long run a militantly Islamist regime prevails in Kabul, some Pakistanis worry that an Afghan government could help destabilize the political situation in Pakistan by training and arming renegade political elements aimed against a Pakistani leadership deemed not sufficiently Islamic.

Where once some in Pakistan, particularly in the military, may have hoped to profit from Afghanistan's internal disunity, the dominant circles in Islamabad became concerned that Afghanistan is likely to fragment under continued civil strife and concluded that Pakistan must assist in state-building. An independent and nonaligned Afghanistan increasingly came to be seen as consistent with Pakistan's unburdening itself of the social, economic, and political consequences of the conflict. For a Pakistan able to maintain its own territorial integrity and improve its economic well-being, restoration of a pacified, stable Afghanistan appears indispensable. A moderate government is seen by most as the key to this stability. With this in mind, Islamabad repeatedly expressed its confidence in the interim Kabul leadership and provided active assistance.[29]

Islamabad has, all the same, also hedged its bets. Should the mujahidin factions controlling the capital prove incapable, Pakistan's leadership could still fall in behind Hekmatyar in his political ambitions if that is the alternative to virtual anarchy. Importantly, the intimate links between elements in Pakistan's military and intelligence service and the more extreme fundamentalist Afghan parties have still to be entirely uncoupled.[30] The first delegation of Pakistani officials to visit Afghanistan to discuss the country's reconstruction with the new government in Kabul was headed by Lt. General Javed Nasir, then the chief of the ISI.

To be sure, by 1993 many ISI middle-level personnel with close ties Hezb-i-Islami had been removed. The ability of elements in the military to act autonomously as they did throughout the war was curtailed for the time being. Yet given the structure of Pakistani military intelligence operations and the personal ambitions of many officers, depending on the character of the government in Islamabad, the ISI could again stand beyond the full control of civilian officials.

In the period since Kabul's liberation, Pakistan has repeatedly offered its good offices to bring about conciliation among the warring Afghan factions. As in the Islamabad agreement, it has seen a broad-based government—one including not only all the mujahidin factions but defeated Afghan elements—as best suited to bring about a solution. At a critical juncture, when two months following the collapse of the communist regime Hezb-i-Islami fighters and their allies were close to defeat at the hands of Kabul government forces, Pakistan intervened in the name of preserving all the major factions.[31] Not anxious to alienate any of the potential major figures, the Islamabad government was also willing to cultivate General Dostam, arranging for him to visit Pakistan several times and travel to Saudi Arabia. The inclusive approach to finding a satisfactory outcome is even more apparent in the willingness of Pakistan to welcome in Peshawar as refugees three former defense ministers in communist regime, along with many others who had served the former Kabul government.

The changed nature of the Afghanistan conflict and needed reassessment in Islamabad of the country's national interests raises the larger issue of what in fact are the actual threats to security in contemporary Pakistan. The possibility of the country being overrun or humiliated by India remains uppermost in the minds of many in leadership positions and the general public. Others contend that foreign intelligence operatives as well as internationally connected arms and drug dealers, having been strengthened by the Afghan war, seriously undermine Pakistan's security and stability. Most definitions of Pakistan's security dwell on the protection of the state—its sovereignty and integrity. In reality, these may be far less in jeopardy than the dangers posed to Pakistan's society that arise from its ethnic antagonisms, rampant population growth, and explosive poverty.

The dangers to Pakistan are, then, far more likely to come from lost battles within rather than from external enemies. They result, for example, from the pitiful public investment in health delivery and educational systems, poor even by Third World standards. Pakistan ranks among those countries lagging most in human development and is grouped with the few that spend at least twice as much on their military as on health and education combined.[32] It places 112 out of 125 countries ranked in terms of literacy and devotes only 1 percent of its GNP to health, leaving 55 percent of the population without access to health care.[33] As well as protections afforded by state action, full realization of civil liberties and human rights, and the security these provide individuals and groups, may require government authority willing to accept restraints on itself.

The issues posed by Afghanistan and Kashmir, a nuclear program, and alleged challenges to Islam often seem to be used to distract the public from what in fact threatens their social welfare and rights in civil society. Indeed, it frequently seems as though the policy-making elites, whether lacking in commitment or bereft of ideas, have conspired to give the Pakistani people exaggerated issues of state security because the leaders are unable or unwilling to address the country's endemic problems. Instead, a potentially alienated public is given state parades and cricket matches, and other pride-building side shows to distract or entertain them. Still more, the country's heavy defense expenditures, justified in the name of national security, draw off scarce resources and further reduce the capacity of decision makers to deal with the society's well-being. Peace and reconstruction in Afghanistan will help, but it will take far more for Pakistan's leaders to face up to the real sources of national insecurity.

Notes

1. The ISI was still believed to have exerted some influence over the negotiations, and was probably not unhappy to have representatives of Pakistan's Foreign Office excluded. *AFGHANews*, Vol. 9, nos. 10 and 11 (June 1, 1993) as reprinted in *Afghan Forum*, Vol. 21, no. 4 (July 1993): 6–7.
2. Late in 1991 Saudi King Fahd pledged a multi-million dollar fund for reconstruction of Afghanistan's schools, hospitals, roads, and power plants and called on other Muslim countries to contribute to a fund. A $7.5 million grant intended for education was designated for religious schools in Pakistan and Afghanistan that had been threatened with closing for financial reasons. *AFGHANews*, November 15, 1991, reprinted in *Afghan Forum*, Vol. 20, no. 1 (January 1992): 16.
3. Indian intelligence sources charge that about 400 foreigners, 200 of them Afghans, have fought alongside the Muslim separatists. *The New York Times*, August 25, 1993. Indian officials also claim to have killed a former bodyguard to the Hezb-i-Islami leader and explosives expert in an armed clash between Muslim militants and security forces. *The News* (Islamabad), August 8, 1993. Hekmatyar denied any connection with the individual. Ibid., August 10, 1993. A religious leader with the Afghan Jamiat-i-Islami once boasted that his party had sent 35,000 Afghan fighters to fight the jihad in Kashmir over the course of the rebellion. *Newsline* (Karachi), February 1993, p. 86.
4. That India might not have to wait too long, at least if more moderate elements were in power, was suggested by the first interim Afghan president, Professor Mujaddedi, who in an interview with All India Radio on May 18, 1992, indicated that the new government "wants to strengthen its age-old relations with India." Foreign Broadcast Information Service (FBIS), Near East and South Asia, *Daily Report*, May 19, 1992, p. 41.
5. Salamat Ali and Ahmed Rashid, *Far Eastern Economic Review*, September 24, 1992, pp. 18 and 20.
6. Mark Fineman, *Los Angeles Times*, April 7, 1992. There is much disagreement over the actual number of Arabs still remaining. See *The Herald* (March 1993), p. 55.
7. *Pakistan Affairs*, Embassy of Pakistan, Washington, D.C., Vol. 44, no. 2 (1990): 1; and FBIS-NES, October 15, 1990, p. 68.
8. FIBIS-NES, September 24, p. 48.
9. *Pakistan Times*, February 12, 1991. Also, *The New York Times*, February 17, 1991, p. E 2.

10. *Asiaweek,* October 5, 1990, p. 11. *Friday Times,* March 19–25, 1992, p. 3, quotes sources that say that more than 10,000 Kashmiris were trained and that they suffered disproportionately high casualties in battle.

11. Ali and Rashid, *Far Eastern Economic Review,* pp. 18 and 20.

12. "Impact of Central Asian Developments on South and West Asia," *Spotlight on Regional Affairs,* report of the Institute of Regional Studies (Islamabad), Vol. 11, no. 4: 41.

13. Ibid., p. 40.

14. Although many Pakistani businessmen had made their way to Tashkent—thanks to direct flights by the Pakistani national carrier—in the months after Najibullah's departure, they (and "tourists" from Pakistan) not only disappointed the Uzbeks with what they had to offer commercially but soon lost their welcome with reportedly loose moral behavior.

15. *The Economist,* December 26, 1992, pp. 42–44..

16. *Spotlight,* p. 36.

17. Charles Hoots, *Middle East International,* no. 430, (July 24, 1992), in *Afghanistan Forum,* Vol. 20, no. 6 (November 1992): 10.

18. FBIS-NES May 21, 1992, AFP from Hong Kong, May 20, 1992. Quoting Uzbekistan's president Islam Karimov. In response some months later, Hekmatyar warned the leadership in both Uzbekistan and Tajikistan to stop interfering in Afghan affairs, claiming that he had evidence of assistance to the ethnically related "unholy coalition of the north." Ibid., October 14, 1992, p. 45, from (clandestine) Radio Message of Freedom, October 13, 1992.

19. *Pakistan Times* (Islamabad) February 6, 1993. One report estimates that during just three weeks in July 1992, Afghan smugglers had supplied local militias in Tajikistan—at cut-rate prices and possibly free of charge—5,000 AK-47 assault rifles, scores of grenade launchers, many anti-tank rifles, hand grenades and other weapons. Boris Rumer and Eugene Rumer, "Who'll Stop the Next Yugoslavia," *World Monitor* (November 1992) in *Afghanistan Forum,* Vol. 21, no. 1 (January 1993): 21.

20. *The News,* August 10, 1993.

21. Pakistan's slowed economic growth in the wake of the U.S. cut-off, the changed opportunities in the Gulf, and the country's intensifying sectarian and ethnic violence were thought by many to have weakened democratic institutions. High unemployment, together with a bitter competition for scarce resources by political and social groups, may have brought particular damage to the system. So too has the corruption laid to Pakistan's political leaders, together with their often shameless political maneuvering and unprincipled alliances. It remains to be seen whether Ms. Bhutto's second government, not having to contend with a hostile president or opposition-controlled provincial assemblies, will be better able secure a democratic system—by being the first elected prime minister to serve out a full term of office.

22. Trade between the pre-breakup Soviet state and Pakistan had been running at roughly $100 million yearly during the 1980s. FBIS-NES, November 16, 1987, p. 69, from Islamabad Domestic Service, November, 12, 1987.

23. Russian sources insist that Hekmatyar runs a camp for Tajik fighters inside Afghanistan and claim that their border troops have captured trainees. The *New York Times*, September 30, 1992

24. Ibid., February 18, 1992.

25. Ali and Rashid, *Far Eastern Economic Review*, pp. 18 and 20.

26. There was particular fear for the safety of Chinese working a large mineral project at Saindak. Earlier, six of them had been kidnapped and held for ransom. *Muslim*, August 3, 1993.

27. *Christian Science Monitor*, May 14, 1992. Also, FBIS, June 8, 1992, p. 54, from AFP, Hong Kong, June 7, 1992, quoting Burhanuddin Rabbani.

28. FBIS-NES, May 1, 1992, p. 36, from AFP, Paris, April 30, 1992. It was only after Islamic forces had taken Kabul that Pakistan acknowledged that, indeed, many Pakistanis had died in Afghanistan, that Pakistan had sacrified lives as well as given diplomatic, political, and moral support to the cause. FBIS-NES, 6 May 6, 1992, p. 42, from an address to the nation by Prime Minister Sharif on May 5, 1992.

29. Pakistan was rumored to have helped block a coup against Rabbani by some of his own allies who felt that he was becoming soft on Hekmatyar. Pakistan was allegedly asked its blessing for the coup, but rebuffed the plotters led by Sibghatullah Mojadeddi, Dostam, Masoud, and even possibly the former communist President, Babrak Karmal. The scheme was supposed to have been foiled when Hekmatyar, presumably with Pakistan's help, caught wind of the plan and informed Rabanni. *Pakistan Times*, June 19, 1993. While the rumors were very likely false, they underline what was seen widely as Pakistan's commitment to the accords reached in Islamabad and Jalalabad.

30. Despite Pakistan's declarations that its territory would not be allowed to be used as a base for launching aggression against Kabul, efforts to cut off the arms flow across the poorly policed and admittedly porous border were often only half-hearted. When 14 truckloads of arms believed intended for Hekmatyar's fighters were seized by Pakistani authorities in early September 1992, it only underlined the massive smuggling in progress, very little of it uncovered. Pakistan undercut its claims to not allow any group to challenge the Afghan government's integrity by failing to close the large mujahidin arms depots near the border from which Hezb-i-Islami and other parties were drawing down stocks. Nor, according to Professor Rabbani, was Jama'at-i-Islami's Qazi Hussein being prevented from supplying the Kabul government's opponents, specifically Hekmatyar. Salamat Ali, *Far Eastern Economic Review*, September 3, 1992, p. 14. Also, Hazoor Ahmed Shah, *Pakistan Times*, September 30, 1992.

31. Former intelligence chief, General Hamid Gul, the long-time friend of the mujahidin, was asked by civilian authorities to intercede personally in order to arrange a late August 1992 cease-fire. FBIS-NES August 27, 1992, p. 43, from AFP broadcast August 27, 1992. Earlier, soon after the April victory of the mujahidin, Gul had been instrumental in arranging a meeting between rival leaders Masoud and Hekmatyar. The Islamabad government continued to use the former ISI head, even if in a unofficial capacity, when it tried to influence those parties that he had once patronized. In February 1993, the General and a delegation headed

by Qazi Hussain Ahmad, Pakistan's Jama'at-i-Islami leader, at the request of Rabbani, visited Kabul in an effort to bring about some reconciliation with Hezb-i-Islami. *Pakistan Times*, February 18, 1993 and *Frontier Post*, February 17, 1993.

32. "Development of, by, and for the People," *The Newsletter* from the International Center for Economic Growth, Vol. 6, no. 3 (January 1993): 6, based on the *United Nations Development Report 1991* (London: Oxford University Press, 1991), prepared by a team led by Mahbub ul-Haq.

33. *The News* (Islamabad), August 8, 1993.

Index